The Bad Object

The Bad Object

Handling the Negative Therapeutic Reaction in Psychotherapy

Jeffrey Seinfeld, Ph.D.

JASON ARONSON INC.
Northvale, New Jersey
London

First Softcover Edition 1993

Copyright © 1990 by Jason Aronson Inc.

10 9 8 7 6 5 4 3 2 1

Library of Congress Cataloging-in-Publication Data

Seinfeld, Jeffrey.
   The bad object : handling the negative therapeutic reaction in psychotherapy / by Jeffrey Seinfeld.
     p. cm.
   Includes bibliographies and index.
    1. Psychotherapy—Complications and sequelae.   I. Title.
   [DNLM: 1. Psychotherapy.   2. Therapeutics—adverse effects. WM
420 S461b]
RC480.5.S416   1989
616.89'14—dc20
DNLM/DLC
for Library of Congress   89-15199

ISBN 0-87668-831-8 (hardcover)
ISBN 1-56821-002-7 (softcover)

Manufactured in the United States of America. Jason Aronson Inc. offers books and cassettes. For information and catalog write to Jason Aronson Inc., 230 Livingston Street, Northvale, New Jersey 07647.

To my wife Rhonda
and my daughter Leonora

Contents

Preface

This volume shows how to help the patient overcome what has been described by Freud as the most serious obstacle to psychotherapy: the negative therapeutic reaction. It is the bad object that is predominantly responsible for this reaction—the treacherous road upon which the therapeutic process often flounders. The patient and therapist enduring the travails of the therapeutic journey often resemble Odysseus and his crew forced to outwit the demons, sirens, witches, and cyclops threatening to thwart the long voyage. In fact, those mythological demons personify the manifold masks of the bad object often described as exciting (but not satisfying), enticing, bewitching, addicting, engulfing, rejecting, punishing, and persecuting.

The bad object is comprised of the actual negative attributes of the parental figures—often a composite of the features of both mother and father along with later significant others resembling them—and the child's fantasies and distortions about these figures.

ix

In this regard, the unsatisfactory experiences with the parental figures give rise to frustration and anger, which color the child's perception of the object. The bad object therefore often becomes more powerful and persecutory than the actual parental figures upon whom it is based, leaving the child with no alternative but to repress or split off the awesome, frightening object. The designation "bad" regarding the object does not refer to a moral valuation, but rather to the child's subjective unsatisfactory experience with it.

Therapeutic progress threatens the patient and the therapist with the terrible wrath of the bad object. The patient is conflicted between his loyalty and fear of the bad object and the longing to enter into a good object relationship that will promote separation from the bad object. It is the threat of loss that releases the bad object from repression, resulting in the negative therapeutic reaction.

Fairbairn believed that the term *salvation* was a more apt designation than that of *cure* for the patient's subjective experience of his need to be rescued from the bad object. There are two fundamental manifestations of the negative therapeutic reaction. In identification with the bad object, the patient attacks his potential relationship to the therapist. In theological prescientific terms, the patient is "possessed" by the bad object. If the therapeutic relationship survives this assault, the bad object is projected into the therapist. In theological prescientific terms, the patient, in his dependence on the therapist, feels that he has sold his soul and entered into a Satanic pact with the bad object. The patient thereby attempts to win back his soul (or "self" in contemporary language), from engulfment by the Satanic bad object, thus promoting the process of separation-individuation in the transference. This volume will provide the clinician with an effective guide in handling the negative therapeutic reaction and carrying the treatment to a successful completion.

The clinical picture of the bad object is described based on a historical overview of the object relations literature, including S. Freud, K. Abraham, M. Klein, W. R. D. Fairbairn, H. Rosenfeld, E. Jacobson, and O. Kernberg. I then present a clinical theory of the bad object and the negative therapeutic reaction. H. Searles and D. W. Winnicott have been the clinicians most inclined to work directly with the bad object transference.

The bad object establishes a systematic clinical theory of bad object transference in order to provide clear guidelines for intervention. Toward this end, the book presents chapters on child therapy, interpreting the bad object transference, and management of the symbiotic transference, along with numerous clinical cases to clearly illustrate effective guidelines for intervention. This work also illustrates how patients with differing clinical diagnoses manifest the bad object transference.

ACKNOWLEDGMENT

I am grateful to Dr. Jason Aronson for his sustained encouragement and enthusiasm for this volume and to Joan Langs, editorial consultant to Jason Aronson Inc., Gloria Jordan, production editor, and Nancy Andreola, copy editor, for their helpful collaboration. I wish to express special gratitude to Dr. George Frank of New York University School of Social Work for his supervision and instruction in the application of ego psychological/object relations theory to clinical practice. I am indebted to Dr. Peter Ferber for the excellent psychiatric consultation he provided in many difficult treatment situations and to Patricia Nitzburg for providing a holding environment at the Jewish Board of Family and Children's Services, where the theory of the bad object transference was applied to clinical practice. I am grateful for the work of Dr. Harold Searles, whose courageous revelations on countertransference sustained me in many difficult treatment situations. I am grateful also to Dr. Shirley Ehrenkranz, dean of New York University School of Social Work, for providing me with support and encouragement, and to all my colleagues at the school for their support and stimulation. My thanks to Dr. Andrea Hadge for her sensitive wisdom about countertransference and to my colleague Robert Berger for his friendship, encouragement, and willingness to share his own clinical experience with the bad object transference. I owe much to my colleague Jane Charna Meyers for her friendship, support, and for some of the case material presented in this volume, and to my colleague Dr. Michael Gropper for his friendship and encouragement, as well as his comments concerning the relationship between my views and those of cognitive/behavioral therapy.

To the many patients who have appeared throughout this volume who, with extraordinary courage and endurance, prevailed through the sturm und drang of the bad object transference, everlasting thanks.

Part I

THE CLINICAL
PICTURE

1

The Negative Therapeutic Reaction

This chapter reviews the literature and describes the importance of the internal bad object in the negative therapeutic reaction. A structural analysis provides the framework for effective clinical intervention.

REVIEW OF THE LITERATURE

Sigmund Freud

Freud (1923) aptly described those patients suffering from what he termed the "negative therapeutic reaction." He states:

> There are certain people who behave in a quite peculiar fashion during the work of analysis. When one speaks hopefully to them or expresses satisfaction with the progress of the treatment, they show signs of discontent and their condition invariably becomes

3

worse. One begins by regarding this as defiance, and as an attempt to prove their superiority to the physician but later one comes to take a deeper and juster view. One becomes convinced not only that such people cannot endure any praise or appreciation, but that they react inversely to the progress of the treatment. Every partial solution that ought to result, and in other people does result, in an improvement or a temporary suspension of symptoms, produces in them for the time being an exacerbation of their illness; they get worse during the treatment instead of getting better. They exhibit what is known as a negative therapeutic reaction. [p. 39]

Rosenfeld (1987) has stated that Freud (1916) first described a negative therapeutic reaction when he mentioned the story of a young woman who had rebelled against her family by running away from home. Later she met a young artist who wanted to marry her. It seemed that just when her life circumstances had begun to improve, she began to neglect the home she and her lover shared, imagined that her lover's family was persecuting her, interfered with her lover's work, and then succumbed to a chronic and severe mental illness. Freud attributed the young woman's behavior to feelings of guilt. He also noted (1918) that in the treatment of the Wolf Man, the patient experienced transitory negative reactions every time the analysis progressed.

As Finell (1987) suggests in his review of the negative therapeutic reaction, Freud became quite pessimistic about the therapeutic reversal of this process. In his paper "The Economic Problem of Masochism," Freud (1924) discussed the negative therapeutic reaction in terms of the patient's unconscious need for punishment related to unconscious forbidden instinctual impulses. Rosenfeld (1987) has stated that Freud believed that the sadism of the superego and masochism of the ego complemented one another in the negative therapeutic reaction. Freud (1924) spoke of the patient as suffering from a severe sense of guilt or conscience and the sadomasochism as derived from the death instinct. In "Analysis Terminable And Interminable," Freud (1937) reiterates his pessimism concerning the effective handling of the negative therapeutic reaction and confirmed its relationship to the death instinct.

Karl Abraham

Abraham (1919) also identified negative reactions of the patient in response to progress in the analysis and pointed to unconscious problems around narcissism and envy. Abraham's astute clinical observations foreshadowed the work of M. Klein. In "A Particular Form of Neurotic Resistance against the Psycho-Analytic Method," Abraham (1919) described those patients who begrudge the analyst any progress in the treatment. Abraham emphasizes the patient's need to feel superior to the analyst and to do the analytic work on his own. The patient is viewed as wanting to be more effective than the analyst, because accepting the analyst's help evoke envy and rage.

Abraham (1919) states:

> In place of making a transference the patients tend to identify themselves with the physician. Instead of coming into closer relation to him, they put themselves in his place. They adopt his interests and like to occupy themselves with psychoanalysis as a science, instead of allowing it to act upon them as a method of treatment. They tend to exchange parts, just as a child does when it plays at being father. They instruct the physician by giving him their opinion of their own neurosis, which they consider a particularly interesting one, and they imagine that science will be especially enriched by their analysis. In this way they abandon the position of patient and lose sight of the purpose of their analysis. In particular, they desire to surpass their physician, and to depreciate his psychoanalytic talents and achievements. They claim to be able to "do it better." It is exceedingly difficult to get them away from preconceived ideas which subserve their narcissism. They are given to contradicting everything, and they know how to turn the psychoanalysis into a discussion with the physician as to who is in the right. [pp. 306–307]

Melanie Klein

Klein (1957) relates the negative therapeutic reaction to a reenactment of the early infantile feeding situation. She states that "this helpful interpretation may soon become the object of destructive criticism. It is then no longer felt to be something good he has received and experienced as enrichment" (p. 15).

Klein states that the patient experiences the analyst as the good object and must devalue his interpretations because of early oral envy and narcissism. The patient becomes guilty over devaluing the analyst (the good object) and may unconsciously prevent any benefit from treatment in order to punish himself for injuring the good object. Klein therefore adopts Abraham's view of narcissism and envy in developing her views on how early object relations are enacted in the transference to the analyst.

Rosenfeld (1987) points out that the study of Klein's work suggests that the most significant negative therapeutic reactions occur when envy remains silent or hidden, due to primitive defenses against it. Klein (1946) elaborated on the primitive defenses against envy in terms of idealization, splitting, devaluation, omnipotence, and reversing envious situations by inducing envy in others. As Rosenfeld points out, the defenses against envy are the same as those Klein described as the very earliest defenses of the ego in the paranoid schizoid position mainly directed against the death instinct.

Like Freud, Klein viewed the negative therapeutic reaction as derived from the death instinct; she was therefore somewhat pessimistic about the potential for reversing it. Klein emphasized that oral envy exists from the beginning of life. She noted that split-off envy manifests clinically as an inability to accept with gratitude interpretations that are perceived in some part of the patient's mind to be helpful. In the negative therapeutic reaction, the patient splits off and projects envy into the analyst and therefore fears his retaliation. Klein believed that the patient's ego could sometimes be strengthened by the repeated analysis of the split-off envy, which would result in a greater feeling of responsibility and tolerance for guilt and depression. Klein believed that if the patient is to overcome the paranoid–schizoid position, envy and the defenses against it must become integrated into the ego.

W. R. D. Fairbairn

Fairbairn (1944) was able to draw upon the dynamics described by Klein (rejection of the good object) without resorting to a theory of the death instinct; instead, he originated a theory of internalized object relationships based upon actual relationships prevailing between the ego structures and their internalized objects as well as between one another. Fairbairn (1958) states:

> [S]ince the nature of these relationships is the ultimate source of both symptoms and deviations of character, it becomes still another aim of psychoanalytic treatment to effect breaches of the closed system which constitute the patient's inner world, and thus to make that world accessible to the influence of outer reality. [p. 380]

Fairbairn's theory of the internal tie to the bad object is actually an elaboration of an idea set forth by Freud in a footnote to his discussion of the negative therapeutic reaction. Freud (1923) points the way toward an object relations theory of the negative therapeutic reaction. Remarking upon the patient's unconscious sense of guilt, Freud states:

> One has a special opportunity for influencing it when this sense of guilt is a borrowed one—when it is the product of an identification with some other person who was once the object of an erotic cathexis. A sense of guilt that has been adopted in this way is often the sole remaining trace of the abandoned love/relation and not at all easy to recognize as such. [p. 40]

Freud's statement is another way of depicting the patient's tie to an internal object through guilt and points the way toward Fairbairn's theory of the tie to the bad object. In Fairbairn's view, the abandoned love (and hate) relationship is internalized, and guilt is experienced when the self component of that internalized relationship threatens to separate from the bad object by the influence of an external good object.

Finell (1987) has suggested that the theory of the negative therapeutic reaction has evolved from initially basing the clinical importance of aggression on the death instinct to focusing recently upon relating aggression to early experiences of frustration and aggression. The shift from the death instinct to early frustration and deprivation is exemplified in Fairbairn's work, which emphasizes the infant's internalization of frustration and deprivation in the context of the internalization of the rejecting relationship with the early object. This relationship is then reenacted in the negative therapeutic reaction as the patient rejects the therapist's potentially helpful interpretations and the analytic progress. In focusing upon early deprivation as opposed to the death instinct, however, Fairbairn nevertheless maintains the classical and Kleinian dynamic emphasis on the clinical importance of aggression in the patient's rejection of the good object.

Edith Jacobson

Jacobson (1964) has also developed a theory of internalized object relations relevant to the negative therapeutic reaction. She states that in early life, positive (pleasurable) and negative (unpleasurable) memory traces are libidinally and aggressively cathected with instinctual energy and thereby split off into positive and negative self and object representation units. Self and object constancy are achieved when the positive (good) and negative (bad) self and object representation units are integrated under the dominance of the positive attributes. Jacobson's theory of internalized object relations integrates classical drive and object relations theory and will therefore serve as a framework for this clinical study of the negative therapeutic reaction.

Kernberg (1980) has suggested that Fairbairn's ego segments attached to internal objects are analogous to Jacobson's (1964) self and object representation units. As Kernberg points out, Fairbairn's ego segments (libidinal ego–antilibidinal ego) are not psychic structures of functions and defenses in the classical Freudian sense, but rather are specific self-representations. I believe that Jacobson's internalized object relations theory becomes more clinically useful if integrated with Fairbairn's theory. Jacobson's libidinally and aggressively cathected split-off self and object representation unit is described in static terms. A synthesis of Fairbairn's and Jacobson's views provides a more accurate rendition of Fairbairn's theory and transforms Jacobson's theory from a static to a dynamic system. Jacobson's all-negative self and object representation unit or aggressively cathected self and object representation unit can be rendered dynamic by speaking of a rejected self-representation and rejecting object representation. In this way, I propose to synthesize Jacobson's self and object representation unit theory with Fairbairn's dynamic object relations theory. This synthesis of the two theories will be shown to serve as a useful clinical model for understanding the dynamics of the negative therapeutic reaction.

Otto Kernberg

In discussing Klein's views on the negative therapeutic reaction, Rosenfeld (1987) has stated the following:

> It is, however, apparent from the study of Klein's work that the most powerful negative therapeutic reactions occur when envy remains hidden or silent, due to the creation of powerful defenses against envy. Defenses against envy include splitting, idealization, confusion, flight from the original object leading to a dispersal of feelings, devaluation of objects and self, violent possessiveness, and reversal of the envious situation by stirring up envy in others through success and possessions. [pp. 100–101]

Kernberg (1975) has elaborated upon these primitive defenses against envy in his theory of borderline personality disorder. Kernberg outstandingly crystallized the clinical concept of a stable borderline personality disorder by synthesizing Klein's views on the paranoid–schizoid position and Jacobson's theory of internalized object relations units. In her theory of the paranoid–schizoid position, Klein (1946) hypothesized the splitting of the good and bad internal breast with primitive idealization of the good breast to protect it from aggression. In his theory of borderline personality organization, Kernberg replaces Klein's internal breast with Jacobson's self and object representation unit. He therefore speaks of an idealized all-good self and object representation unit split off from the devalued all-bad self and object representation unit. In the transference, the patient defends against the envy associated with the negative therapeutic reaction by maintaining a primitive idealizing transference. Therefore, Kernberg believes that the borderline patient who unrealistically idealizes the therapist is also undergoing a negative therapeutic reaction but defends against it by splitting it off from the therapeutic relationship. The patient may not directly devalue the therapist; rather, he may express the negative therapeutic reaction indirectly in self-destructive behavior outside of the sessions, for example, or in destructive external relationships.

Kernberg (1980) suggests that borderline pathology is closely associated with the rapprochement subphase of separation–individuation, a view Mahler herself had previously stated (1975). In Kernberg's view, the borderline patient is ego fixated in the rapprochement subphase in the sense of denying the discovery of his separateness and clinging to an illusory tie to the all-good symbiotic mother. Kernberg emphasizes that the borderline patient does not experience a true symbiosis but maintains the illusion of oneness to the all-good object by defensively splitting off the good and bad object relations unit. His theory therefore posits a relationship between the negative therapeutic reaction and separation from the object.

Masterson (1976) further elaborates upon the relationship between the negative therapeutic reaction and fear of separation. He contends that the borderline patient was rewarded during the rapprochement subphase for passive, regressive, dependent behavior and rejected for his autonomous strivings. Therefore, separation from the object is equated with abandonment by the object. The negative therapeutic reaction is the result of the fear of separation. Progress in the analysis would imply to the patient that he is separating from the analyst-mother and will therefore be abandoned. The negative therapeutic reaction is therefore a cry for the preoedipal symbiotic mother.

The negative therapeutic reaction has also been understood, in terms of separation–individuation theory, as an effort to ward off regressive symbiosis with the preoedipal symbiotic mother. Olinick (1964, 1970) has emphasized the negativism of the negative therapeutic reaction. He sees this negativism as a defense against the loss of self that is feared in the relationship to a depressive preoedipal maternal love object who demands fusion with the patient. Asch (1976) has also considered the negative therapeutic reaction as a defense against a regressive pull to the symbiotic mother as activated in the transference.

Finell (1987) has emphasized that the patient who is undergoing a negative therapeutic reaction experiences both a longing for fusion with the preoedipal object and a conflicting wish for separateness. In the dynamic view of the negative therapeutic reaction, this impossible conflict between the wish for fusion and the wish for separateness is central.

The Structural-Deficit View

The structural-deficit view of the negative therapeutic reaction emphasizes the lack of actual positive object experiences in the patient's early life that would serve as receptors for the taking in of later positive object relations. From the structural-deficit viewpoint, the patient who undergoes a negative therapeutic reaction suffers from an impoverishment of internal positive self and object representations based upon an actual lack of good external object experiences. Adler (1985), Blanck and Blanck (1979), Giovacchini (1982), and Kohut (1984) have referred to some patients' lack of positive self and object representations. The structural-deficit viewpoint does not emphasize the importance of aggression, the conflict around fear of fusion or fear of separateness, or the bad object; rather, it emphasizes the patient's deficit of positive object representations, resulting in the lack of evocative memory of postive object experience. The failure in object relations would therefore predate rapprochement; the positive object experience would be viewed as lacking from the earliest months of life (Adler 1985).

STRUCTURAL ANALYSIS

The Closed Internal Psychic System of Structural Deficit and the Internal Bad Object

The foregoing review of the literature suggests two general views of the negative therapeutic reaction, one based on a dynamic conflict model, and the other based on a structural-deficit model. The structural-deficit and conflict models should not be viewed as mutually exclusive. Rather, I contend that the negative therapeutic reaction *always* involves both structural deficit (of positive self and object representations) and conflict (the bad object situation).

In the negative therapeutic reaction, both the structural deficit and the identification with the bad object account for the patient's inability to accept the good object. From the perspective of the structural deficit, the therapist as a potential good object is perceived as alien, strange and unfamiliar. If the patient is so impoverished in positive object experience that he is hardly receptive to accepting the therapist as a good object, then the internal bad object does not need to be strongly activated to defend against the potential good object because there is little threat involved. Nevertheless, even in those cases of severe structural deficit, clinical observation will reveal evidence of the internal bad object situation. If the patient's positive self and object representations are strong enough to create the possibility of a hoped-for good object relationship, then the internal bad object situation will have to be activated to abort the hoped-for good object relationship. Therefore, the patient's active and aggressive rejection of the therapist indicates that the positive self and object representations are sufficiently strong to threaten the projection of a hoped-for good object in the transference. The patient who seems more indifferent to, than aggressively rejecting, of the therapist experiences such an impoverishment of positive self and object representations that the internal bad object situation does not need to become strongly activated in rejection. However, even the patient who is severely impoverished in positive self and object representations must be assumed to experience some sort of positive self and object representations no matter how weak or fragile, or he would have no motivation to come for treatment.

The patient who undergoes a negative therapeutic reaction has experienced both a lack in actual external positive object experience and the rejection of his need for such experience. The lack of positive object experience results in the deficit of positive self and object representations. The rejection of his need for positive object experience results in his internalizing the rejecting experience and rejecting his own need for the positive object. Therefore, the negative therapeutic reaction comprises the patient's unreceptivity to an alien, unfamiliar positive object reinforced by his active rejection of his own need for a positive object in identification with the original external rejecting object. In this way, structural deficit and the internal bad object reinforce each other.

THE BAD OBJECT'S REJECTION
OF THE INTERNAL GOOD OBJECT

Viewing Jacobson's internal object relations theory from a dynamic perspective provides a clinical model for understanding the bad object's rejection of the internal good object. As discussed earlier, Jacobson actually speaks of split-off libidinally and aggressively cathected self and object representation units. In synthesizing her view with Fairbairn's dynamic model, we speak of the negative self and object representation unit actively rejecting the positive self and object representation unit. This dynamic structural model suggests in clinical terms that the patient, in identification with the original rejecting object, rejects his own need to *internalize* a positive object. In synthesizing Fairbairn's and Jacobson's theories, I will extend both. For instance, Fairbairn states that the patient, in identification with the bad object, rejected the influence of an external good object. Fairbairn's internalized object relations theory was primarily concerned with the bad object situation. Only late in his writings did he refer to an ideal good internal object projected into external reality. However, he never established a theory of the development of an internal good object and how it might relate to the bad internal object situation. By synthesizing his views with Jacobson's theory, I am suggesting that the internal bad object situation rejects not only the external good object but also the *internalization* of the good object.

The concept of the development of an internal good object is described in the work of Jacobson (1964) and Mahler (1975) in the ego psychology theory of object constancy. Furthermore, their work suggests that impairment in self and object constancy is central to severe psychopathology. However, American ego psychology has basically attributed failure in self and object constancy either to an ego defect, possibly constitutionally determined (Blanck and Blanck 1979, Giovacchini 1982, Masterson 1981), or to the mothering object's rewarding dependence and rejecting autonomy (Masterson 1976), thereby impeding the integration of positive and negative self and object units. Thus, in Jacobson's writings, the libidinally and aggressively cathected units are viewed as split off from one another. In synthesizing Jacobson's American ego psychology and Fairbairn's British object relations theory, I propose that the negative self and object representation unit splits off the positive self and object representation unit. Stated in clinical terms, the patient, in identification with the original external bad object, rejects his own need for an internal positive comforting object. Furthermore, the deficit in actual positive object experience results in an unreceptivity to the taking in of a strange and alien positive object. This dynamic internal object relations structural analysis can serve as a model both for the negative therapeutic reaction and for the severely disturbed patient's impairment in self and object constancy.

THE WISH FOR FUSION AND
THE WISH FOR SEPARATENESS

As previously mentioned, Kernberg (1975) and Masterson (1976) have emphasized the patient's longing for fusion and fear of separateness, whereas Olinick (1964) and Asch (1976) have emphasized the patient's fear of fusion and longing for separateness. This seeming contradiction may be resolved by a close review of Mahler's theory of rapprochement. Mahler (1975) states:

> The rapprochement struggle has its origin in the *species-specific* human dilemma that arises out of the fact that, on the one hand, the toddler is obliged, by the rapid maturation of his ego, to recognize his separateness, while, on the other hand, he is as yet unable to stand alone and will continue to need his parents for many years to come. [p. 229]

In this statement, Mahler emphasizes that the discovery of autonomy is inevitably associated with the discovery of vulnerability. In Mahler's view of rapprochement, the youngster discovers his own separateness from the object, and this intrapsychic autonomy gives rise to vulnerability and the need for reunion with the object. In the reunion with the object, the youngster plays at still being symbiotic with the mother. The secure-enough playful symbiosis enables the child to tolerate the vulnerability associated with separation. I would therefore suggest that the parental object can impede the child's autonomy by rejecting the child's vulnerable need for a holding object as well as by rejecting his autonomy strivings.

The Masterson formulation that the child experiences a rewarding of regressive dependency needs and a rejection of autonomy does not pay sufficient attention to distinguishing dependency needs that serve autonomy from those that impede it. This dilemma can be resolved by Fairbairn's concept of the exciting bad object. In other words, the dependency that is rewarded by the external parent is the dependency on the exciting object. In such instances the child's vulnerable need for a human holding object to provide comforting, soothing, mirroring, and empathy is rejected and instead the exciting object is offered in place of the holding object. Food, toys, sexual stimulation, money, and so on can all be offered to compensate for the vulnerable self's estrangement from the holding object. The child becomes insatiable in his need for the exciting object because it cannot possibly gratify his need for an internal holding object. The external parent becomes a means to the end of the exciting object. Before long, the parent may complain that the child is insatiable and wants his needs met upon demand. The insatiable need for an exciting object will inevitably lead to feelings of disappointment and rejection, thereby reinforcing the tie to the internal rejecting object. I will illustrate these dynamics with a brief clinical vignette.

Case Example

A single mother of a 7-year-old child worked full-time and allowed the child to travel to and from school by herself and to remain alone after school. The child felt extremely frightened and vulnerable. Upon returning from school she would go to a neighbor's house, saying that she was afraid of being alone and asking whether she could stay with them until her mother returned. The mother became angry and told her to stop acting like a baby. She rejected her crying and fearfulness but bought her toys to compensate. The child, in identification with her mother, split off the vulnerable self's need for a holding object. She increasingly demanded toys, and before long she and her mother were constantly fighting. The child became a precocious "street kid," expressing all of her dependency needs through orally demanding, rageful behavior.

The mother brought the child for therapy, complaining that she was "spoiled" and that she had "created a monster" by buying the child whatever she wanted. However, the rewarding of the child's dependent, regressive behavior tells only a part of the story. The dominance of the rejecting object and the activation of the exciting object created a psychic fortress, closing any possibility of an internal holding or mirroring object. The activation of the exciting object created an insatiable need which in turn activated the rejecting object.

As Finell (1987) states, the patient in the negative therapeutic reaction is caught between the wish for fusion and the wish for separateness in his interpersonal relationships. The interpersonal situation reflects the internal object relations configuration of the hoped-for good object transformed into an exciting object into a rejecting object into a rejected object into a hoped-for good object once again. The patient's need for a hoped-for good object gives rise to the fear of fusion. The latter anxiety can be understood as the unconscious bad object's fear of losing the self component to the good object. Fear of fusion may therefore be an unconscious fantasy of the patient's bad object. The fear of fusion is reflected in the transformation of the hoped-for good object into an exciting object. The self's insatiable need for an exciting object is also an expression of the self's estrangement from the good holding object. The insatiable need for the exciting object will inevitably give rise to feelings of disappointment and anger toward the object. The wish for separateness is now manifested in viewing the object as rejecting and rejecting it in turn. The rejection of the object will result in feelings of object loss and depression, giving rise to the need to fuse with the object. These transformations of the internal object relate to the patient's being caught between the longing for fusion and wish for separateness.

In the foregoing discussion, this author remarked upon Klein's and Kernberg's views that some patients can defend against the negative therapeutic reaction with primitive defenses such as idealization and splitting. The patient's capacity to maintain an idealizing transference by splitting off the negative reaction suggests that the positive self and object representations are strong enough to withstand the rejection of the bad object. Kernberg (1975) and Masterson (1976) view primitive idealization or a symbiotic transference as a pathological destructive defense and neglect the possibility that a prolonged idealizing or symbiotic transference may further strengthen positive self and object representations and repair the structural deficit. In a later chapter I will discuss in depth the dilemma of supporting or interpreting the idealizing or symbiotic transference.

THE IDENTIFICATION
WITH THE BAD OBJECT

Internal objects refer to the patient's unconscious and/or conscious fantasies about significant early objects (Klein 1945). An important factor in the identification with an internal object is that the patient fantasizes about himself and the external object world from what he perceives to be the attitude or feelings of the early object. The patient can therefore perceive himself as he imagines his parental objects viewed him. From this perspective, the self component of the patient becomes the object of the internal object. In the negative therapeutic reaction, the patient identifies with the early bad object and feels the terror and rage that he had perceived the original parental object would feel at the threat of separation from the patient.

Hitchcock's film *Psycho* offers a dramatic example analogous to the dynamics of the negative therapeutic reaction. The leading character, Norman Bates, sometimes disguises himself as his mother, thereby becoming the bad object. Whenever a strange woman, a potentially good object, appears at the hotel and threatens to take Norman away from the internal mother, Norman, as the bad mother, becomes terrified, jealous, and enraged. Dialogues occur between Norman and himself as his mother in which the latter commands him to stay away from the strange woman, a hoped-for good object. Norman, putting himself in his mother's place, kills the good object.

Of course, a patient who actually acted out the role of the bad object as Norman Bates does in the movie would be deemed psychotic, given the loss of reality testing, judgment, impulse control, and so on. Nevertheless, if we think of the identification with the bad object not in terms of the patient losing reality testing and actually believing he is that object, but rather only in terms of unconsciously feeling the rage, terror, and jealousy of the object, then the film can be understood to depict the identification with the bad object in the negative therapeutic reaction.

The internal bad object is based upon both the actual attributes of the original external parental object and the level of cognitive, psychosexual, and ego development at the time of internalization which also played a part in how the child understood or fantasied about the actual external object.

The next chapter describes the negative therapeutic reaction in terms of early developmental phases and the reenactment of these phases in the evolution of the patient–therapist interaction.

2

Manifestations of the Bad Internal Object

Searles (1961) described four phases of patient–therapist interaction in intensive psychotherapy of the severely disturbed patient as a framework for understanding the various manifestations of the negative therapeutic reaction. Searles's phases not only describe the sequential phases of patient–therapist interaction during the treatment process but also reflect early levels of object relations enacted in the transference–countertransference situation. Therefore, each specific phase of patient–therapist interaction also refers to the patient's developmental level of object relations and clinical diagnosis. Searles sequentially described the phases of patient–therapist interaction as (1) out-of-contact, (2) ambivalent (pathological) symbiosis, (3) therapeutic symbiosis, and (4) resolution of the symbiosis. A long-term treatment case will illustrate the dynamics of the negative therapeutic reaction at each phase of patient–therapist interaction.

21

THE OUT-OF-CONTACT PHASE

In this initial phase of treatment, Searles (1961) describes the patient and the therapist as isolated in their own psychic territories until the patient gradually permits the therapist entry into his psychic space. Searles cautions the therapist against imposing his own internal world on the patient and speaks to the value of the therapist's tolerance of the patient's isolation. By permitting the patient to be alone in the presence of the therapist (Winnicott 1958), the therapist communicates his empathic understanding of the patient's need for protection against impingement, and the patient thereby begins to trust the therapist enough to permit the psychic entry of the therapist into his world.

The out-of-contact phase is especially relevant to the negative therapeutic reactions of the severely disturbed borderline patient who is predominantly experiencing a structural deficit of positive internal self and object representations. These patients do not know how to relate to the therapist as a positive empathic object. Lacking in positive object experience that can serve as a receptor for internalizing the therapist as an empathic holding object, the patient experiences the therapist as an alien creature from another psychic planet. Given the incapacity to expect any help from human object relations, the patient is for the most part indifferent to the therapist. The deficit in internal positive self and object representations is, of course, not absolute or the patient would never come for treatment. Many of these patients are referred for or pressured into treatment by external sources or circumstances, but it can be assumed that the patient's continued attendance indicates that some part of him wants help. When faced with a problem or crisis in their lives, however, these patients often become indifferent to the therapy and cancel or forget their appointments. As one patient said, "When a serious problem arises I never even think of you. I forget that you exist, even that the building you work in exists. I must do something about the problem. Time to act. Sitting and talking is a waste of time, preventing me from doing whatever it is I need to do to take care of business."

These patients are unable to reflect upon themselves or upon other people. They are the patients described by Ogden (1986) as using "reality as a defense against fantasy" (p. 219), or by McDougall (1980) as "anti-analysands." As Ogden points out, the dialectical process between fantasy and reality is broken down, with reality dominating and foreclosing imagination. The patient lacks a sense of self as subject of experience. He does not experience himself as the author of his thoughts, feelings, and circumstances but rather experiences thoughts, feelings, and circumstances as happening to him. He is not the subject but rather the object of his life. McDougall (1980) points out that these patients are quite similar to the classic schizoid patient in the sense that they are concrete, reality bound, disconnected from human object relations, and more related to inanimate objects. Unlike the classic schizoid, however, the patients in question are highly impulsive and do not use the defense of isolation of affect. Often they become enraged and disppointed in their object relations. McDougall refers to them as anti-analysands because of their capacity to go through the motions of treatment while remaining unaffected by the therapist's empathy and interpretations.

In the treatment situation, the out-of-contact patient will describe life events as stories that have happened to him. If the therapist explores the patient's motivations or the internal life of other participants in the story, the patient will often simply tell another story. Such patients are often extremely reality- and action-bound. They experience a strong sense of inevitability about any problem that arises and about their immediate reactions. There is no reflection between the problem and the reaction. The patient reacts with an immediate solution to any given problem, thereby avoiding the sense of vulnerability that could arise if he were to reflect upon himself in his situation.

A patient reported that she had finally begun to develop a subjective sense of self after many years of intensive therapy. "It's as if all of my life I reacted automatically to anything that happened—just existing and reacting on automatic. I just took the first answer at hand, never thinking about the long term or about how my solution of today

would sit in six months. Just reacting to the crisis. It was easier then. I
didn't realize how difficult anything was. Consequences didn't occur
to me. Didn't think about anything."

All patients experience some degree of an initial out-of-contact
phase in the patient–therapist interaction. For instance, a patient
whose predominant mode of object relating is ambivalently symbiotic might begin treatment sometimes with out-of-contact relatedness and at other times with ambivalent symbiotic relatedness, with the ambivalent symbiosis quickly becoming the
dominant mode of relatedness. In the case of the out-of-contact
patient—also referred to as "the patient using reality as a defense
against fantasy" (Ogden 1986, p. 219) and as "the anti-analysand
patient" (McDougall 1980)—the out-of-contact phase does not
spontaneously give rise to symbiotic relatedness; rather, the patient remains out of contact. The structural deficit of positive
object representations results in the patient's being unable to project a hoped-for good object into the therapist. These patients
have given up hope for rapprochement, reparation, or resurrection
of the internal good-enough human object, usually because of the
extreme abuse or neglect, or both, that they experienced in early
life. They bring to mind T. S. Eliot's line from "The Wasteland"
when he speaks of rats' alley and dead men who have lost their
bones. *Rats' alley* refers to the internal psychic world, a wasteland
in which the internal bad object, the orally destructive rat, has
even devoured and chewed the bones of the internal good object,
leaving no hope for resurrection, rapprochement, or reparation.

The patient's discourse resembles the narration in a Kafka novel
where the character is faced with a senseless, absurd, and meaningless reality that inevitably crushes him. Like those characters, the
patient experiences himself as facing a world populated by shallow
people who fulfill their pragmatic roles and functions to the point
of meaningless absurdity; the patient experiences himself and others around him as abstractions who could be distinguished just as
easily by initials.

The patient compensates for his internal psychic wasteland and
the lack of a hoped-for good object by compensatory attachments

to nonhuman exciting objects. Drugs, alcohol, food, money, clothing, or nearly any nonhuman object can serve as the focus of an addictive compulsion to compensate for the lack of a human holding object. The insatiable need for things, in turn, generates crises around such things enslaving the patient in an inevitable vicious cycle of crisis, need, reaction.

The negative therapeutic reaction in these patients is manifested through the crisis-need-reaction cycle. In other words, the patient constantly creates crisis in his life, which evokes urgent need, which gives rise to immediate, desperate reactions, which bring about further crisis, which evokes urgent need, and so on. The patient faced with such severe crises and desperate, urgent need simply has no time, no interest, no use for therapy. The vicious cycle of crisis, need, reaction leaves no room for the therapist. As one patient put it, "I have no time for this. Too much is happening. I've got to get out of here and take care of things."

The patient's reality, behavior, and crisis-bound life becomes the negative therapeutic reaction that closes the therapist out of the internal psychic system. The patient constructs a real crisis, in the context of which the therapist is useless, impotent, and ineffectual. It is important to note that these patients' crises are real and not merely imaginary; however, the patient has constructed his reality in accord with the internal object world. This particular view, which has been an important development in recent object relations theory (Ogden 1986)—that of the mental construction of reality and the interpenetration of the patient's internal world and the environment—will inform most of the clinical vignettes in this book. This view does not presuppose that the internal world is more important than external reality, or that external reality determines the internal world; rather, it focuses upon a complex interpenetration of internal and external worlds through projective and introjective identification.

If the out-of-contact patient does begin to internalize the therapist as a positive object, then the crisis-need-reaction cycle becomes increasingly intensified in the negative therapeutic reaction in order to eject the therapist as useless, impotent, unimportant. The active rejection of the therapist as a positive internal object makes the shift from the out-of-contact phase to ambivalent symbiosis.

AMBIVALENT SYMBIOSIS

The patient who has reached the phase of ambivalent symbiosis in object relations has a strong enough positive self and object representation unit to project a hoped-for good object into the transference. The internal bad object situation aborts the hoped-for good object by constructing an insatiable need for the good object, which invariably becomes an exciting and rejecting object. The self-component feeling rejected will then reject the exciting object. The self then becomes a rejecting self, the object a rejected object. The rejecting self-rejected object leads to the inevitable depression associated with object loss, resulting in the wish for merger with the hoped-for good object, resulting in the exciting and then rejecting–rejected object configuration. All of the foregoing shifts occur with the inevitability of a mathematical formula. The patient's rejection of the internal hoped-for good object must be understood both from the self component's fear of losing the bad object and the bad object's fear of losing the self component, as already described in Chapter 1.

The hoped-for good object could be likened to the myth of the hero. Campbell (1949) discusses a theme that reoccurs throughout the myths of humankind related to the search of the hero for a reunion with a lost good object. In the reunion adventure, the hero repeatedly encounters gods, goddesses, demons, and witches who attempt to impede his journey toward reunion. Homer's *Odyssey* is a typical reunion adventure of this kind. Odysseus is separated from his son, Telemachus, and wife, Penelope, by the Trojan war. The epic poem recounts his journey home and the various demons, witches, and temptresses he must cunningly outwit in order to reunite with his wife and son. James Joyce, in his great novel *Ulysses*, updates and relocates the *Odyssey* adventure to pre-war Dublin. The hero, Bloom (symbolizing Odysseus as the father-husband), seeks reunion with his wife, Molly, and the symbolized son, Daedalus. The reunion is thwarted not by supernatural demons, witches, and temptresses, but rather by ordinary characters in everyday Dublin who are perceived as similar to Homer's demons and witches, in the narrator's stream of consciousness. Therefore, in the Joyce novel, they are depicted as the narrator's internal bad objects, which impede the reunion with the hoped-for good object. The theme centering around the thwarting of the reunion with the hoped-for good object by bad internal objects, is the basic dynamic of the negative therapeutic reaction in ambivalent symbiosis. This epic myth is reenacted in the transference–countertransference situation as the hoped-for reunion with the good object becomes activated in the transference, and the bad internal object world seeks to thwart the reunion.

Once a break is established in the closed-psychic system, the patient will experience the classic borderline rapprochement transference of rapid oscillations between clinging and distancing. Searles (1961) has referred to the rapprochement merry-go-round as an *ambivalent symbiosis*. His use of the term *symbiosis* implies a regression not to the symbiotic phase of total fusion of self and object representations, but rather to extensive use of projective identification (Grotstein 1985). Mahler (1975) describes this phenomenon when she speaks of the rapprochement youngster who wants to separate from mother and projectively identifies this wish into her. This interaction is central to the ambivalent symbiosis of rapprochement.

The patient clings to the therapist in dependence. The clinging leads to a fear of loss of autonomy, so that the patient then distances with aggression. He distances by transforming the hoped-for good object into an exciting, then rejecting, then rejected object. Distancing leads to depression and fear of object loss, which causes the patient to cling again in dependence. This transference phenomenon can be termed ambivalent symbiosis (Searles 1961) or rapprochement clinging/distancing (Mahler 1975). From an objective standpoint, clinging reflects the activation of the all-bad self and object representation unit. From the subjective standpoint, clinging and distancing reflect the transformation of the hoped-for good object into the exciting, then rejecting, then rejected object.

Searles (1961) has commented that this phase has the feeling tone of sexuality and aggression, and patient and therapist often feel that they drive each other crazy. The dependent self expresses both an oral, active need for the exciting object and a passive, vulnerable need for the holding object in the transference. The therapist can therefore serve as a bridge in the integration of the split-off dependent selves and good and bad (exciting) objects during ambivalent symbiosis. Although self and object units are split into all good and all bad, the all-bad self and object unit still predominates because the patient still cannot maintain the all-good self and object unit over long periods. Antidependent resistance continues to view the hoped-for good image of the therapist as a threat to fragile autonomy and must therefore reject the positive image of the therapist by transforming it into an exciting object. This ambivalent symbiotic phase is also characterized by the patient's putting third parties between himself and the therapist to create distance. Therefore, in the transference, the patient might become jealous and obsessed with the therapist's involvement with other objects, or he might preoccupy himself with other objects.

THERAPEUTIC SYMBIOSIS

Therapeutic symbiosis begins to predominate in the transference when the idealized positive self and object representation unit becomes stronger than the negative self and object representation unit. Searles (1979) has posited that the therapeutic symbiosis is a regression to preambivalent object relatedness prior to the splitting of the object into all good and all bad. I believe Searles may have considered therapeutic symbiosis as preambivalent in response to the American object relations view that symbiosis is reflective of splitting and therefore defensive and antitherapeutic. American object relations (Kernberg 1975, Masterson 1976) contends that symbiosis in the borderline patient cannot be preambivalent to symbiotic fusion of self and object representations, but rather refers to a defensive splitting of the all-good object relations unit into the transference and the all-bad object relations unit into the external object world. In this author's view, it is no longer necessary to posit a preambivalent symbiosis in the borderline patient in that Grotstein (1985) has convincingly demonstrated that splitting and projective identification are far more than mere pathological primitive defensive maneuvers and can be understood as normative developmental psychic operations by which the infant constructs meaning to raw sensory data experience. Although I differ with Searles on this minor issue of whether symbiosis is preambivalent, I do strongly agree with his view that symbiotic relatedness can be therapeutic. In a later chapter, this theoretical issue of splitting and therapeutic symbiosis will be discussed in greater depth.

Searles (1961) states that the feeling tone of therapeutic symbiosis is one of maternal care and love, with the receding of sexual and aggressive trends. In the phase of therapeutic symbiosis, there is a full reemergence of the vulnerable and fearful regressive, dependent self, in the care and protection of the idealized holding therapist. The patient and the therapist can sometimes interchange transferential positions, according to Searles (1961): The patient assumes the role of the omnipotent mothering object and the therapist assumes the role of the vulnerable child. During this phase, the feeling tone between patient and therapist is akin to "you and me against the world," also suggesting that the bad internal object situation is projected into the external world that the "you and me" are against. Searles (1961) has remarked on the great difficulty in distinguishing whether the manifestations of the therapeutic symbiosis are a true preambivalent relatedness or a folie à deux between the participants that splits off and denies aggression between them. Possibly it is not an either–or situation, but rather one in which symbiosis is therapeutic in terms of allowing the patient an opportunity to internalize a positive self and object representation but a folie à deux in terms of denying and splitting off aggression.

The therapeutic symbiosis marks the gradual integration of the active oral and passive vulnerable split-off dependent self. The vulnerable self becomes increasingly less withdrawn and passive as it actively asserts the need for the holding object. The patient can

thereby begin to integrate the good holding object and bad exciting object. In his discussion of the regressed transference, Winnicott (1960b) also describes how the therapist gradually becomes
more of a holding object for ego care and less of an object for the
gratification of instinctual needs. He says that the patient's need
for primary ego care gains ascendance over instinctual need gratification.

Winnicott (1960b) says that regression in the transference permits emergence of and contact with the true self by the holding
therapist. Winnicott speaks of two aspects of the true self: the true
self as fragile, vulnerable to internal and external impingement,
and the true self as spontaneous, omnipotent, and alive. These two
aspects of the true self engage in two aspects of the transference.
The true self as vulnerable to impingement relates to the therapist
in the transference as an omnipotent holding object. Kohut (1971)
refers to the phenomenon as the idealizing self–object transference.
The second aspect is that the true self in omnipotence seeks with a
spontaneous gesture, the gesture of acceptance from the holding
object. He refers to this phenomenon as the mirroring self–object
transference.

The true self, which is analogous to the passive, withdrawn,
regressed self (Guntrip 1969), has become disconnected from the
holding object because of traumatic failures in empathy and holding and because of antidependent bad object attacks against
vulnerability, fear, and dependence. Winnicott says that the true
self is on ice, in cold storage, buried and withdrawn beneath the
conflicts of active oral sadomasochistic infantile dependence (ambivalent symbiosis). In disconnection with the holding object, the
true self remains infantile, weak, vulnerable, and fearful. Stolorow
and Lachmann (1980) refer to this phenomenon of the true self as
a "developmental arrest." The true self is in need of a holding
object to thrive and to grow. Empathic communication with the
fragile, vulnerable true self's need for holding protection or omnipotent self-expression is what facilitates the emergence of the
true self in the therapeutic symbiotic transference.

In integrating Winnicott's view with ego psychology, it can be
seen that the true self in cold storage is the patient's separation–

individuation potential and the self-representations associated with that potential. Winnicott's view that the true self is in need of a protective holding object in therapeutic regression to facilitate growth and development is closely akin to Mahler's belief that the child needs to continue to be dependent upon the parental object long after the discovery of his separateness in order to grow through the rapprochement crisis on the way to object constancy. During this phase of therapeutic regression, the emerging true self is highly vulnerable to impingements of all sorts and to failures of empathy on the therapist's part. The rapprochement crisis is a psychological birth and marks the advent of the subjective self, the awareness of separation and loss of symbiotic omnipotence. The subject is at his most vulnerable to impingement and is in the greatest need of a holding object to support his growth. This phase still marks the splitting of all-good and all-bad self and object representation units, but now the all-good idealized unit is increasingly activated and dominates the all-bad unit, which is split off and projected into the external object world. The patient can now increasingly maintain a positive image of the therapist to comfort himself. Over time, the patient internalizes the therapist as a comforting object.

As the patient increasingly internalizes the positive object–therapist, he becomes less dependent upon the therapist and other external objects. The patient now becomes both comforter and comforted. In unconscious fantasy, he becomes the internal good breast object. In becoming his own good object, the patient has achieved a narcissistic adaptation in which he denies his dependence on and envy of the external good object. In this way, the narcissistic symbiotic fantasy that one contains the good object inside oneself serves the denial of dependence on and separateness of the external object. The continued presence of the therapist enables the patient to protect himself from the persecutory bad object during the therapeutic symbiosis. At first, he needs the actual contact with the therapist as a good object to reinforce and strengthen the internal positive self and object unit that protects him from the persecutory bad object. With the increasing internalization of the positive object, he develops a narcissistic adaptation that serves to defend him against dependence, greed, and envy toward the external object.

The clinical diagnosis of narcissistic personality applies to the patient who can fantasize that he is the good breast or comforter, holder, and mirror as well as the comforted, held, and mirrored. For this patient, external objects serve to reinforce the fantasy that he is the good breast, as the needy, dependent self is sometimes projected into the external other. At this point the patient can psychically play at the fantasy that he is the good object rescuing the weak, fragile self from the bad object. In order to psychically play in the good object position, the patient must have had enough early life experience with good object aspects of the real external object in order to arrive at a strong enough representation of the positive self and object to serve as a basis for psychic play. If the real early experience with good aspects of the external object are lacking, then the patient is enabled to develop the positive self and object representations through the treatment in the out-of-contact ambivalent and therapeutic symbiotic phases. Internalization of the therapist as a positive object begins once the patient has secured a strong enough positive representation of the therapist nurturing, comforting, or mirroring the self. The fantasy that the patient has incorporated the good breast is active in the sense of the patient psychically playing at comforting, nurturing, mirroring himself and putting himself simultaneously in the position of comforter–comforted.

RESOLUTION OF SYMBIOSIS

Searles (1961) refers to the final phase of patient–therapist interaction as the resolution of the symbiosis. He says that this phase is not the tail end of the treatment process, but is of prolonged duration, sometimes longer than the combined previous phases. Searles says that the feeling tone of this phase is one of increasing conflict between symbiosis and separation–individuation.

The emergence of aggression is now of central importance, in that the aggression serves separation–individuation. Jacobson

(1964) states that the splitting of all-good and all-bad self and object representations gradually gives way to the child's increasingly investing all badness in the object representation and all goodness in the self representation. The libidinal investment in the all-good self representation endows the self with narcissism and libidinally cathects self, ego interests, ambitions, and ideals. The aggression invested in the object representation serves autonomy and separateness from the object. Clinically, in the resolution of the symbiosis, I suggest that this all-good self–all-bad object unit appears in the disillusionment that occurs in the transference. As I discussed in the previous section, the patient takes a good part of his idealization into himself. He thereby begins to idealize his own ego interests and self representations. The patient who takes part of the idealization of the therapist into the self can also be viewed as fantasizing that he possesses the good breast within himself, thereby developing the capacity to comfort himself. The internal bad object is then projected into the therapist. The patient now experiences a full-blown negative therapeutic reaction, which can be seen as having great therapeutic value as the patient objectifies the bad object through the transference.

How the patient *unconsciously* enacts the position of the bad object as he experiences the terror of losing the child self component to the good object therapist has already been discussed in Chapter 1. The patient's unconscious identification with the bad object is especially relevant through ambivalent symbiosis. In the resolution of the symbiosis, the patient discovers the bad object in the transference by perceiving the therapist as engulfing, frightened of losing the patient, rejecting autonomy, and jealous of the patient's other interests, relationships, and activities. The patient attempts to create the therapist as bad object through projective identification, and the therapist may, more or less unknowingly, enact the role of the bad object in the countertransference. In projectively identifying the bad object in the transference and introjectively identifying the good object in the self, the patient now works at actively separating from the bad object that is jealous and fearful of losing him. This phase of the resolution of the symbiosis is relevant to Searles's view that the patient becomes the analyst to the analyst. The patient will fully project the bad internal object into the therapist only if he has experienced him as an idealized good object during symbiosis. Fairbairn (1943) stated that the patient will release his repressed internal bad object only if the therapist can be a good-enough object in reality. For a prolonged period, the therapist must permit the patient's analysis of the bad object in the transference. However, it must also be remembered that in internalizing the idealization of the object, the patient denies dependence, greed, and envy in relation to an external good object while also splitting off the all-good and all-bad object. Kernberg's views on the narcissistic transference are relevant here. The therapist must eventually interpret the splitting off of idealization from dependence, envy, and greed into an external object. In this way the therapist increasingly enables the patient to integrate the good and bad self and object units.

INTENSIVE THERAPY WITH A BORDERLINE PATIENT: A LONG-TERM CASE REPORT

This long-term case illustrates the negative therapeutic reaction in the various phases of the patient–therapist interaction. The patient entered treatment with an ambivalent symbiotic level of object relations, so the initial out-of-contact phase was brief and peripheral. (Other case reports in later chapters will focus on patients with structural deficits for which the out-of-contact phase is crucial in discussing the negative therapeutic reaction from a developmental perspective.) The patient was initially seen three times a week; after four years, sessions were held twice weekly.

Kernberg (1975) has provided the definitive definition of intensive therapy for borderline patients. Kernberg considers intensive psychotherapy to involve no fewer than two weekly sessions; the initial focus is on interpreting the primitive defenses in the here-and-now transference activations, eventually leading to genetic reconstructions. Interpretations of the transference require a position of technical neutrality but are limited by the need to establish parameters of technique (Eissler 1953).

Justine

Justine had grown up in an intact working-class family, the youngest of three sisters. Her parents were in their forties and her siblings were already adolescents at the time of her birth. She was not a planned-for child. All of her sisters had histories of significant psychiatric illness and hospitalization.

The patient's mother was the dominant force in the family. She was embittered by economic burdens and often took out her rage on the children, physically abusing them with household objects. She had no work or activities outside the home; although she met their material needs she didn't know how to care for them emotionally. The patient's father, a manual worker, was withdrawn and depressed. Her sisters devalued and criticized him, but the patient developed a close and lasting attachment to him. She would go to him for security and comfort and to escape the violence and chaos of the family and felt in turn, that she could lift him out of his depression and give him something to live for. All the other women in the family were abusive toward her, and she related their abuse to jealousy of her attachment to her father. When she was 9 years old, her father fondled her genitals twice.

Justine was hospitalized during the oedipal phase for a serious medical problem that she believed was a punishment from God. She fully recovered but was left with a slight limp, which she felt was a visible sign of her evil. Her father also became ill when she was in the oedipal stage and she worried about his health throughout her childhood.

She had a stormy adolescence, characterized by sexually abusive relationships with males, clinical depression, suicidal gestures, and rageful assaults by her mother. She was hospitalized twice in late adolescence, each time for several months. Hospital reports and treatment summaries diagnosed her as latent or pseudo-schizophrenic and as a severe borderline personality.

Justine began long-term therapy after being discharged from the hospital. The therapist helped her apply for college admission and for financial aid, and generally provided her with support so that she was able to take a minimum of required courses each semester to graduate. She met a kind, supportive, but passive man, married several months later, and became pregnant.

Following the birth of her child, Justine experienced a mild post-partum depression. She recovered somewhat during the child's symbiotic phase but then became seriously depressed with suicidal ideation and homicidal impulses toward the child. She sometimes felt like throwing him out the window, smothering him, cutting him up into little pieces, and stabbing him. During this period, Justine could not tolerate any separation from her husband outside of their regular routine. She would panic if he wanted to do something outside of work or the marital relationship. For a time, she would telephone him at work, demanding that he come home at once because she could no longer manage the child. The husband did most of the household chores, including the shopping and laundry. It was with the onset of these symptoms that the first therapist, who had seen her for twelve years, referred her to a second therapist.

The second therapist helped her verbalize her homicidal feelings instead of acting on them. The treatment focused on helping her maintain an angry stance instead of becoming depressed and was helpful in that it prevented the patient from abusing her child as well as significantly lessening her clinical depression. The therapist had taken an active, directive approach by encouraging the patient to find a baby-sitter and to join recreational activities and a support group. She initially did not like the therapist because of his "autocratic" approach, but she grew to idealize him for forcing her to be independent. The patient's functioning remained marginal although she made appreciable gains in the important area of caring for her child. After treating the patient for two and a half years, the second therapist referred her to me.

Out-of-Contact Phase

Justine was an attractive but somewhat hard-looking woman. Her hair was dyed jet black, in striking contrast to her fair complexion. There was a certain tension in her movements when she was angry. I would sometimes see her hard, frozen face dissolve into a tender, affectionate, or loving expression, in complete contrast to her prior impermeability. At other times she would become vulnerable, frightened, and childlike, in striking contrast to her angry or maternal expressions. She could then become beautiful, seductive, and sophisticated. I emphasize these affective transformations to illustrate the radical transformation of self-representations in the patient's ambivalent symbiotic relatedness.

When I suggested that we meet twice weekly, Justine was pleased. The patient had initiated the treatment session by idealizing Dr. N., her former therapist, and devaluing me. She reported that at first she had not liked Dr. N. because he was autocratic and had refused to see her more than once weekly or to permit her to call when she was upset. She had come to appreciate his approach, however, because he had forced her to be independent. She thought that if he had not terminated with her, he most certainly would have cured her. She thought that maybe she had driven him away by expressing so much anger, but he had assured her that she did not have that much power, and that his reason for terminating was solely his move to another town. At the same time, she wondered why he had not offered her the option to continue, and she questioned his response that she would be better off seeing a therapist in her own area. These thoughts prompted her to want to go to his office and shoot him, although she insisted that she would never do so. She questioned my ability to help her, given my social work training, and she noted that her previous therapists had been psychologists. She responded contemptuously to both my silence and my comments. When I was silent, she would say that she felt I was intimidated by her, afraid that if I opened my mouth, she'd jump down my throat. When I spoke, she said that my comments did not measure up to Dr. N.'s. If she was upset or agitated, she said that Dr. N. had known exactly how to calm and reassure her, whereas I did not know what to do with her. She considered calling Dr. N. to ask whether she could return to him, but she decided to give me a try since he had recommended me. She then figured that he could not really have known what sort of therapist I was since he had never been my patient. Maybe she should tell him.

I commented that she might be idealizing Dr. N. and devaluing me in order to avoid becoming involved in therapy with me, perhaps because she had risked involving herself with Dr. N. and he had left. She arrived for the next session saying that she had thought about what I had said about using Dr. N. to avoid becoming involved with me, and she thought I might have a point. Her statement was the first indication that she had begun to internalize me as an object by thinking about what I had said.

For my part, I was feeling like an unwanted child being repri-manded by a rejecting mother. This countertransferential feeling is clinically relevant, especially in light of the presenting problem: The patient sometimes wanted to get rid of her child by murder-ing him. As Searles (1986) has stated:

> But I have found, in my work with a reliably long succession of patients now, that such an experience of myself in the work, comes in course of time to reveal at its core, the experience of myself as being an unwanted little child in relation to the patient. . . . In case after case, I become impressed, inevitably, with how much the patient is sounding like a mother who is reproaching and blaming her small child, giving him to feel that, had he only not been born, her life would be a paradise of personal fulfillment. [p. 211]

This transference–countertransference phenomenon indicates that the antidependent self, in identification with the rejecting internal object, is attacking the unwanted vulnerable, dependent self projected into the therapist. The therapist is viewed as a threat to the closed internal system. The patient's antidependent self fears that the therapist, as a supportive object, might awaken the neediness and vulnerability of the dependent self, thereby under-mining what little fragile autonomous adaptation the antidepen-dent self has been able to achieve. Through projective identifica-tion, the antidependent self rids the personality of the dependent part of itself that might want the therapy.

After the interpretation of the idealization of the former thera-pist as a defense against involvement with me, the patient began to discuss her problems concerning her child. She reported that when the child was about 9 months old, she started to have murderous impulses toward him. She said that the child's vulnerability "set something off" in her. She would look at the child and think of how vulnerable, dependent, and helpless he was. She would feel the impulse to stab and smother him. At 9 months of age, the child was in the practicing phase. It was earlier suggested that separa-tion–individuation and greater autonomy is initially associated with a heightened sense of vulnerability and dependence. At this age, the child was beginning to toddle away and to show the subphase-appropriate interest in the other-than-mother world. At the same time, he began to make greater demands on the patient, cried more often, and was a bit more aware of his mother's presence, so that he sometimes protested when she left.

In thinking of murdering her child, the patient defended against experiencing a dependent relationship with him that would awaken both the merger and separation anxiety of the dependent self representation. The patient rejected me as well in order to avoid a dependent relationship in which merger and separation anxiety would emerge. Therefore, she projected the vulnerable, dependent self on both her child and me. By adopting a rejected, rageful, antidependent stance, the patient maintained her closed internal world as a schizoid compromise. It was safer for the patient to feel like murdering her child than to feel the wish to be close to him and to admit that he was beginning to move away from her. I am not suggesting that the patient did not experience anxiety, guilt, and depression about her murderous impulses—she most certainly did, sometimes to an unbearable degree. However, guilt and depression were still more acceptable to the antidependent self than was the dependent relationship that prompted merger and separation anxiety. This state of object relations affairs illustrates Guntrip's notion that guilt and depression can be a defense against the underlying fundamental ego weakness of merger and separation anxiety.

THE ANTI-DEPENDENT DEFENSE AGAINST OBJECT LOSS

When the therapist interpreted the patient's conflicts about separation from her child for the first time since the treatment began, nearly a year earlier, the patient responded emotionally, with crying and sadness. Searles (1986) has suggested that the borderline patient splits off the sadness and grief of object loss in denial of separation–individuation.

At around this time, I was planning to take a brief vacation that would require the first interruption in the treatment. The patient verbalized sexual mutilation and murderous impulses toward me. The murderous impulses were interpreted as antidependency impulses against feelings of loss, dependence, and separation anxiety. I asked her whether she would miss me. She became visibly unsettled and said that it was much more difficult to disclose positive feelings toward me than it was to talk about such negative feelings as wanting to murder or mutilate me. I suggested that in her relationship with me, with her husband, and with her child, she used angry distancing to avoid her positive, dependent feelings. In the next session she stated that she had been thinking about what I had said concerning her positive feelings—that she in fact had thought about little else since—and she thought that I was right: For some reason she felt it was dangerous to experience positive feelings.

Searles (1958b) suggested that a central dynamic in the severely disturbed patient relates to the patient's and his mother's avoidance and terror of positive feelings in their relationship. He suggested that in the treatment relationship, the negative transference serves as a defense against the emergence of positive feelings toward the mother. Searles is not saying that hate or negative transference is not real and important in its own right; rather, he is emphasizing that the avoidance of positive feelings and dependence is even more primary. His idea is very close to Fairbairn's notion that the antidependent self uses aggression to split off and reject the dependent self. In other words, Fairbairn and Searles are emphasizing the defense against symbiotic dependence.

The American object relations interpretation of the foregoing clinical data would have a different emphasis. The patient's murderous rage toward her child and toward me would be viewed as abandonment depression and rage over being confronted with separateness. The child's moving away and my vacation would be viewed as disrupting the rewarding all-good object relations unit and activating the withdrawing all-bad object relations unit. The child's moving away and my vacation would be viewed as interfering with the patient's defensive fantasy that she was symbiotically united with her son and with me. The murderous rage would be seen as her response to feeling abandoned by the child and by me.

In my own view, the patient constructed symbiotic insatiable need and resulting abandonment depression in order to reject the internalization of a positive relationship to the object. I have termed this the out-of-contact phase despite the fact that the patient continually established contact through angry rejection, because for the most part she was able to avoid internal contact with the positive object.

Ambivalent Symbiosis

The interpretations of the antidependent defense resulted in a breach of the closed system. The patient began to think between sessions of what I had said about her fear of positive feelings, and she felt unsettled. Therefore, she was beginning to internalize the therapist. The beginning of the internalization marked the onset of the next phase of the treatment, that of *ambivalent symbiosis*.

While away on vacation, I sent her a postcard. Giovacchini (1982) suggests that sending cards during vacations to patients with primitive mental states is a nonverbal interpretation of the impairment of object constancy. Blanck and Blanck (1974) believe such a technique promotes object constancy in the unstructured patient. Justine responded to the card by looking at it daily for comfort and reassurance, but she also thought of throwing it away in order to avoid dependence on me. The card became symbolic of the internal object therapist. The fact that she did not throw it away and that she comforted herself with it pointed to an increasing idealization of the therapist. She also experienced simultaneous positive and negative feelings toward me. This momentary ambivalence struck her as strange and overwhelming; she felt as if she were "going crazy." I have repeatedly found that when borderline patients first begin to experience occasional moments of ambivalence, as opposed to their chronic states of splitting, they often feel that the therapist is driving them crazy. This author believes that the effectiveness of nonverbal interventions (such as sending a card) can be measured by whether they promote ambivalence as opposed to intensified splitting.

At around this time in the treatment, the patient's father died. She initially responded with rage, wanting to break his bones into tiny pieces and castrate him, but then she became numb. Although she was no longer angry at his loss, she started to see the world as a dangerous, malevolent place, and she feared going out and being robbed, assaulted, or raped. She also became highly sensitive to noise, which she felt was driving her crazy.

In the patient's internal object world, the father object representation served as a buffer between herself and the bad, noisy, persecutory objects that represented her mother and sisters. In her fantasy, an omnipotent symbiotic union with her father protected her from the female persecutory objects. This protection related to her having omnipotent symbiotic control over her father so that she had no need to be close to or dependent upon her mother or sisters. The fantasy of her union with her father was centered upon her father being exclusively and totally devoted to her so that he would do whatever she wished and never abandon her. This fantasy of union with the internal father was acted out in her childhood relationship with the external father and in her current relationship with her husband. As long as she had her father, she did not need her mother and could remain distant from her; thus a major function of the symbiotic fantasy was to protect her from her mother's persecution, rejection, and abuse.

Klein (1940) has pointed out that the patient whose aggression is dominant over libido will experience the loss of an external object as a threat to the internal object. Rage at the actual loss of the external person is also directed against the internal representation of the external lost object. There is therefore a threat of losing the internal as well as the external object. Klein (1940) states:

The poignancy of the actual loss of a loved person is, in my view, greatly increased by the mourner's unconscious phantasies of having lost his *internal* "good" object as well. He then feels that his *internal* "bad" objects predominate and his inner world is in danger of disruption. We know that the loss of a loved person leads to an impulse in the mourner to reinstate the lost loved object in the ego (Freud and Abraham). In my view, however, he not only takes into himself (reincorporates) the person whom he has just lost, but also reinstates his internalized good objects (ultimately his loved parents) who became part of his inner world from the earliest stages of his development onwards. These two are felt to have gone under, to be destroyed, whenever the loss of a loved person is experienced. [p. 353]

The patient, whose internal good object representation was only tenuously maintained even before the loss of her father, lost the internal father as well and felt at the mercy of the internal bad objects (her mother and sisters). She projected her aggression and the bad internal objects into the external world and therefore saw the outside as dangerous and violent and tried to separate from the bad persecutory objects by a schizoid withdrawal into her apartment, from which the bad objects were projectively excluded. However, she then experienced the bad objects as invading her apartment. She would listen for noise from loud female neighbors and, upon hearing it, feel that they were trying to drive her crazy. Listening for the noise reflected her need to seek out the bad, persecutory mother in that a bad object was still better than no object at all. The loss of the external and internal father set off intensified dependency needs toward the mother. The patient's fantasy of omnipotent control over her father protected her from an even more dangerous dependence upon mother. To be close to her intrusive, controlling, rejecting mother threatened the patient with both engulfment and rejection.

I made myself more available to the patient during this crisis, telling her that she could call between sessions and request extra appointments if necessary. For the next few months, the patient experienced an intense struggle over internalizing or rejecting the therapist object. When she felt persecuted and impinged upon by noise, a representation of the bad internal object, she found that she could significantly comfort herself by thinking of me and using my image as a buffer against the persecutory object world. She would be able to calm herself for a considerable time in this way, but then an antidependent reaction would be set off against the internal connection between her vulnerable self and therapist holding object. Fearing symbiotic merger with me, she would think of me involved with my family members, colleagues, or other patients and experience intense jealousy that I did not belong exclusively to her. She would hold onto these fantasies and become enraged at me, thinking that these other objects received the best of me while she merely got the leftovers—a couple of hours a week of my undivided attention. She would then begin to lose her positive image of me and would feel alone and depressed. In her jealousy, she projected her own internal objects onto the actual persons in my life and fantasized my being involved with her internal objects and abandoning her. The internal objects were her mother and sisters, projected into the people in my life.

Searles (1986, p. 229) states that "jealousy of the internal object" is an indication of symbiotic relatedness in the transference. The patient distances himself from the therapist by placing an internal object between them. Likewise, the patient would also put her own internal objects, her former therapists, between us in an attempt to create jealousy in me and distance in the symbiosis. When she was angry at me, she would say, "I never think of what you say between sessions. For some reason, what you say never stays with me. I think about what my previous therapists said all the time, and it helps me through the day. I never forgot what they said to me, and I still draw on them for help."

At other times she would say that she deliberately thought all day of her previous therapist and had dialogues in her head with him so that she did not have to think of me. The quality of her thinking of the previous therapist was clearly different during the ambivalent symbiotic phase than it had been during the out-of-contact phase. Before, she had thought of him as an external object, and she compared her treatment with him to her current treatment with me. Now, during symbiosis, she related to him as an active, current internal object with whom she had internal dialogues during the day. In the earlier phase, the relationship with her former therapist had been used to protect her from involvement with me as an actual external object. In the symbiotic phase, her relationship to the therapist as an internal object was used to protect her from involvement with me as an *internal* object. It was an antidependent defense against internalization of the therapist object.

Continued interpretations of the patient's conflict over internalizing me led to a focus upon her treatment of the internal object therapist. She became quite conscious of when she comforted herself with my image, when she aggressively attacked my image, when she displaced my image with another image to create distance, and when she altogether dismissed my image from consciousness. The pattern that emerged was as follows: feeling vulnerable or deprived, she would fantasize being held by me for comforting and soothing. The fantasy of being held promoted libidinal arousal, and she'd fantasize orally incorporating my phallus. The therapist was thereby transformed from the hoped-for good object into the exciting object. She would then become frightened over losing her autonomy as a result of insatiable dependence, so she would establish distance with anger, usually through jealousy over an internal object. Once distant, she would experience object loss and depression and then need to reconnect and cling. This pattern was viewed as a rapprochement merry-go-round. The therapist's tolerance of both dependence and distancing served as a bridge to integrating the all-good and all-bad self and object units. In terms of Jacobson's theory, the activation of the dependent self (clinging and dependence) related to the idealized all-good self and object unit and the activation of the anti-dependent self (angry distancing) related to the devalued all-bad self and object unit.

As already mentioned, the patient would think of her previous therapist in order to create distance in the symbiosis. She would think about how her previous therapist had forced her to be independent, had not permitted her to call him or to schedule extra appointments, and had discouraged her from discussing dependency and libidinal needs in the transference. She thought of me as encouraging her dependency and libidinal arousal because I had urged her to verbalize both passive and active libidinal transferential needs. Therefore, in the transference, she viewed me as a bad, exciting, and symbiotic object in that I encouraged her to verbalize libidinal needs but did not gratify them. She viewed me as wanting her to be a passive, dependent female and to be libidinally addicted to me to serve my male ego. She would at times mistrust my motives in permitting her to be symbiotically related to me and in encouraging her to maintain a positive image of me. She did notice that when she felt better about me and maintained a positive image of me, she also felt better about herself. But she would then insist that she could not trust me as much as she had her previous therapists because they had concentrated on forcing her to be independent and had discouraged dependence and regression.

It can be seen that underlying the antidependent defense is the exciting bad object transference, as Fairbairn suggests. If the therapist attempts to be an available libidinal holding object to the patient and to interpret the antidependent defenses against internalization of the therapist object, the patient will inevitably mistrust the therapist and experience him as the exciting, symbiotic object. In the countertransference, it is uncomfortable and ego alien for the therapist to contain the borderline patient's exciting, symbiotic transference object. To put it simply, the therapist does not like the patient to think of him as a sexually stimulating, symbiotic, autonomy-thwarting parental figure. It is far more ego syntonic for the therapist's sense of professional identity to be viewed by the patient as rejecting dependence and libidinal arousal in the transference and encouraging, even forcing, separation–individuation. However, as will be seen in this and other case discussions, the emergence in the transference of the therapist as the crazy, incompetent, symbiotic, sexually stimulating parent is an essential aspect of the treatment. The patient must experience the therapist as the exciting, symbiotic, crazy parent in order to separate and individuate from the symbiotic parent in the transference. I suggest that the American object relations approach, which focuses on confronting the rewarding, dependent unit in the transference, could sometimes be a defense against the emergence of the symbiotic parent transference.

What I have in mind here refers to Kernberg's recommendations (1975, 1980, 1984) that the therapist confront the patient's primitive idealizations and merging fantasies as unrealistic and as defensive in order to achieve a therapeutic alliance with the patient. My concern is that such an alliance will not be therapeutic but will be based on the patient's antidependent identification with the therapist to avoid the emergence of symbiotic needs in the transference. Early confrontations of the patient's symbiotic and idealizing needs will serve to abort the emergence in the transference of the crazy, symbiotic parental object. The therapist would thereby become an antidependency identification object who supports the repression of the patient's dependence upon the symbiotic object. In such instances the patient's anger toward the therapist might not be the result of the spontaneous activation of the all-bad object relations unit, but instead might be the consequence of the therapist's rejection of the patient's symbiotic needs.

Searles (1986) has also commented on Kernberg's writings as reflecting distancing from the patient's symbiotic needs in his statement that Kernberg appears to view the patient's plight from a cool, Olympian view. The focus of establishing a therapeutic alliance (Zetzel 1966), and a working alliance (Greenson 1965) can sometimes be a countertransferential issue in work with the borderline patient. In other words, the therapist finds it more comfortable to his professional identity to view himself as a real object promoting a therapeutic alliance. Therefore, the therapist's efforts to avoid regression and dependence in the transference could be an avoidance of the crazy, exciting object transference.

The genetic reconstruction of the transference in this case provides an important illumination of the object relations dynamics in symbiotic relatedness. The patient recalled going to her father for holding, comforting, and soothing and then becoming libidinally aroused, just as in the transference activation. In going to her depressed, withdrawn father for comfort, she also felt that she comforted him. She felt that she brought her emotionally dead father to life by comforting and libidinally arousing him. In fact, her father had been raised in an orphanage, had hardly known his own mother, and had suffered extreme emotional and maternal deprivation in early childhood. The father was in desperate need of a mother to bring him to life and to lift his depression. The patient, who was named after the father's mother, was both child and mother to her father, as he was both parent and child to her. She was the vulnerable and libidinally aroused child seeking both comfort and libidinal gratification from the strong, holding, exciting father. She was simultaneously his holding object, providing him with comfort, and his exciting object, libidinally arousing him from his emotional deadness and depression. Searles (1986) states:

> [A]ll these processes in the patient's childhood regularly involved his becoming the object, beginning in early childhood or infancy or even before birth, of transference reactions on the mother's (and/or father's) part, from her own mother and/or father (or sibling, or whomever) to the patient. Typically, the more ill the adult patient is, the more sure we can be that such transference-responses on the parent's part were powerfully at work remarkably early in the patient's childhood. I have written a number of times of the schizophrenic patient's childhood in this regard, and I am aware that a number of other writers have done so. We are only beginning to mine this rich lode of psychodynamics. [pp. 211–212]

Searles is suggesting that the borderline patient as a child was the object of strong transferential feelings on the part of his parent. In other words, the child was unconsciously a parent to his parent. As I have shown, there is evidence that Justine was unconsciously the mother to her own father. As mentioned earlier, she, at times, also viewed her own child as a persecutory object. Therefore, this transferential legacy was clearly handed down through generations.

I suggest that an essential ingredient of true symbiotic relatedness in the transference is the activation of the simultaneous contradictory roles. In other words, the patient will experience himself simultaneously as both child and parent and will experience the therapist simultaneously as both child and parent. I first experienced this strange symbiotic quality of relating with Justine when she would call me to reconnect after an angry outburst. In this dialogue, she would sound like the parent reassuring me that I was not an unwanted child, while at the same time she sought reassurance from me that *she* was not an unwanted child fearing the abandoning parent. I, in turn, felt simultaneously reassured and reassuring in the countertransference.

Once the closed internal system is breached and symbiotic relatedness is initiated, a new quantumlike law of transference is established. Opposite, contradictory object relations units will coexist in the transference. The patient will simultaneously experience the activation of child and parent images in relation to the child and parent object image. Which dimension of the transference is perceived will depend upon the standpoint of the observer. In other words, the patient can be viewed as the child relating to the parent therapist or as a parent relating to the child therapist. An observer (or the participant observers, the patient and the therapist) will usually have only one perception, because we are not accustomed to perceiving contradictory object relations states as coexisting. This state of object relations affairs is similar to light being both a wave and a particle in a physical experiment depending upon the standpoint of the observer. The relationship between symbiotic object relations and the laws of quantum energy are related to the subatomic world, which is described by physicists as symbiotic in terms of a physical oneness of the subatomic universe in which individual entities do not exist. I propose that in symbiotic relatedness, there is a change in the laws of object relations. In ordinary object relations activations in the transference, the patient either activates a single self and object representation unit. The patient might experience either the self representation *or* the object representation and project the other self representation *or* object representation into the therapist. In the symbiotic transference activation, the patient will simultaneously experience both a self representation and an object representation and will project into the therapist both of the corresponding self and object representations. In other words, the patient experiences himself as both child and parent to the child and parent images projected into the therapist. Kernberg has discussed rapidly alternating object and self representations (Kernberg 1984), but his idea differs from mine in that I am suggesting simultaneous activations of self and object units.

The borderline patient's difficulties with separation–individuation are directly connected to the symbiotic relatedness. In separating and individuating, the borderline patient feels not only that he will be abandoned by the parental object but also that he is abandoning his needy child-parent. Thus the patient's efforts at separation–individuation are doubly burdened.

Such was the case with Justine. At around this time of intense, ambivalent symbiosis, she went on vacation, leaving me for the first time. Although she was the one leaving, she nevertheless felt intense separation anxiety, as if I were leaving her. In our last session before her departure, she had trouble saying goodbye and leaving, and I had the distinct impression that this difficulty had as much to do with her need to reassure me that she was not abandoning me and that she still cared for me, since it had to do with her own separation anxiety. She told me that she planned to write to me, and she asked me to respond. When I dropped her a card when I was on vacation, I usually wrote no more than a line. This time, however, when I responded to her letter, I wrote a few lines. The content was innocuous; I merely commented that I was pleased to hear that she was getting along with her family and enjoying the vacation.

Shortly thereafter, Justine called me to say that she felt terrible and that the vacation was turning out badly. She had started to miss me terribly and couldn't wait to come home. She wanted to cut her vacation short and come directly to my office from the airport. When we explored what had precipitated the vacation's going sour, it became apparent that the precipitant had been my letter! She had apparently read the fact that my letter was a bit longer than usual as an unconscious communication on my part that I felt abandoned and wanted her to return at once. She was not conscious of the letter as the precipitant, but once I pointed out that she had started to become depressed only hours after receiving it, she saw the connection. The letter had activated the transference to me as the child-father feeling abandoned and needing her to return. Her unconscious was highly attuned to any sign that I might have some difficulty in permitting her to separate. Searles (1972) has pointed out that the transference is not projected into thin air, but is elaborated upon real aspects of the therapist. Furthermore, the patient will internalize the therapist's unconscious messages. I was consciously aware of missing the sessions and wanted her to do well and manage the vacation. However, I suspect that I unconsciously wanted her to miss me as well and to have some difficulty separating. The extra lines communicated my own split-off ambivalence about her individuating from me. She internalized my need to have her not individuate so easily, in addition to her own separation anxiety, and was therefore ready to return immediately to her father-child, who needed her. Once I encouraged her to continue the vacation, she became calmer and was able to stay a few more days.

I want to stress that although the patient accurately detected an unconscious communication from me to return, this nevertheless should be understood as the real aspect upon which the transference is elaborated. The borderline patient in symbiosis is often keenly attuned to the object's unconscious and elaborates the transference on the basis of that reading (Searles 1972). Once the patient perceived that I did not consciously encourage her to return, the transferential need to rescue the abandoned child-father was temporarily eliminated from the transference equation, and she was able to manage her own separation anxiety.

The borderline patient's need to establish such strong antidependent defenses is related to the capacity for symbiotic relatedness which is so burdensome and threatening to his autonomy. The capacity for borderline symbiotic merger is the result of the idea, discussed by Searles (1986), that the borderline patient, in earliest childhood, was the object of his parents' intense transference of feelings toward their own parental objects.

The Therapeutic Symbiosis

During this phase of treatment, Justine presented a dream that marked the beginning of a less ambivalent therapeutic symbiosis. She dreamt that she and I were out walking when she accidentally fell into a deep hole in the street, but I caught and saved her. Her association to the dream was that she had begun to trust me not to let her fall apart or fall into a hole or a bottomless pit. Guntrip (1969) presents numerous examples of the vulnerable, passive, regressed self as fantasizing returning to a small, womblike enclosure, such as a hole, and not being able to get out and make contact again with people. Guntrip says that regression is destructive and dangerous unless the patient can regress to a holding object–therapist. He suggests that regression with a holding object is therapeutic and provides opportunity for regrowth, whereas regression into a vacuum becomes mental illness. The dream signified that the patient was beginning to trust that I would hold her in regression and not allow her to sink into a bottomless pit.

Justine gradually found that if she maintained a positive representation of me, it was easier for her to feel separate from the actual external therapist. The idealized all-good self and object unit became increasingly dominant in the transference. She viewed us as the best of therapy teams during this phase, and she lived to talk to me. If she was depressed or anxious about something in her external life, I could calm her with just a few words. Her need to call me between sessions and to request extra appointments lessened somewhat; she could comfort herself merely by maintaining a positive image of me. The all-bad object unit seemed to have been split off into the external environment, and there was a quality of "you and me against the world." For instance, when she would tell me that someone had been insensitive to her, she would conclude by saying, "But I can't expect everyone out there to be like you and me." This phase can also be understood in terms of Kohut's (1971) idealizing transference, in that the patient merged with the strength of the idealized self–object therapist.

The external world generally bothered the patient much less during this phase, and she was also able to relate in a prolonged positive fashion to her husband and child. Her murderous impulses toward her son, and occasionally toward her husband as well, had lessened considerably. In the transference, she began to verbalize fears that I would abandon her if she continued to improve and became autonomous. She was able to recall numerous childhood incidents when she had felt that her mother had responded by emotionally abandoning her when she tried to be independent. There was also a lessening of sexuality and aggression in the transference as she integrated the active and passive libidinal self and the exciting and holding libidinal object.

The height of this phase occurred when the patient disclosed that for the past eighteen years she had punched herself in the stomach every morning, while thinking of all the trouble she had made for herself. She said that she had never told any of her therapists, including me, about this behavior because she did not want to relinquish it. When she punched herself, she identified sadistically with the puncher as well as masochistically with the victim. Months later she realized that she hit herself in the stomach where her father would always massage her. Therefore, the punching reflected the sadomasochistic relationship between the antidependent and vulnerable selves. The antidependent self punished the vulnerable self for the dependent, libidinal relationship to the father. Of course, this self-punishment also related to guilt over oedipal strivings. The patient said that because she had told me of this behavior, she would never be able to do it in the same way again because now she would think of me whenever she began to hit herself. Her prediction proved true in that she returned to hitting herself only on rare occasions when she was intensely angry with herself, and she finally stopped the behavior completely. In telling me of her self-punishment, she took a major step in internalizing me as a positive object and in placing her dependent self in my protection as a holding object.

During this phase of the treatment, Justine experienced a severe trauma in her external reality. Nevertheless, she was able to hold herself together and to take appropriate and sensitive care of her child. She found that she was stronger and more capable of managing her anxiety than she had thought.

With increasing frequency she would say that she felt good about herself as long as she felt connected to me, but she realized that she would like to feel good about herself separate from me. She would complain on occasion that I made her dependent, but for the most part she now viewed her dependence upon me as helping her to feel better.

She began to talk about wanting to go to work. She complained that she was living only for therapy, that the sessions were the most important part of her life. She wanted to have something other than therapy in her life.

The Resolution of the Symbiosis

Justine decided to enroll in a vocational training school, attended for a few weeks, and then dropped out, saying that it was "too much" for her. She at first feared that I'd be angry at her for quitting and that I'd give up on her. When I did neither, *she* became angry at *me* and blamed me for not making her independent enough to succeed and for the fact that she was so disappointed in herself for quitting. She again complained that I had caused her to be too dependent, and she again said that her previous therapist had helped her more by limiting her dependency needs and forcing her to be independent. She was seriously considering calling him and requesting a consultation in order to get a second opinion from him as to the value of her therapy with me. She said that she thought she might ask whether she could return to him for therapy. At this point I attempted to persuade her not to return to him but to consult a third party if she wanted a second opinion. I now consider this a mistake. In any event, it served to increase her threats to return to him. At one point she asked whether I would give her an ultimatum that I would refuse to see her again if she went to him, adding that if I gave her such an ultimatum, she would not go. I replied that I would give her no ultimatum; she could see him and return to me if she wished.

She finally went to see her former therapist and complained about how dependent I had made her. She said that after four years of treatment with me, she felt worse instead of better. She asked whether he would see her in therapy if she chose to leave me. He advised her not to act impulsively and offered to see her again if she felt a need to discuss the matter further. He also raised the possibility of her seeing both of us for a time.

Justine continued to threaten to leave me to see another therapist for the next year and a half of her treatment, but she did not return to her former therapist for a second consultation and chose to continue the work with me. Whenever she was angry or disappointed, however, she would seriously consider calling him. Searles (1965) states that the patient's wish to transfer to a new therapist is typical of the resolution of the symbiotic phase.

> It is worth noting, further, that if the therapeutic relationship is to traverse successfully the phase of resolution of the symbiosis, the therapist must be able to brave not only the threats of suicide or psychotic disintegration on the patient's part, and of the professional and personal destruction to himself which might be a correlate of such outcomes; he must also brave the threat, which seems at times to be of a comparable order of magnitude, that the patient will, after these arduous years have passed and the home stretch is in sight, change therapists. It is as though the patient, by presenting the therapist with this threat of separation and finding that the latter can face it squarely without resort to panicky efforts to re-establish their erstwhile mother/infant symbiosis, gains the reassurance that the therapist will allow him to become a person in his own right. . . . [p. 549]

Searles notes as well that it is not at all unusual for patients entering the phase of symbiosis resolution to actively seek out another therapist. He states:

> Another thing which the patient tends to do, when his recovery has proceeded far enough to become a formidable threat to his personal identity, is press for a change of therapists. If he succeeds in this, he will thereby be shielded, for a considerable time longer, from the recognition of how much he himself has changed, for it will be all too easy for him to assume that any shift which he now detects in his functioning in the therapeutic sessions, and elsewhere, is due solely to the contributions of this different therapist. [p. 461]

Searles (1965) believes that resolution of the symbiosis is characterized by disillusionment about the therapist's omnipotence. He explains that in order to separate, the patient must make the therapist helpless and impotent. He explains that the patient becomes more autonomous in an atmosphere where the therapist feels increasingly helpless. No one, neither an adult patient nor a helpless child, would want to give up a perfect, omnipotent therapist or parent.

Nothing I said could relieve the patient's intense disappointment about her training program. Whereas months before I could have calmed and comforted her with a simple phrase, the same words now had no effect. She threatened to commit suicide or to leave me for another therapist, and I felt utterly helpless. I tried every intervention and technique that had worked in the past, but to no avail. I began to feel as if I were with another person, as if there had been some radical change in her, and I at first saw this change as negative given the fact that I could no longer help her.

She congratulated me upon being the first therapist to show her that therapy did not work. She had always had a certain faith in therapy, and this faith had helped her to maintain hope, but I had destroyed her faith in therapy. She now realized that no one could help her but herself, and if she wanted anything, she had better go and get it. Her favorite saying became "No one will help me but myself." She went out and found a part-time job, at first only for one day a week. Rather quickly, however, she added additional hours every few weeks. She also decided to run for election, to become a part-time paid staff person in her support-group center. When she was elected, she panicked and asked me what I thought she should do. I replied that it was her choice and that whatever she decided would be all right. She complained that the former therapist would have become very involved in the intricacies of the decision, and she would have left him knowing what to do. Meanwhile she continued to complain about my neutral stance, even after she took and maintained the position. In the transference she continued to call me incompetent and crazy for encouraging her to be dependent, and she decided that she would no longer call me between sessions except in the event of a dire emergency and that she would reduce her sessions from three to two a week. In addition, she would no longer depend upon her husband to do household chores. She was tired of being a passive female depending upon the strong male, and she would no longer remain passive and weak to feed the male ego. She was making the object all bad and herself all good to promote her autonomy. She took back into herself all of the goodness she had previously invested in the object, and she thereby narcissistically cathected her own ego interests and ambitions. Likewise, by making the object all bad, she used aggression in the service of autonomy. Jacobson (1964) writes:

> We remember that at first the child wants to take in what he likes and to spit out what he dislikes; to ascribe to his self what is pleasant and to the "strange" outside object what is unpleasant. In other words, he tends to turn aggression toward the frustrating objects and libido toward the self. Hence frustrations, demands, and restrictions, within normal bounds, reinforce in principle the process of discovery and distinctions of objects and self; they throw the child back upon his own resources and stimulate progressive forms of identification with the parents, which open the road to realistic independent achievements. Enhancing the narcissistic endowment of his ego, they promote the eventual establishment of secondary ego and superego autonomy. [p. 56]

As the patient blamed significant past and present objects, especially me for her problems, she felt thrown on her own resources to pursue independent functioning. At this point her aggression was no longer rage but rather neutralized in the service of autonomy. The good internal object was truly becoming a part of herself and no longer a foreign introject she had trouble maintaining. The antilibidinal self was now promoting autonomy in a constructive fashion. This phase of resolution of the symbiosis closely resembled Jacobson's description of the child's development of an identity.

At first Justine had often become enraged and threatened to return to the previous therapist. I had responded that the decision was hers. On a couple of occasions she stormed out of sessions saying she was going to call her previous therapist, but she did not, and she always returned. She would also say that she sometimes felt that she came to sessions to help me and not herself, and she would remind me that our sessions were for *her*, and that she would not use them to build my ego or to help me. I considered this statement an important transferential effort to separate from the depressed child-father who needed her to remain dependent in order to comfort and help him. She increasingly began to describe her father as weak and depressed, and she realized that she empathized with him and tried to help him at her own expense. It became clear to her that she sometimes tried to help me as the father-child by her dependence and that now she was trying to separate both as the dependent child needing the strong father and as the mother object helping the father-child. She became unwilling to discuss her libidinal feelings in the transference. Blanck and Blanck (1974) have noted that resistance can be understood as a developmental step in serving autonomy. Furthermore, in the transference, the patient was now unwilling to be the exciting object for her emotionally dead and depressed father-child.

Her anger toward me gradually subsided as she began to feel pride and narcissistic gratification at her independent functioning. She no longer saw the therapist object as either deified or devalued, but rather as both good and bad, with the good outweighing the bad. She became more tolerant of my imperfections; she said that she had read an article that said that even Freud was only human, so I could be, too. She also became more tolerant of her own imperfections. She recalled memories in which her mother had rejected her vulnerability and imperfections, and she remembered her mother taking her to school the first day. The patient had cried and her mother had told her to stop acting like a baby. Years later, the patient learned that when her mother had returned home, she herself had cried uncontrollably over the separation. But her mother would always appear invulnerable in front of her children. The only feeling she had ever expressed was rage. Behind the closed door of her room, however, she had often cried. As a child, the patient had seen her mother as a rock. The patient's granitelike facial expression suggested her antidependent identification with the rock-hard mother.

The patient reported that all of her therapies and her activities at the support-group center had seemed disconnected, but she had now begun to see their continuity. The various episodes of her life had begun to come together like pieces of a puzzle, and she now understood the connections. She was beginning to develop "a cohesive sense of self" (Kohut 1971).

After she had been working at her part-time job for a year, she experienced ill fortune. First she lost her job because the firm closed. She became dependent again and began to call me for support and then reject it. With her other therapists she had always felt a sense of hope, but because of my ineffectiveness as a therapist, she was now losing this hope. Searles (1977) stated:

> Hope is generally assumed to be a "good" emotion, just as hate is assumed to be a "bad" one. We, as adults cling to our cherished illusions that our hope is innately as good—as pure, as virtuous—as is that of the infant or little child who, at least so our concept would have it, is hoping that his momentarily absent good mother will imminently return. The realm of hope seems to us a last repository of such innate goodness as human beings possess. One of the harshest maturational tasks the individual must accomplish, to become truly adult, is to realize and accept that his hope is "impure" in two vast ways: first, it is not unitary in nature but multifarious and permeated with ambivalence, with conflict . . . and, secondly, many of these hopes are devoted not to loving, but rather to destructive ends. [p. 479]

Weeks after Justine lost hope, she decided to make use of her college degree and took a professional licensing exam, which she passed. She went on to obtain part-time professional employment, which, as she felt stronger, gradually increased to full-time.

Conclusion

The resolution of the symbiosis in the case of Justine involved the projective identification of the all-bad object into the transference. The patient resisted internalizing the good object because of both the self component's fear of loss of the internal bad object and the internal bad object's fear of loss of the self (to the good object). Once she had sufficiently internalized the good object during therapeutic symbiosis, she projectively identified the bad object into the therapist. The therapist was then perceived as transformed into the bad object that is jealous and fearful of losing the self component. The projective identification of the internal bad object into the transference permitted her to objectify and practice separation from the internal bad object. She was then able to transform other external objects into the all-good object and to perceive the bad-object therapist as jealous and fearful of losing her.

During the resolution of the symbiosis and at a time when her child was ill, the patient became quite attached to his pediatrician. She actually had not had extensive contact with the physician, although he was supportive, sensitive, and available during a period of crisis. For a good while afterward she would think of him frequently and would discuss him at length during our sessions. She idealized the pediatrician in the same way that she had idealized me during the therapeutic symbiosis. Now when she discussed her previous therapists, she would idealize them for the more positive aspects of their treatment of her. It will be recalled that during ambivalent symbiosis, she had idealized them predominantly for their attributes as bad objects. She now idealized them for their acceptance, sensitivity, and availability rather than for their rejection, insensitivity, or unavailability. Whenever she discussed one of the idealized figures in the treatment, she would allude to the present bad-object therapist's perceived jealousy or dislike of her attachment to them. She would say "I'll discuss them anyway, even if you don't like it." In this way she practiced an attachment to the all-good object in the face of the all-bad object's jealousy and fear of loss. As she began to separate from the internal bad object, she could integrate good and bad objects and self-components.

I have been treating Justine twice weekly for the past nine years. She is currently employed full-time and has been able to continue to function despite significant environmental and economic hardships.

3

American Object Relations Theory and Self Psychology

This chapter will review American object relations theory and self psychology from the perspective of the bad object. The ensuing discussion will focus on the respective theories of the symbiotic transference. The author explains the therapeutic value of the symbiotic regressive transference based upon the theory of the bad object.

AMERICAN OBJECT RELATIONS THEORY

Primitive idealization manifests itself in the therapy as an extremely unrealistic, archaic form of idealization. This idealization appears to have as its main function the protection of the therapist from the patient's projection onto him of the negative transference disposition. There is the projection onto the therapist of a primitive all-good self and object representation, with a concomitant effort to prevent the "good image" from being contaminated by the patient's bad self and object representations. [Kernberg 1975, p. 96]

61

Kernberg (1975) recommends early and constant confrontation of primitive idealizations and clinging in the transference. He emphasizes the unrealistic and primitive nature of the borderline patient's idealizing transference, which he distinguishes from the less regressive idealizations of neurotic patients. He speaks of the necessity of repeatedly confronting unrealistic transferential idealizations that often mask underlying paranoid anxieties and primitive rage toward the transference object.

Kohut (1971) and Stolorow and Lachmann (1980) have objected to Kernberg's view that primitive idealization is a destructive primitive defense and have instead argued that primitive idealization and merging phenomena can be viewed as a developmental arrest. Their position is similar to Searles's view that the symbiotic transference can be preambivalent and therapeutic. I will later discuss in depth Kohut's and Searles's views. I agree with Kernberg that primitive idealization and merging phenomena reflect splitting. However, I disagree with his conclusion that the borderline patient's symbiotic transference is merely a destructive defense. As presented in the beginning of this chapter, Kernberg argues that primitive idealization protects the patient's good object from the aggression associated with the all-bad object relations unit.

Kernberg (1975, 1980, 1984) says repeatedly that primitive idealization and splitting in the transference protect the good object or therapist in the transference. He emphasizes that such splitting results in the keeping apart of the good and bad part object units, thereby impeding self and object constancy. I would suggest that before the patient can integrate the good and bad part object relations units, the good object relations unit must be sufficiently strong and internalized not to be overwhelmed by the bad object relations unit. The activation of the therapeutic symbiosis in the transference reinforces the internalization and strengthening of the all-good self and object representation unit. If the patient is not able to maintain the activation of the idealized all-good self and object unit because the all-bad self and object unit is dominant and aborts the hoped-for good object, the patient will experience a pathological ambivalent symbiosis and a negative therapeutic reaction.

Even M. Klein (1946), who recognizes the importance of negative transference, has stated that primitive idealization of the good object by the young child often serves the function of protecting the internal good object by shielding it from aggression. I would add that in this way, primitive idealization may aid in the process of internalizing a good object. From this point of view, splitting and primitive idealization in the symbiotic transference can be viewed as both adaptive and maladaptive. It is adaptive when it serves to reinforce the internalization of the positive object; it is maladaptive when it serves to impede integration of the internal good and bad part object relations units. Later chapters will provide examples of when the therapist should empathize and support the patient's need to internalize the idealized all-good object and when the therapist should interpret the defensive splitting apart of the good and bad objects.

Kernberg (1978) and Masterson (1978) have argued that there is no therapeutic symbiosis in the transference of most borderline patients. They believe that symbiosis as a stage is entirely resolved by the rapprochement subphase, which they consider to be the precise point of ego fixation or level of ego regression of most borderline patients. Therefore, they believe that primitive idealizations or merger phenomena are manifestations of projective identifications or are a denial of the firmly established boundary between self and object representations. Basing his views on Jacobson's theory of the development of the self and object representation world, Kernberg (1980) argues that the psychotic patient's level of ego regression involves a refusion of self and object representations that account for the psychotic symptoms. Kernberg states that the borderline patient has arrived at rapprochement, that phase during which boundaries between self and object representations are forever fixed. The symbiotic transference is merely a denial, through projective identification and splitting, of that reality. A careful reading of Jacobson (1964) does not support the view that self and object representations are absolutely delineated by rapprochement. She states:

Child analysts seem to agree that up to the age of three, conscious fantasies of merging with love objects are within the margin of

normal development. Even when the child has progressed to a full
awareness of himself and of his love objects as individual entities,
his dependency on the mother for the satisfaction of most of his
instinctual needs and the execution of his ego functions is still
bound to prevent the complete separation of maternal and self
images. [p. 41]

Masterson also elaborates on the borderline patient's internalized object relations. Basing his views on Mahler's developmental
theory, Masterson (1976) suggests that the borderline patient
experiences two split-off internalized object relations representation units. He refers to them as the *rewarding* part object relations
unit and the *withdrawing* part object relations unit. The rewarding
unit reflects the rapprochement mother's rewarding of dependent,
clinging, regressive behavior, and the withdrawing unit reflects
the mother's emotionally withdrawing from the child's autonomous striving. According to Masterson's theory, borderline pathology stems from the rapprochement mother's rewarding dependent, clinging, regressive behavior and rejecting the child's
autonomous, individuated strivings. Masterson regards the transference activation of the rewarding unit as a defense against the
activation of the withdrawing unit and against associated abandonment depression.

Mahler's theory of the rapprochement subphase does not completely support the American object relations view that primitive
idealization, dependence, and clinging are destructive defenses
against autonomy or that rewarding of dependence and rejecting
of autonomy are the direct cause of borderline pathology. Mahler
(1975) states that symbioticlike clinging and idealization reflect
the child's reunion with the mother subsequent to discovering his
own intrapsychic separateness. In reconnecting with the mother
and in reassuring himself as to her continued availability, the child
experiences the security that she will not abandon him. Therefore,
the child's reunion with mother can serve separation–individuation. There is also an emphasis in Mahler's work on the vulnerability of the rapprochement youngster and on what may be called
the need for a continuing playful symbiotic relationship with the

parent to serve as a foundation or home base for autonomy. The child's autonomy strivings could be thwarted by the parental object's rejection of his dependence or vulnerability as well as by the direct rejection of his autonomy.

SELF PSYCHOLOGY

Kohut (1971) and Stolorow and Lachmann (1980) have argued that primitive idealization is not a defense but rather reflects a developmental arrest.

As Bach (1985) has shown, Kohut's concept of the self–object elaborates upon how the parent or therapist serves a tension-regulating function, thereby enabling the child to achieve a state of psychophysical well-being. Here tension regulation refers not to gratification or frustration of the instinctual drives, but rather to the regulation of mood, affect, and self-esteem. The acceptance by the self–object of the child's mirroring and idealizing needs is essential for the achievement of self constancy. Kohut (1984), like Fairbairn and Winnicott, has also discussed how the parental object serves two functions—that of self–object and that of the target object of drive tensions. The target object of preoedipal drive tensions is referred to by Fairbairn as the "exciting object," related to an excited, oral, needy, dependent self component.

Bach (1985) has pointed to the similarity of Winnicott's holding-object relationship, Kohut's narcissistic or self–object transference, and Searles's preambivalent symbiosis. I would add Fairbairn's good object to this analogous depiction of the object that serves a tension-regulating function, enabling the child to achieve the state of psychophysical well-being and regulating mood, affect, and self-esteem. Searles (1986) has remarked on the similarity between his own views of the symbiotic transference and Kohut's concept of the mirroring transference. In particular, Searles refers to his earlier introduction of the symbiotic identity partner and to Kohut's 1971 monograph (*The Analysis of the Self*).

The following passage from Kohut's (1971) writings on the self–object transference is similar to Searles's earlier writings:

In this narrower sense of the term the mirror transference is the therapeutic reinstatement of that normal phase of development of the grandiose self in which the gleam in the mother's eye, which mirrors the child's exhibitionistic display, and other forms of maternal participation in and response to the child's narcissistic exhibitionistic enjoyment confirm the child's self-esteem, and, by gradually increasing selectivity of these responses, begin to channel it into realistic directions. As was the mother during that stage of development, so is now the analyst an object which is important only in so far as it is invited to participate in the child's narcissistic pleasure and thus to confirm it. [p. 116]

As Giovacchini has stated, Searles's writings in the 1950s on the intensive therapy of schizophrenic patients anticipated many of the current views on the treatment of severely disturbed patients. He (1978) and Searles (1986) argue that symbiotic relatedness occurs in the borderline transference and has therapeutic value for separation–individuation. Searles, for instance, agrees with Kernberg and Masterson that the borderline patient's level of ego regression is in the separation–individuation phase, but the self and object representation boundaries are not so clearly defined and remain more flexible than Kernberg assumes. Searles has remarked upon the similarity of his own view of therapeutic symbiotic transference and Kohut's concept of a self–object transference.

Guntrip (1969) defined the central problem in psychotherapy of the severely disturbed patient as how the therapist can reach beyond the antidependent defense and engage the undeveloped, vulnerable true self in a holding relationship. Kohut (1977) describes empathy as the medium through which the vulnerable self of the patient can be reached by the self–object therapist. He states:

The child that is to survive psychologically is born into an empathic responsive milieu (of self-objects) just as he is born into an atmosphere that contains an optimal amount of oxygen if he is to survive physically. And his nascent self "expects"—to use an inappropriately anthropomorphic but appropriately evocative term—

an empathic environment to be in tune with his psychological need–wishes with the same unquestioning certitude as the respiratory apparatus of the newborn may be said to "expect'" oxygen to be contained in the surrounding atmosphere. When the child's psychological balance is disturbed, the child's tensions are, under normal circumstances, empathically perceived and responded to by the self–object. The self–object, equipped with a mature psychological organization that can realistically assess the child's need and what is to be done about it, will include the child in its own psychological organization and will remedy the child's homeostatic imbalance through actions. [p. 85]

Kohut's theoretical views concerning the therapeutic value of empathy to the development of the cohesive self are analogous to Winnicott's poetic statements concerning the importance of the holding environment for the development of the true self. Winnicott (1960a, p. 49) states that holding:

Protects from physiological insult.
Takes account of the infant's skin sensitivity—touch, temperature, auditory sensitivity, visual sensitivity, sensitivity to falling (action of gravity) and of the infant's lack of knowledge of the existence of anything other than the self.
Includes the whole routine of care throughout the day and night, and it is not the same with any two infants because it is part of the infant, and no two infants are alike.
Follows the minute day-to-day changes belonging to the infant's growth and development, both physical and psychological.

THE PATIENT'S REJECTION OF THE SELF-OBJECT'S EMPATHY

The author takes as his point of departure, Kohut's views concerning the treatment of the borderline patient. Kohut (1984) describes the borderline state as a covertly psychotic personality organization constituted by a peripheral defensive structure surrounding a central hollowness because a nuclear self was never established in infantile development. He contends that psychoanalytic treatment could not bring about a workable long term self–object transference that would activate processes of a nuclear self. He cannot imagine a therapist or patient tolerating the chaos and primitive anxieties engendered by the prolonged, archaic transference. He states further:

> I am aware of the fact that I may simply be describing my personal limits as a psychoanalyst and thus my acceptance of the existence of psychoses and borderline conditions. . . . Be that as it may, however, my clinical experience suggests that the analytic dissolution of defensive structures that have been formed behind a persisting hollowness in the center of the patient's self cannot be achieved— even in cases where the central hollowness is perceived as painful by a would-be analysand. [p. 9]

Kohut later makes it clear that he established a differential diagnosis between severe narcissistic personality disorders and the borderline states based on dynamic structural considerations pertaining to the transference and not on behavioral or symptomatic considerations. The differential diagnosis is based on whether the patient is able to establish a workable self–object transference when provided with the opportunity in the analytic setting to re-experience the self–object of childhood. If the patient can establish a workable self–object transference, Kohut says he should be diagnosed as a narcissistic personality, if not, he should be diagnosed as borderline (p. 219).

Kohut recommends a highly structured, educative, goal-setting, directive, and supportive orientation in the treatment of the borderline patient. The patient is helped to manage his defensive structure adaptively. Here, he reiterates his earlier position (1971, pp. 12–14) that the borderline patient is in need of an educational, supportive form of psychotherapy because of his inability to maintain a self-object transference.

Basch (1980), in his manual of psychotherapy informed by self-psychology principles, discusses differential diagnosis and treatment of the borderline patient. He states that a cohesive sense of self that can withstand stress will only emerge if the infant's early development provided enough security in the self–object relationship. Borderline patients usually receive such inadequate response to their need for mirroring that the nuclear self never develops. These patients are threatened by psychotic decompensation and react to affective feedback and empathy not as supportive but rather as a danger that threatens to overwhelm their fragile egos. He states: "Thus many borderline patients cannot and will not enter a therapeutic relationship. Insofar as therapy can serve them by sheltering them from emotional stress, they will tolerate a therapist, but will quickly distance themselves, if, for the purpose of furthering their therapy, he attempts to insinuate himself into their lives as a meaningful figure" (p. 123).

Here again, the nature of the relationship with the therapist is used to establish the diagnosis and the choice of treatment. Basch (1980) concludes that the narcissistic patient can establish a workable self–object transference but the borderline patient usually cannot. He believes that most borderline patients cannot make good use of intensive psychotherapy, and he therefore recommends a reality-oriented, educative, supportive mode of treatment.

Kohut and Basch have explicated the problem to which this book is devoted: the severely disturbed patient's rejection of the therapist's empathy and his inability to sustain a meaningful therapeutic symbiosis or self–object transference. Both Kohut and Basch are saying that the borderline patient is unable to respond or to take in the therapist's empathy. Instead, the patient becomes overwhelmed by unspeakable anxieties or aggressively distances. Kohut refers to the patient's hollow self. I attribute the hollow self both to the patient's lack of positive experience with the external object world and to the patient's identification with an internal rejecting object that perpetuates the hollow self by rejecting the therapist as a new positive object. I contend that Kohut's pessimism in the treatment of the borderline patient is the consequence of his neglect of the internal bad object.

Searles (1986) has remarked that Kohut described the good-object role of both mother and therapist in the development of the cohesive self but neglected the therapist's role as the bad mother. He states:

Although it may feed the analyst's narcissism to experience himself as being a lovingly empathic mother nearly all the time, the emergence of the patient's adult feeling capacities, including his assertive and aggressive capacities, requires that the analyst have much readier access to his own "bad mother" kind of responses than one would believe from reading Kohut. [p. 382]

Kohut describes only idealized self and object images in the intrapsychic realm; he mentions the grandiose self and the idealized parental image. He speaks of the self–object as external, specifically human: parents, siblings, grandparents, peers, and admired and admiring others. Grotstein (1986) has suggested that Kohut's external self–object is a result of the projective identification of an internal object into the external object. In any event, the external self–object is also a good object in Kohut's writings.

The narcissistic personality who can activate and sustain a stable self–object transference is reflecting a secure enough hold on the internal good object. This view is a clinical application of Grotstein's idea that the good external self–object is the result of the projective identification of the internal good object. In such cases, the good internal object would be prominent over the bad internal object to the point at which the internal bad object does not seriously disrupt the self–object bond. Kohut (1984) points out that narcissistic patients do resist the activation of the self–object bond, but empathy for the resistance usually overcomes it. Kohut recommends empathically demonstrating to the patient how the resistance served to protect the enfeebled sense of self from narcissistic injury at the hands of faulty self–objects. As the self–object transference becomes stabilized, it is disrupted, for the most part, only by traumatic or nontraumatic failures in empathy on the part of the therapist self–object. The therapist can reestablish the self–object bond by empathizing with the patient's disappointment and by identifying how the current failure in empathy recalled, to the patient, past failures in empathy on the part of the self–object.

I would say that the external self–object bond reinforces the internal positive self and object representation unit over the negative self and object representation unit. In this sense, splitting and projective identification serve to strengthen self and object constancy. Traumatic and nontraumatic empathic failures by the therapist tend to temporarily activate the bad object and antidependent self. If traumatic failures in empathy predominate in the treatment, they would reinforce the negative self and object representation unit and work against object constancy. If most of the therapist's failures in empathy are nontraumatic and are ameliorated by the therapist's empathy, they will serve to integrate positive and negative self and object representation units. Self and object constancy are thereby furthered.

Kohut (1977) describes narcissistic patients for whom one pole of the bipolar self has been irreparably damaged by traumatic failures in empathy by the original self–objects and is no longer available for activation in the self–object transference. In such cases, the other pole can be activated in the transference and can compensate for the damage to the self structure. In my view, the damaged pole of the bipolar self is unavailable for the activation of the self–object transference, not just because of extreme trauma in the past at the hands of external self–objects; rather, the traumatizing self–objects of the past have been internalized as bad objects, and actively and currently reject the "damaged" pole of the self's need for a self–object.

The self–object, or symbiotic, transference always reflects the splitting of internalized self and object representation units. The activation of a mirroring or idealizing transference reflects the dominance of the positive self and object representation unit. In considering the self–object transference as a manifestation of splitting, I agree with Kernberg. However, I disagree with his view that splitting and projective identification in the self–object transference are always destructive to self and object constancy. When the positive self and object representations have become sufficiently internalized to dominate over the negative self and object representation unit, a limited period of splitting in the transference can serve to reinforce self and object constancy by providing a foundation for integrating self and object representation units under the dominance of the strengthened positive unit. Therefore, I agree with Kohut (1971, 1977, 1984), Giovacchini (1986a), and Searles (1986) on the therapeutic value of symbiosis. Splitting is destructive of self and object constancy both when the negative self and object representation unit dominates over the positive self and object representation unit (ambivalent symbiosis) and when the dominance of the positive self and object representation unit becomes too prolonged and does not give way to integrating the positive and negative units.

In the case of the narcissistic personality, Kohut's approach attempts to bypass the pole of the bipolar self that is dominated by the bad internal object situation and to strengthen that pole in which the good internal object situation dominates. The damaged pole can be understood as a pocket of borderline pathology. Kohut believes that the damaged pole cannot activate a stable self–object transference but instead will manifest further self fragmentation and regression. I propose that the damaged pole, under the dominance of the internal bad object, activates a specific transference, that of ambivalent symbiosis. Activations of the positive self–object transference will immediately be followed by activations of the bad object transference as the antidependent self rejects the internalization of the positive-object therapist. What we will see is rapid oscillation of the all-good and all-bad self and object representation units. The self fragmentation is a manifestation of the internal bad-object situation. In a later chapter, this author will discuss one of Kohut's cases in which the mirroring pole of the bipolar self is irreparably damaged so that Kohut works with the more available idealizing pole. It will be demonstrated that the mirroring pole is a pocket of borderline pathology under the dominance of the internal bad object.

As Kohut and Basch have stated, the borderline patient cannot, unfortunately, be cured by empathy alone. Empathy serves an important therapeutic function in terms of mobilizing the vulnerable dependent self's need for mirroring and idealizing from the holding object. What is being said is that empathy activates the positive self and object representation unit. However, the internal bad object situation that immediately rejects the positive self and object representation unit must be directly and repeatedly subject to interpretation. In the borderline patient who cannot maintain a self–object transference, both poles of the bipolar self are governed by the internal bad object.

The dependent self's need for mirroring relates to the child's need for support for his individuation and autonomy. The vulnerable self's need for an idealized object refers to the child's need for dependence upon a strong, reliable other as he discovers the vulnerability associated with autonomy. Initially, as it was shown in Chapter 1, vulnerability and autonomy are inevitably closely interrelated in rapprochement, the fixation point for the borderline personality. As I pointed out earlier, the borderline patient experienced rejection at both of these poles of mirroring/ autonomy and idealizing/vulnerability because of how closely they are associated in rapprochement. Therefore, both poles are under the influence of the internal bad object, which rejects the self–object bond. The poles of the narcissistic personality are more separate because, as I will show later, those patients are fixated at a later point in ego development, on the way toward object constancy, when the poles of vulnerability and autonomy are more distinct.

A CLINICAL THEORY OF
THERAPEUTIC SYMBIOSIS

I propose that the phase of therapeutic symbiosis can be divided into two parts. Initially, the vulnerable self is increasingly related to the therapist as holding object. The internal positive self and object representation unit is increasingly dominant over the negative self and object representation unit as long as the external therapist is highly available to reinforce the strengthening of the positive unit. During this early phase of therapeutic symbiosis, the patient feels increasingly less vulnerable to the persecution of the bad object. As one patient said, "So long as everything is all right between you and me, I feel that all is well with the world." The good internal object serves to neutralize the bad, persecutory, rejecting object. In unconscious fantasy, the patient experiences himself as loved and protected by the good breast.

In the latter part of therapeutic symbiosis, the patient internalizes and identifies with the positive object image of the therapist to the point at which he is no longer so dependent upon the external therapist. This would be Kohut's phase of self–object transference and transmuting internalization of the self–object functions. In Kohut's terminology, the patient can now increasingly comfort, soothe, and mirror himself, regulating his own affect, mood, and self-esteem. In unconscious fantasy, he is now the good breast and the oral self, the comforter, sympathizer, mirror, and holder, as well as the comforted, empathized with, mirrored, and held. In Jacobson's terminology, these self-representations are expanded to take in the idealization of the object, and ego interests, ambitions, and narcissism are thereby strengthened. All goodness is taken into the self; all badness is projected into the external object world. The grandiose self (Kohut 1971), the fantasy of the internal good breast (M. Klein 1940), and the idealized self-representation (Jacobson 1964) are all analogous concepts related to the latter part of therapeutic symbiosis.

Freud (1925) stated:

Originally the property to be decided about might be either "good" or "bad," "useful" or "harmful." Expressed in the language of the oldest, that is, of the oral, instinctual impulses, the alternative runs thus: "I should like to eat that, or I should like to spit it out;" or carried a stage further, "I should like to take this into me and keep that out of me." That is to say, it is to be either *inside* of me or *outside* of me. As I have shown elsewhere, the original pleasure-ego tries to introject into itself everything that is good and to reject from itself everything that is bad. From its point of view what is bad, what is alien to the ego, and what is external are, to begin with, identical. [p. 183]

Freud's statement of normative early psychic mechanisms can be translated into object relations terms: The child tries to take in or internalize the good object and reject or externalize the bad object. In the model I'm developing of the negative therapeutic reaction, the borderline patient manifests an inversion of the normative developmental process. Instead of taking in the positive object relations unit and rejecting the negative object relations unit, he takes in the negative object relations unit and rejects the positive object relations unit. In Fairbairn's terms, he is attached to the internal bad object. The out-of-contact phase and ambivalent symbiosis are manifestations of the pathological inverted symbiosis in terms of the attachment to the bad object and rejection of the good object. Symbiosis becomes therapeutic when the patient adopts the normative but primitive developmental position of taking in all that is good and rejecting all that is bad. In this way, the patient can establish a psychic foundation to eventually integrate the good and bad object relations unit.

In normative symbiosis, the parent serves, for a time-limited period, as an extension of the child. Winnicott speaks of this phase in terms of the parent fulfilling the child's wish in such a way that the child experiences himself as creating the fulfillment. In Kohut's terminology, the parent mirrors the grandiose self of the child. Infantile omnipotence is seen as promoting development. Both Giovacchini and Searles have stressed that in pathological symbiosis, the parent does not assume the position of an extension of the child or of a self–object; rather, the parent turns to the child as a self–object or as an extension of the parent. Instead of providing the child with comforting, soothing, and mirroring, the parent turns to the child for those same needs. Therefore, the child is viewed by the parent as a transferential object. In this way, the child internalizes the parent's perception of himself as an object (of the parent). He becomes an extension of the parent and accepts or rejects himself based upon his perception of the internal object's acceptance or rejection of him. It is through experiencing the object as an extension of the self, or as a self–object, that the child arrives at a subjective sense of self. The borderline patient's lack of subjective sense of self is related to his experience of himself as an extension, transference object, or mirror of the parent.

4

Clinical Cases
in the Literature

This chapter will illustrate how the perspective of the bad object
serves as an effective explanatory model to further existing theoretical frameworks. Toward this end, cases from Basch, Kernberg,
Kohut, and Masterson will be reviewed.

MICHAEL BASCH:
THE CASE OF MRS. ELBOGEN

Basch (1980) reports that Mrs. Elbogen was a socially prominent
woman in her mid-30s. She was referred by her physician for
treatment of a serious drinking problem (pp. 110–118). She saw
him in consultation but did not at first follow through for treatment, denying the seriousness of her problem. Basch states that
"she spoke disparagingly of psychotherapists who make patients
slavishly dependent on them, something she did not intend to have
happen to her" (p. 111).

Basch did not defend his work but instead inquired about her life. At first she responded factually, but then she became bitter as she discussed how her parents, husband, suitor, and friends were to blame for her dissatisfied state. She did not intend to continue to see Basch. Several months later, however, she was involved in a traffic accident while intoxicated. In order to be treated leniently by the court, she agreed to seek help at an alcoholic treatment facility and then to pursue psychotherapy. She sought Basch as a therapist.

Although she was materially secure, the patient's background was full of emotional deprivation. Her parents traveled extensively to pursue business affairs, and the children were left with a series of babysitters. The patient reported having been a lonely child, constantly tortured by her older brothers. Although she was surrounded by numerous toys, she did not enjoy play and was not attached to any other child or pet. Primary school was marked by her inability to learn and by her inability to get along with peers or teachers.

As an adolescent she was repeatedly expelled from boarding schools because of her inability to fulfill scholastic requirements. She could not concentrate and was anxious about failure, so she'd behave as if she didn't care, and rebel.

After completing high school, she married a socially prominent man, and although they appeared in public to be the ideal couple, behind closed doors they quarreled constantly. She took a lover, and was indifferent when her husband left her. But when her lover later refused to marry her, she fell apart and began to drink heavily. She called her physician with somatic complaints at all hours of the night. At this point she was referred to Basch for the initial consult.

Basch attempted to see her in intensive psychotherapy three times weekly. Her typical attitude in treatment was that "nothing ever works out for me" (p. 114). She resented coming to see him, believing that since she was no longer drinking, her problems were resolved. Her mood was tense and angry, and she spoke in an accusing tone, as if Basch were to blame for her problems.

Basch tried to involve her in intensive treatment but concluded that:

The patient was definitely not a candidate for dynamic therapy, but I did my best to support her defenses and to strengthen them where I could. Usually she was angry about something, and I would try to help her see the significance of her anger and to gain a realistic perspective on the situation that caused it. One day she came in furious at a hairdresser because he had missed an appointment. She felt that it was a slight that she could avenge only by taking her business elsewhere, and she was already agitated over the prospect of having to find someone new. [p. 115]

Basch encouraged her to spare herself the agitation of finding someone new until she at least learned what had happened. She was later informed by a reliable source that on his way to work the hairdresser had saved a child from drowning. She did not broach this spontaneously in the next session; Basch had to inquire about it. Inconveniences continued to be taken as personal attacks, and recollection of the dramatic event with the hairdresser was not effective. Basch argues that patients such as Mrs. Elbogen do not benefit from repeated exposure where their emotional liability is concerned. He writes, "To say the least, this was not a satisfying therapeutic encounter for me. One cannot help being affected by the experience of being ineffective and of seeing one's efforts misunderstood" (p. 115).

Shortly afterward, the patient reduced her three-times-weekly therapy to once a week and then discontinued treatment when she met an older, fatherly man who devoted himself to her care. The treatment had helped the patient to behave less impulsively and self-destructively and to make a more positive object choice. Basch learned in later follow-up with the patient's husband that she had continued to refrain from drinking and was not engaging in self-destructive behavior. Although her husband was shielding her from life's hardships, she remained tense, angry, and highly over-sensitive to minor slights from him, to which she would react by disappearing into her room for days at a time. Nevertheless, she maintained her general level of adjustment.

Comments on Mrs. Elbogen

This patient is similar to cases which I have treated in terms of her chronic tense, angry mood, her sensitivity to imagined slights, and her generally negative attitude. Basch's view of the patient's history is similar to my own understanding of the background of such patients. He emphasizes that the patient was emotionally neglected, and that material provisions were given to compensate for the neglect. In my point of view, the borderline patient is not simply rewarded for dependence and rejected for autonomy, as described by the American object relations school. I agree with Basch that such patients experience rejection of their need for the good self–object.

I also agree with Basch's remarks concerning the patient's difficulty in establishing a meaningful self–object transference. As he points out, she had difficulty perceiving any of her external objects in a positive light. Basch states that he attempted to support and strengthen her defenses. However, her predominant defense was that of splitting the object into all bad. Her severe splitting caused her to view the external object world from a paranoid-schizoid position. Support of her defenses would thereby serve to strengthen the internal bad-object situation.

Basch suggests that the patient took inconveniences as personal attacks. I would add that the attack reported in the case actually emanated from herself, the internal bad object projected onto the hairdresser as a way of attacking her by standing her up. Basch describes the patient's early parental objects as abandoning, and neglecting her. The early bad object who abandoned and neglected her remains alive and active in her mind and is projected into any external object whose behavior may—even only remotely—fit the description of the object who abandons her. In viewing the object as all bad and abandoning, she rejects the external object in turn. In so doing, she remains attached to the bad object by eliminating the possibility of finding and internalizing the good object. In my view, the therapist must interpret the splitting and projective identification of the bad object immediately, emphasizing how the patient inevitably turns the hoped-for good object into a bad object. In later chapters, how therapists can intervene with patients such as Mrs. Elbogen will be described.

Recall that in the initial consultation, the patient referred to therapists as making patients slavishly dependent upon them. Shortly thereafter, however, she spoke of dependent relationships with family and friends who had disappointed her. Could she have been referring to two different types of internal self and object dependency units—one that is dangerous, slavish, and unacceptable, and another that is disappointing but less dangerous and more acceptable? This question might have been important to the overall treatment outcome in that Mrs. Elbogen dropped out of therapy once she became involved in a dependent relationship with a protective older man. This relationship was more acceptable than the slavish dependence she feared in therapy.

Basch points out that the patient's fatherly mate provided her with material comforts, but she nevertheless constantly imagined that he was slighting her, and she would withdraw to her room for days. It seems to me that her relationship to him was governed by her internal relation to the rejecting object. It will be recalled that the patient's parents had neglected her emotionally and had provided her with material objects to compensate for their absence. In her relationship to her mate, she imagined herself to be rejected by projectively identifying the rejecting internal object into him. Perceiving him as emotionally rejecting her, she would withdraw and remain alone, just as she had been left alone by her parents. At the same time, she had material objects to compensate for her abandonment, just as she had had in childhood. The material security, in both instances, also enabled her to deny vulnerability and the need for autonomy. Therefore, the relationship to the new protective mate was in compliance with the internal rejecting object.

She concluded treatment with an antidependent compromise. She maintained a general level of adjustment within the limitations of her borderline condition and established an external relationship with a mate that was in compliance with the internal rejecting object. Her adjustment was adaptive in the sense that she was able to stop her self-destructive behavior.

HEINZ KOHUT AND A CASE OF RESISTANCE

In his last book, Kohut (1984) reports on a case to specifically illustrate self psychology's views on resistance and defense (pp. 115–116).

The case concerns a middle-aged lawyer who is described as a narcissistic personality. The patient came from an intact family and had one younger brother. His mother was described as a rigid, cold person who had run the family in strict, regimented, military fashion, but at the same time provided for the family's material needs. Kohut emphasizes that she was not sadistic and could, on occasion, give of herself emotionally if her own needs were being met. She therefore had not completely failed the patient as a self–object. She was attached to the patient's brother, who was more physically graceful and attractive than he. She provided this sibling with much mirroring for his physical grace, but she also dominated him. The patient had received little in the way of mirroring from his mother, but he also was able to avoid her intrusiveness. He viewed her as "a little crazy" and walled himself off.

Kohut describes two traumatic experiences that the patient had suffered at his mother's hands. Once he awoke from a nightmare in which he had fallen from a tall building. He woke his mother for comfort, but she dragged him outside to look for the tallest building in the neighborhood. She took the terrified child to the top of that building so that he would no longer be afraid. The second trauma was a more chronic occurrence. His mother had given him enemas every morning throughout his childhood to regulate his bowel movements.

The patient's father was quite successful in business and enjoyed life outside of the family. He escaped from family life in order to avoid his wife's domination, and he remained an unavailable figure for his children. The patient recalled a significant event from his childhood in which his father had been romping playfully in the basement with the children when his mother appeared, gave the father a cold, fixed stare, and the father timidly wandered off.

The patient's mother had denigrated both the father and their son but had idealized her own father. He was ambitious and hard-working and had made a success of his life. In old age he became feeble. The mother criticized his weakness and old age but still idealized the power, strength, and resolve of his youth. The family spent summer vacations at the grandparents' home, so the patient got to know his grandfather during the vacations and also from his mother's stories. During these vacations, the mother felt that her own needs were being met by her parents, so she was more relaxed and giving.

Kohut suggests that the patient was irreparably traumatized by his mother's lack of empathy throughout his life. The patient had given up his need for mirroring, but the idealizing pole of the bipolar self still searched for the idealized parental image and was therefore available to be activated in a self–object transference. Kohut reflects that the patient experienced less traumatic rejection of his idealization needs at the hands of father and grandfather. Because the latter had been an especially idealized figure, the patient still strove to further the cohesiveness of his sense of self by activating the grandfather image to idealize in the transference. Idealization would serve to compensate for the thwarted mirroring needs.

Kohut (1984) describes the following therapeutic process to illustrate self psychology principles of understanding and managing resistance. His patient informed him of a newfound ability to relate with greater warmth and responsiveness to the colleagues in his law office and to his wife and children. He also expressed greater warmth and positive regard toward Kohut than he had ever shown before. The patient gratefully attributed his newfound relatedness to the analyst; he believed that it had developed not only from insight, but also from the way in which the analyst spoke to him and empathically explored current situations before providing him with reconstructions of his past or explanations of his behavior. The patient added that on occasion, when he related more empathically to others, it occurred to him that the analyst would be pleased with him and that he had adopted the analyst's manner and general attitude (pp. 121–122).

Kohut continues:

The next session began, almost with the patient's first words, with
an attack on psychoanalysis. Analysts were dogmatic, [the patient]
said, forcing their opinions on their patients. Some analysts were
sicker than their patients—for example, an analyst about whom he
had read in a newspaper article had been psychotic, involved with
the law, and was ultimately put into prison, where he died. After
listening quietly to this tirade for awhile, I remarked that this
broadside against analysis was in striking contrast to the spirit in
which the previous session had ended and I wondered whether
there was not some meaningful connection between these two
antithetical attitudes. Specifically, I commented that his attack on
me must, in some way, be connected with his gratefully telling me
that, via an identification with me and in anticipation of the pleasure
I would experience when learning about his progress, he had been
acting in an increasingly relaxed and mature way. [p. 122]

Kohut describes how the patient immediately associated to a
memory of his days as a law student. He had participated in a
mock trial as attorney to the defendant. He led the audience and
participants on a false trail of evidence only to announce, to the
astonishment of everyone, that he had purposely misled them in
order to drive home a point about the case.

Kohut comments that the patient's recollection indicates that
the defense of turning passive into active—or attacking the other
when he feared that he, himself, was in danger of being attacked—
was a long standing character trait. He points out further that the
patient begins to activate mirroring needs in the transference by
anticipating the therapist's pleasure in learning of his positive
identification with him and of his progress. However, anticipating
rejection from the therapist as he had previously been rejected by
his mother, he turns the tables on the therapist and analyzes
analysis and ridicules analysts. Kohut points out that the turning
of passive into active is an ingrained characteristic of the patient's
personality, as was evidenced in his memory of the mock trial.
Kohut believes that the patient's mirroring needs are no longer
available to be activated in the transference, because he has turned

passive into active in order to protect himself from his mother's intrusiveness and rejection.

Kohut discusses two dreams of the patient to support this view. In the first dream, the patient is lying in front of a motel, trying to sleep, and in his restlessness becomes partly uncovered and uncomfortable under the critical, rejecting gaze of the passersby. The dream suggests the patient's anticipation of rejection of exhibition-istic mirroring needs.

In the second dream, the patient is standing on a podium at an attorneys' convention. He is awarded a camera, and to the stunned surprise of the audience, turns the camera on them and snaps a picture. So, instead of allowing himself the pleasurable acclaim of the audience, he turns the tables and mirrors *them*. Kohut contends that the patient walls off the exhibitionistic grandiose self by turning passive into active, an adaptive response to protect his self-esteem in the anticipation of rejection.

Comments on Kohut's Case

It is true that the patient is unable to activate a mirroring self–object transference because of his vulnerability to rejection and intrusiveness. Kohut rightfully stresses that the patient's turning of passive to active is an ingrained personality trait and a defense against the need for mirroring. However, the patient's inability to activate a mirroring transference is not based primarily upon an enfeebled pole of the bipolar self. Rather, the need for mirroring is being rejected by the internal rejecting object. The ingrained personality trait of turning passive to active is the clinical mani-festation of the internal rejecting object.

Furthermore, Kohut even provides historical evidence of the antidependent identification with the rejecting object, although he nowhere explicitly states that the turning of passive to active is an identification with the rejecting mother. Rather, he comments that the ingrained personality trait is a defense against the rejecting, intrusive mother. The historical evidence for the antidependent identification refers to the patient's childhood trauma after report-ing the dream of falling from a building. The child had presented his vulnerable self to his mother for comfort, but his vulnerability had been explicitly rejected. She had forced him to deny vulnerability by turning passive to active. Therefore, his ingrained personality trait of turning the tables on the object is an expression of the antidependent self in compliance with the internal rejecting object.

Kohut's view of the impaired mirroring transference is that the patient began to activate it as was manifested in his experiencing pleasure in the patient's positive identification with him. The patient anticipated rejection and intrusiveness; he anticipated that the analyst would repeat the traumas of the original external self–object. He therefore walled himself off by the ingrained personality trait of turning passive to active, by analyzing and ridiculing analysis and aborted the mirroring transference.

In this view, Kohut neglects both the internal bad object and its activation in an ambivalent symbiotic transference. He states that the patient expects him to reject and intrude upon him as the original self–object had. However, in fact the patient has projectively identified the rejecting, intrusive mother onto the analyst and is now perceiving him as rejecting and intrusive. The patient, in turning passive to active, describes analysts as rejecting their patients' ideas and imposing their own ideas on the patients; he goes on to discuss a newspaper report of a psychotic analyst who was imprisoned. Kohut acknowledges that the patient is displacing anger from the analyst onto analysis in anticipation of rejection and intrusion. Kohut also reveals that the patient perceives his mother as crazy. Perhaps the patient is unconsciously perceiving Kohut as the psychotic, intrusive, rejecting mother-analyst. By turning the camera on the analysis, by analyzing the analyst, the patient has begun to analyze his crazy, rejecting, psychotic mother in the transference. The patient has activated a particular self and object representation unit in the transference, that of the antidependent self-rejecting object.

Searles (1975) has discussed how the severely disturbed patient will sometimes attempt to activate a transference in which he becomes the therapist. In such instances, he projectively identifies the crazy, bad internal object into the therapist and attempts to cure the crazy object through his criticisms of the object's intrusiveness and rejections. In this form of ambivalent symbiosis, the patient attempts to subtly induce in the therapist a faulty response. In this way the patient expresses his ambivalence about maintaining his tie to the original crazy object or establishing a healthier, more positive object relationship. He hopes that the therapist will respond with less rejection and intrusiveness than the original object had, and that the therapist will be responsive to the patient's criticisms and thereby allow the patient the sense that he is curing the bad internal object. Once the patient feels a degree of success in curing the internal bad object, he can increasingly permit the vulnerable needs (in this case, for mirroring) to come to the fore in relation to the cured internal mirroring object. In this way, the antidependent rejecting object gradually gives way to the positive mirroring self and object images. This shift does not occur all at once; rather, it takes place through the rapid fluctuations of positive and negative self and object images of ambivalent symbiosis.

Kohut's narcissistic patient expressed a high level of internalization of the positive object through identification. The positive internalization was immediately followed by rejection of the positive internal object through denigration of analysis. The more disturbed borderline patient exhibits internalization, not through such high levels of identification, but rather through thinking of the therapist for a fleeting moment in a comforting or admiring way. I emphasize *for a fleeting moment* because the patient will then reject the positive internal object either by turning it all-bad or by obliterating it from consciousness by forgetting. Kohut believes that the patient rejects him because he has thought of pleasing him via the positive identification. I do not believe it was primarily the thought of pleasing the therapist that prompted the patient to reject him, but rather it was the *internalization* of the therapist as a positive object through *identification* that promoted the rejection. The patient was in compliance with the internal rejecting object by rejecting his own vulnerable need for an internal mirroring object. By turning the tables on the therapist, he allowed the internal mother to take him to the top of the roof again to deny vulnerability. Sitting on "top of the world," he could look down upon the therapist from his superior position. He rejected a positive mirroring relationship from a sadomasochistic relationship to the rejecting internal mother. However, in his criticisms and analysis of the rejecting mother, he also exhibits the hope of analyzing the bad object into a good one. Therefore, if the therapist were to assume the transference position of the bad object by allowing the patient to express his beliefs that the therapist is crazy, untrustworthy, and a charlatan, and the therapist would remain empathic and not reject the patient, the patient would come to trust the therapist and allow his mirroring needs to emerge in the transference. Subjectively, the patient would feel as if he were curing the crazy mother of her inability to mirror (Searles 1975).

Kohut states that he empathized with the patient's view of analysis as dogmatic and intrusive, and he comments upon the displacement of anger from the analyst to analysis. He considered the idealization pole of the bipolar self to be more accessible for transference activation, and he therefore accepted the position of the idealized grandfather image instead of pursuing the resistances to the mirroring image. Kohut points out that in the case of the narcissistic personality, if one pole of the bipolar self is not accessible, the other pole can be activated to compensate for the damaged self structure. In this author's view, he is thereby performing a psychic bypass over the borderline internal bad-object pathology, and his case reports indicate that this technique is effective for the narcissistic personality structure. However, the more disturbed borderline patient experiences ego fixation precisely at the point at which vulnerability (idealizing dependence) and autonomy (mirroring of individuation) are inherently interrelated. The rapprochement discovery of separateness is invariably associated with vulnerability. Only as the child becomes less vulnerable in his autonomy can we speak of a sharp division between mirroring and idealizing needs. The sharp division implies that either the self or the object has been more strongly idealized. The narcissistic patient presents a more or less stable mirroring or idealizing transference. The rapprochement youngster experiences rapid fluctuations between idealization of the self and object. When autonomy strivings predominate, the self is idealized. However, autonomy involves vulnerability, leading to idealization of the protective object. The borderline patient, like the rapprochement youngster, experiences idealizing and mirroring needs in rapid succession in the positive side of the ambivalent symbiotic transference. Both his autonomy and his vulnerability were rejected by the original external object, so that the internal rejecting object dominates over vulnerability and autonomy.

Therefore, in the treatment of such patients, there is no accessible pole of a bipolar self available to engage in a self–object transference. Rather, there is a self-representation that experiences vulnerability at autonomous strivings. The internal rejecting object rejects both autonomy and vulnerability. Therefore, the patient activates an ambivalent symbiotic transference with rapid fluctuations of vulnerability, autonomy, and antidependent rejection. The therapist must be able to accept both the good and the bad object transference activations in rapid succession. The internal bad-object situation must be identified and interpreted for the patient if he is to internalize the good object to the point at which he can activate a stable self–object or therapeutic symbiotic transference. Self psychology can be advanced by integrating it with the theory of internalized object relations, particularly taking into account the bad internal object.

OTTO KERNBERG:
THE CASE OF A DEMANDING PATIENT

Another patient who was seen in expressive psychotherapy demanded an increase of his hours in an extremely angry, defiant way. Over a period of time it was interpreted to him that it was hard for him to tolerate the guilty feelings over his own greediness, and he was projecting that guilt onto the therapist in the form of fantasies of being hated and depreciated by him. It was also interpreted that his demands to see the therapist more often represented an effort to reassure himself of the therapist's love and interest in order to neutralize his mistrust and suspiciousness of the therapist's fantasied hatred of him. The patient seemed to understand all this but was unable to change his behavior. The therapist concluded that the patient's oral aggression was being gratified in a direct way through these angry outbursts, and that this development might contribute to a fixation of the transference. The therapist told the patient of his decision not to increase the hours and at the same time presented as a condition for continuing the treatment that the patient exercise some degree of control over the form and appropriateness of the expression of his feelings in the hours. With the modification of technique in effect, a noticeable change occurred over the next few days. The patient became more reflective, and finally was even able to admit that he had obtained a great satisfaction for being allowed to express intense anger at the therapist in such a direct way. [pp. 85–86]

Kernberg explains, "The very fact that the therapist takes a firm stand and creates a structure which he will not abandon tends to enable the patient to differentiate the therapist from himself, and thus to undo the confusion caused by frequent exchange of self and object representations by the patient" (p. 87).

Kernberg emphasizes that the patient's request for extra sessions was based upon his wish to deny his view of the therapist as hating him and was intended to neutralize his mistrust of the therapist. Kernberg also remarks that guilt over his greed caused the patient to projectively identify his greed and rage into the therapist.

Comments on Kernberg's Case

The patient requested extra sessions because he was unable to maintain a positive image of the object, so he wished to reinforce that image by increasing his contact with the external representative. The angry and demanding way in which he requested the extra sessions reflects his internal conflict about taking in a positive object image. Therefore, he requests more contact in a manner that drives the object further away.

Here we can see that the patient projectively identifies hate into the therapist. The projection of hate into the object allows the patient to maintain a rejecting image of the object. A question can be raised about the therapist's threatening to discontinue the treatment unless the patient ceased his verbal assault. Kernberg says that the patient settled down and acknowledged the oral sadistic gratification he experienced by the attacks. One's concern is that the therapist is enacting the transference of the rejecting object and becoming the external ego, controlling the patient from the outside. Being controlled by an external object might be far less threatening to such a patient than internalizing the object. As will be seen in later vignettes, when the severely disturbed patient begins to internalize the therapist as a positive object, he begins to feel that the object is in control of his mind.

The vignette focuses on the patient's fear of loss of the all-good object, but he is equally afraid of merging with the good object. As Finell (1987) has pointed out, in the negative therapeutic reaction, the conflict between the longing for fusion and the wish for separateness is central. The patient in this vignette requests the extra contact in an angry and demanding way. The request for extra sessions expresses the longing for fusion, while the anger reveals the wish for separateness. In interpersonal terms, the patient seeks closeness while pushing the therapist away. In internal-object terms, the patient transforms the hoped-for good object into an exciting object (the insatiable need for extra contact) into a rejecting object. In his fear of merger with the hoped-for good object, he creates the exciting object that must inevitably become a rejecting object. Through the relationship with the rejecting object, he can fulfill the wish for separateness by creating distance with anger. The resulting fear of object loss will inevitably give rise to the wish for merger with the hoped-for good object, again giving rise to the vicious cycle of the wish for the hoped-for good object, the fear of merger with the exciting object, the transformation into the rejecting–rejected object, the fear of loss of the good object, the wish for merger with the hoped-for good object, and so on. Interpreting all aspects of this vicious cycle may result in the patient's internalizing the therapist as a positive object (therapeutic symbiosis) and then separating from the internal symbiotic object. The second part of this book will describe how the therapist interprets the vicious cycle of the longing for merger and the wish for separateness.

JAMES MASTERSON:
THE CASE OF CATHERINE

In two of his books, Masterson presents the case of Catherine. He treated Catherine for four years, once weekly during the initial two years and twice weekly for the third and fourth years. He notes (1976) that 22-year-old Catherine was referred by a colleague. She had received her college degree a year earlier but was now aimlessly running around, unable to make a decision about her life. On one hand, she was not able to live at home; on the other hand, she could not stay away. She lived like a nomad, temporarily with friends before moving on. She also had a pattern of having two boyfriends at the same time; one served as a caretaker, and the other as a sexual outlet. At the time of treatment she had Charlie, who would care for her material wants and for whom she felt affection but no sexual interest. Fred served as a sexual outlet, but she did not like him. When she was accepted by the college to which she had applied for graduate study, she elected not to go and instead sought psychiatric help.

Catherine's father, a successful broker, was a self-centered and domineering personality, and the family revolved around him. The patient's mother was described as dependent, helpless, and fearful, catering to the father's outbursts. Masterson comments that the patient had early shifted her dependency needs from the inadequate but engulfing mother to the strong father. Therefore, her father, and men in general, were cast in a symbiotic mothering, and not oedipal, role. The patient recalled that her father had been very interested in her as an infant and young child, but his interest had decreased as she grew older. She reported that the trouble had started when she began to walk and talk. He was oversolicitous about her material and physical well-being but completely oblivious to her interests and feelings. He indulged her with gifts more appropriate to his own interests than hers, and he sulked if she pointed this out. He was annoyed at her plans to live and work in the city and complained when she did not visit on the weekend. When she did visit, however, he ignored her.

Masterson records the tone of much of the treatment in his notes on the first sessions. He writes:

> Catherine immediately demonstrated the extraordinary transference fluctuations that occur in borderline patients by reporting that my writing as she spoke in the previous interview made me seem mechanical and non-personal and made her feel like crying. My writing, which took my exclusive attention away from her and exposed her to separation anxiety—anxiety about loss of the object—interrupted the projection of the wish for reunion fantasy—RORU—[The Rewarding Object Relations Unit] on me and triggered the WORU [the Withdrawing Object Relations Unit]. To set reality limits to this projection I stated I was doing my job and when I queried whether she felt this way before she recalled that when her father shouted at her she would cry instead of standing up to him, because, if she stood up to him, "We'll kill each other." She then reported hating his attacks, wishing him dead, but nevertheless loving him. She also reported memories of his attacking her, pulling her hair, throwing shoes at her. Catherine had thus defined the arena of therapeutic action. [p. 124]

Much of the treatment that followed involved Masterson's encouraging her to stand up for herself with her father and boyfriends, and interpreting her avoidance of responsibility as abandonment depression. He placed much emphasis on analyzing her father, showing how her father had made her dependent and continued to thwart her autonomy. He reports that during the seventh, eighth, and ninth interviews, he dealt with the patient's avoidance of finding her own apartment. He confronted her by saying that her nomadic behavior was symptomatic of her whole problem; she was avoiding dealing with anxiety about committing herself. She did not respond. He repeated the statement. She responded that "it must come from her overprotective parents but there is nothing wrong with that." He challenged her statement. The patient remained silent and cried. He then pointed out her resistance to facing the conflict with her mother and father, as evidenced by this response to his challenge of her stereotyped view. Suddenly she replied, "Today you said something that's

both familiar and unpleasant and you are getting closer to home"
(pp. 124–125).

After such interviews, the patient would run to one of her
boyfriends for comfort or sex. When she told Masterson this, he
confronted her repeatedly with how she was seeking out the
rewarding object in order to escape from what he was showing her
of the withdrawing object.

Masterson repeatedly confronted Catherine's negative transference as a displacement of what she was learning about her father or
as anger at him for forcing her to face her father as the withdrawing object. For example, when she said that she had had a cold
feeling about him all week, that he didn't care about her, Masterson interpreted that this was a transference projection of feelings
about her father that she had just begun to investigate (p. 130).

Masterson says that the patient suffered the abandonment depression of the WORU once she was faced with her parents' real
attitudes. She projected the WORU into the psychotherapy rather
than acknowledge her disappointment in her parents and she then
distanced herself from the therapy. She wanted to end the depression by terminating therapy and finding a man to depend upon
(pp. 133–134). Masterson made this comment about halfway
through the treatment, and it proved to be prophetic.

At the conclusion of the treatment report—which showed the
patient increasingly asserting herself with her father and boyfriends and becoming more autonomous—Masterson reports that
the patient worked through her abandonment depression and the
WORU and turned her life around. He states that she met a man
and after six months they decided to live together. His capacity for
intimacy was greater than hers, but she was aware of her own
limitations in loving and focused on this problem in therapy.
Finally she terminated treatment, intending to continue the work
on her own (pp. 159–160). Masterson concludes that Catherine
turned around, asserting herself with her father and on her job and
stopping the acting-out behavior with men. She married the man
she had been living with and worked as a teacher.

In Masterson's later book (1981), we find a follow-up on
Catherine. Masterson reports that she had returned to treatment

after two years and that he realized only then that her apparently appropriate termination was actually an episode of acting out. Catherine's relationship with her husband was fine. He was overly generous, constantly encouraging her to buy things, but he was also rather rigid and domineering, with little capacity for self-awareness or empathy. Masterson states, "This precarious balance was maintained for 18 months, until she broached the subject of having a baby and moving to a house in the suburbs." Her husband refused and Catherine reacted with depression and rage. "Shortly thereafter she met a fellow teacher who was everything her husband was not: responsive, emotional, in touch with his own feelings. She began an affair with him" (p. 207).

Masterson says that in terminating the treatment, Catherine had acted out a defense against separation/individuation by maintaining the idealized rewarding representation of the mother, while splitting off the abandoning representation. By marrying a man who enacted the good idealized father role, Catherine could maintain the fantasy of an all rewarding symbiotic relationship.

He points out that the fragile marital relationship fell apart with her wish for a baby. She then projected the abandoning object into her husband and the rewarding object into her new lover. The lover demanded that she either give up her husband or their affair. She could not take responsibility for herself or her wishes, so she returned to Masterson (p. 208).

In a series of consultation interviews, Masterson empathized with the environmental and intrapsychic difficulties presented in the conflict between the marriage and the affair, but he suggested that the motivation for the consultation was the same as that for the affair: she was disappointed in both her husband and her lover, since neither would take responsibility for her welfare. She now turned to Masterson in the hope that he would rescue her.

Masterson concludes:

Within a very short time, it became clear that she really had no more motivation to work on the problem now than she had when she left treatment, that she really didn't want to do anything about giving up this fantasy and becoming responsible for herself. I

pointed out that to continue treatment knowing that sort of motivation would be to collude with it, and I thought it would be better
if she stopped until she could make some decision. After several
interviews she agreed to stop, saying that she thought she would
end the affair since she didn't really want to make any decision
regarding treatment; i.e., working to become independent. I have
not heard from her since. [pp. 208–209]

Comments on Masterson's Case

Searles (1979) has discussed how the schizophrenic patient sometimes talks to himself (or his internal object) instead of to the
therapist in order to create distance. Searles also remarks that the
therapist can become self-absorbed in various subtle maneuvers to
distance the patient. In the opening sessions, Masterson makes
notes, and the patient complains of his distancing. Masterson does
not discuss countertransferential schizoidlike distancing maneuvers in the face of the patient's merging needs. His focus is on the
patient's intense fluctuating transference and the need to limit the
projection of the rewarding object in the transference.

For much of the treatment Masterson directs the patient to
stand up to her father. He creates a split in the transference by
presenting himself as the father object who supports autonomy
and rejects dependence and by analyzing the real external father
as rewarding dependence and rejecting autonomy. He brings
home to her the withdrawing image of the external father, confronting her time and again with her father's rejection of her
autonomy. When she becomes angry at him, he invariably interprets her anger as a displacement of her rage at her father.
This technique is faithful to Masterson's theoretical view that
borderline pathology results from the external object's rejection
of autonomy and promotion of dependence. Masterson never
explores with the patient the issue of whether her father also
rejected her vulnerability and dependence. The father is aloof and
disinterested when Catherine complies to his demands to visit him
on weekends but Masterson ignores the father's schizoid detachment.

Masterson views Catherine's dependency needs completely from the perspective of a retreat from abandonment depression. His interpretations and confrontations focus upon the patient's father as an external object rewarding dependence and rejecting autonomy in their real interpersonal relationship. Of course, the patient should be shown how external objects in the present and past impede autonomy; however, the patient also needs to see that she identifies with such objects and does to herself what they do to her. The patient's description of external objects also cannot be taken at face value; often the external object is distorted by the projective identification of the internal object. Masterson originally describes his patient's husband as having a greater capacity for love, of teaching her about love and providing her with an emotionally sustaining relationship. It could be said that Masterson's description of the husband at this point is based on the patient's projective identification of the hoped-for good object into the external husband.

In his next discussion, Masterson describes the patient's husband as being overly generous in meeting his wife's insatiable material needs, but also as authoritarian, emotionally unempathic, rigid, and insensitive. It seems that the patient is exhibiting extreme splitting of the internal object. Yet Masterson seems to take the description of the external object at face value. Catherine's various descriptions of her husband clearly illustrate the sequential transformations of the internal bad object. The husband is initially described as a hoped-for good object in his capacity for intimacy. When Catherine returned to Masterson, we find the husband now transformed into the exciting object, who showers her with material gratification, and then as the rejecting object, who refuses her a baby, and finally as the rejected object, who is authoritarian, rigid, and insensitive. The cycle then begins again, with the hoped-for good object being projectively identified into the sensitive, empathic lover. Perhaps it is possible that the hoped-for good object will next be transformed into an exciting, then rejecting, then rejected object.

The transformation of the hoped-for good object into an exciting object is under the direction of the internal bad object. The hoped-for good object is a positive self–object or holding object in the sense of promising empathy, holding vulnerability, and mirroring autonomy. The internal bad object aborts the good object by creating the omnipotent need to sadomasochistically control the exciting object. The internal bad object attacks the patient's vulnerable, dependent need for a good holding mirroring object. The internal bad object ridicules the patient's vulnerability and dependence as weakness. The unconscious commandment of the internal bad object is that the self component should be in omnipotent sadomasochistic control and never vulnerable toward the object. The self component is not permitted to care about the object but instead is directed to use it as a means to gratification. The impossibility of achieving omnipotent control over the object creates the inevitable disappointment and frustration and transformation into the exciting, rejecting, rejected object.

Masterson does not permit the patient to develop an ambivalent and therapeutic symbiotic transference. After each session, the patient runs to her boyfriends. Masterson asserts to her that she is trying to run from the withdrawing object image with which he had confronted her to the rewarding object. She is running to an external symbiotic object because Masterson explicitly rejects the symbiotic transference. Her need for him as a symbiotic object was evident in the first sessions, when she requested that he stop taking notes and provide her with his undivided attention and empathy. He set the tone of the rejection of her symbiotic needs by his immediate effort to confront her with the unrealistic need for the all-good, rewarding object relations unit. Given his rejection of her symbiotic needs, it is no surprise that she increasingly enacted those needs with external objects until she left treatment. Even if Masterson had not put his note-taking between himself and the patient, or if he discontinued doing so in response to her protest, she would have increasingly demanded his undivided attention until he inevitably disappointed her, at which point he would have been transformed into the rejecting–rejected object. If the therapist does not immediately confront and reject the exciting object transference, then the inevitability of the rejecting object transference arising out of insatiable need can be clearly demonstrated to the patient. The therapist interferes with this process if he becomes the rejecting object instead of waiting for the patient to transform his image into rejecting and rejected. In this way, the therapist can interpret the way in which the exciting, rejecting, and rejected configurations serve the bad object to defend against internalizing a positive self–object or holding object symbiotic transference. The patient can thereby enact all of these transformations within the transference instead of acting them out with objects external to the treatment.

5

The Dynamics
of the Bad Object

The following case discussions will elaborate on the bad object's rejection of the internal positive self and object representation unit. They will show how oblivion to the therapist and acting-out behavior in the severely borderline patient can be a manifestation of antidependent regression to the practicing subphase of separation–individuation in order to reject the vulnerable, libidinal self-holding object unit of rapprochement.

KIM

This case report focuses on the first three years of Kim's intensive twice-weekly treatment. Kim is a 22-year-old, white, Irish-American female.

Kim was referred to me by a colleague after she had had five years of twice-weekly psychotherapy. He reported that Kim never developed a workable transference and maintained a pattern of missing appointments without calling to cancel. She abused alcohol and illegal drugs at periodic intervals and did not work or attend school. The therapist was concerned about Kim's lack of progress and inability to function. She expressed no motivation to change and used therapy sessions to boast about antisocial and destructive behavior. For instance, she boasted of tempting a friend, struggling to conquer a drug habit, into again using illegal drugs. She also engaged in behavior that threatened her own and others' safety. Although she did not have a driver's license, she would "steal" her mother's car when drunk. The therapist had therefore recommended residential treatment or psychiatric hospitalization out of concern for her safety, but Kim and her mother refused.

He reported that over the first three years of her treatment, he tried to engage her by understanding her world view and empathizing with her feelings that current and past significant objects failed her. He stated that although she viewed him as supportive and as "the only one on her side," her acting-out behavior increased and her already poor functioning worsened. Her attitude was "Who can blame me for messing up with all I've been through." He attempted to interpret how she held on to a victimized position for fear of growing up, but to no avail. He increasingly confronted her self-destructive behavior and fear of autonomy, but she replied that she had no interest in autonomy and was not concerned about her self-destructiveness. During this period he recommended residential treatment or hospitalization and referred the case to me. He felt that he and Kim had reached a therapeutic impasse, and they agreed that she should see another therapist. He did not discontinue the treatment because he was giving up on her, but rather because of his concern for her well being and his hope that a new therapeutic experience might help her.

I scheduled Kim for twice-weekly appointments, and for the first 15 months of her treatment she regularly missed sessions without calling to cancel.

History

Kim was an only child in an intact family. Kim's mother alternately neglected and overindulged her. During Kim's first years of life, her mother often ran out of the house to escape a psychotic husband, leaving Kim in the hands of her maternal grandparents, who lived in the same apartment building. The mother would promise to return later in the evening, but she sometimes stayed away for days at a time. Kim therefore had repeated experiences of awaking to find herself abandoned by her mother. She grew to hate falling asleep if her mother was present, and she had frequent tantrums, insisting that her mother sleep with her. During latency she would cry until taken to bed with her parents. She slept in the parental bed until puberty. Thus her difficulty was not simply an overindulgence of dependency, but was rather an overindulgence following earlier neglect and abandonment. Kim did not have tantrums simply to avoid the separation from the parental objects at bedtime. For her, going to sleep meant waking up abandoned. She therefore attempted to gain omnipotent control over her parents in order to avoid the vulnerability associated with abandonment anxiety.

Kim's psychotic father had delusions that he was Jesus Christ and that demons possessed him. He underwent psychiatric hospitalization, and his condition was finally stabilized with psychotropic medication.

Kim's mother went to work when Kim was 3 years old, leaving her at home with her father, who was on disability. He would ignore her as he read the Bible or sat in a catatonic-like stupor. If she disturbed him with her romping and playing, sometimes designed to get his attention, he would beat her. He attempted to intimidate her with physical force, but she refused to submit and would defy him, trying never to cry.

The family was always concerned that since Kim resembled her father in physical appearance, she was destined to suffer from the same psychiatric illness. When she quit high school and did not work, they became unhappily convinced that she was on the same path as her father.

Throughout childhood, Kim was on a merry-go-round in her relationships with her family members. First she would side with her mother against her father. When her mother upset her, she would go to her father and side against her mother. When her father upset her, she'd go to her grandfather and side against everyone. When her grandfather upset her, she'd go to her grandmother and side against her grandfather.

As an adolescent, Kim took no interest in learning at school but instead "hung out" with peers and smoked marijuana daily. She dropped out of high school at the age of 16. Her father died a year later. Kim felt indifferent about his death. She began to have paranoid episodes when she used marijuana, so she began to abuse alcohol instead.

On the Run in the Transference

When this therapist started to treat Kim, her life had little structure. Her mother who was busy working two jobs and was involved in a very active social life would see me on occasion as a collateral but was unwilling to commit herself to regular treatment. Kim did not sleep at night but remained awake until she was exhausted. Often she would sleep through the day, but even this was not a stable pattern.

Kim could not tolerate being alone and had a set of telephone pals. She had an insomniac paraplegic friend whom she could call at any hour. She enjoyed going on drinking bouts with her peers, but they were becoming somewhat less available as they grew older.

Kim's chief complaint was that "everyone" becomes busy with his own life and eventually abandons her. Therefore her internal rejecting object was a busy object who put her last. The internal object was based on her real mother, who was frequently too busy for her.

Kim acted out the antidependent defense against internalizing the positive therapist object in identification with the busy rejecting object. In the first 15 months of her treatment, when Kim could be busy with friends, she'd forget her sessions, becoming oblivious to the therapist.

In therapy and on telephone contacts, Kim would recount past and present adventures with peers. She was constantly on the run, physically and mentally. I often felt as if my mind raced to keep up with hers. She did not seek mirroring in terms of admiration of her adventures. She usually seemed unaware of my presence, so long as she knew I was still there. On the telephone, racing through events, she might suddenly stop to check that I was still there. She would describe her adventures in minute detail, as if she were reliving them in the telling. My position as an object was that of a witness as opposed to an admirer. Her mode of interaction in the transference–countertransference brought to mind Mahler's practicing subphase of separation–individuation. She described (1975) the practicing youngster as on the run, elated by his own physical activity and dexterity, oblivious to mother so long as he could assure himself of her presence by returning for periodic refueling. Kim therefore displayed mirroring needs on the primitive, practicing level of checking back for the object's continued presence as she raced through her adventures.

Kim would sometimes request that I return her call at a certain hour. When I called, her mother would say that she had "disappeared again" and that it was "anyone's guess" as to when she would return. Her need to check back would prevent her from staying away for long. In this sense, she became oblivious to the object until the need to check back emerged.

In her adventures, Kim sometimes assumed an invulnerable position. She could take a subway alone through two boroughs at midnight, oblivious to concern for her safety. She would "steal" her mother's car and drive while drunk. In such instances she had some degree of control (and luck) in that no harm came to her. Mahler (1975) describes how the practicing child sometimes darts off, oblivious to danger, forcing the mother to give chase. In the transference–countertransference, I often felt that I had to give chase and stop Kim. Sometimes I did so by informing Kim's mother that Kim had endangered herself and others. At other times, I attempted to persuade Kim's mother to hospitalize her for a brief period.

Kim showed the first sign of internalizing a positive object image of the therapist by writing about me in her diary. She wrote for the first time about missing her father and wishing that she had a father like me. Her vulnerability and autonomy emerged as she became concerned that her life was "going nowhere" and wished that she could work or attend school.

The Closed, Invulnerable Position of the Bad Object

About four months into the treatment, immediately following the internalizing of a positive object image (with associated vulnerability and autonomous strivings), she cut her wrist with a razor (not a suicide attempt). As she watched the blood flow, she felt invulnerable and powerful. After this act, Kim became submissive and apologetic. She even agreed to a psychiatric evaluation, something she had always refused because she was not a "nut case" like her father. She pleaded with me not to drop her as a patient, and the overall quality of her behavior was very much like that of Justine, who would attempt a rapprochement after verbally attacking me.

Kim's self-destructive act could be viewed in terms of Basch's statement that the borderline patient becomes overwhelmed and is unable to tolerate the insinuation of the therapist into his life as a meaningful person. This description is correct. However, I do not think that the patient is overwhelmed because of an enfeebled self; rather, the self-mutilation is an antidependent attack against the vulnerable, libidinal self's expressed need for an internal holding object. The antidependent self thereby reestablishes a closed, internal, invulnerable position.

Dwelling on the Rejecting Object

The first phase in Kim's transference evolution, termed by Searles the out-of-contact phase, was marked by the practicing phenomenon of obliviousness to the therapist while on the run. The internalized object relations were dominated by the activation of the all-bad self and object representation unit. Her external object world was more bad than good in reality. Kim's mother was often too busy and preoccupied with her own problems to provide her with the attention and care she needed. Her friends were self-absorbed and related to one another on a need-satisfying level. However, Kim was constantly preoccupied with how her friends and family rejected, exploited, and did not care about her. She would dwell on the rejecting object and rejected, unimportant self-image throughout the day and so would remain in a depressive, victimized position. When her mother or a friend disappointed her, she would fluctuate between rage and depression. When the all-bad self and object representation unit became activated by the external relationship to her mother, she would run to her peers. When disappointed by one peer, she would run to another. Even when the external object did not in reality reject her, Kim interpreted the situation as rejection. When she was away for a couple of days, she would call her mother and ask, "What are you doing?" When her mother replied that she was watching television, Kim would say, "So you *are* too busy!" and hang up before her mother could respond. She would expect her mother to sit up all night to comfort her after she was rejected by a boyfriend. When her mother finally said that she had to get some sleep because of work the next day, Kim would activate the all-bad self and object unit and become enraged and depressed. She would bolt from the room, blaming her mother for not caring. She would demand that her mother get her beer or cigarettes at midnight and when her mother refused, she would accuse her mother of not caring and run out of the house. All of this is not to say that the external objects did not often treat Kim badly; on the contrary, they often did. But Kim had her own need to perpetually activate the all-bad self and object unit.

Kim's running from mother to peers, then from one peer to the next, recapitulated her running from one family member to another in childhood. She was on a practicing merry-go-round, always on the run but going nowhere. While running to the next object she felt elated, reflecting the internal activation of the libidinal self-exciting object representation unit. Regarding the practicing subphase, Mahler (1975) says:

We might consider the possibility that the elation of this subphase has to do not only with the exercise of the ego apparatuses, but also

with the elated escape from fusion with, from engulfment by,
mother. . . . We need not assume such behavior is intended to serve
these functions when it first emerges, but only that it produces
these effects and can then be intentionally repeated. [p. 71]

By perceiving the object as all bad and fleeing, Kim was defending against her merger needs. The flight was an antidependent
rejection of the need to internalize a positive object. Making the
object all bad served the escape.

After the act of self-mutilation, Kim became involved with a
young man who was addicted to "crack" (cocaine). He possessed
the "bad" qualities of both Kim's parents. Like her mother, he was
always too busy with his friends to provide her with attention. He
often stood her up if an opportunity to use cocaine unexpectedly
arose. When they did meet, he would comfort her with bottles of
beer, just as her mother had given her bottles (of milk) in place of
herself until she was 7 years old. He would then take care of her,
undressing and showering her and putting her to bed. Like her
father, he was constantly in a drugged stupor and would experience sudden fits of rage.

Kim saw very little of this boyfriend, but she would dwell on
his rejecting or exciting image all day. She would thereby elaborate upon her worthlessness in relationship to his rejection. She
imagined that he rejected her because she was not pretty, because
she was too needy; she'd fantasize that he was with another girl.
She decided that if she kept her distance and rejected him, he
would become interested in her. She put this plan into action by
not returning his calls and standing him up. She proved to be
partially correct, as he would often chase after her. As soon as she
responded, however, he would distance himself. He became
another object on her merry-go-round. When she was angry at
her mother, she would run to him. She would then return to her
mother when he disappointed her.

The bad objects in her life were interchangeable. In dialogues
with me, she would begin discussing how the boyfriend rejected
her, then switch to how her mother and friends mistreated her. In
this way, she kept the bad, rejecting object—rejected self-

images—constantly activated. Her internal bad objects resulted in narcissistic disequilibrium of depression and rage. She would therefore drink or use drugs and go for a joyride in her mother's car or a midnight subway adventure in order to activate the dependent, exciting object images. She would then experience elation.

During all this time, throughout the first of fourteen months of her treatment, she seemed relatively out of contact with me. She would recount her adventures and seemed to expect nothing from me but my continued presence. She refueled by making sure I was still there after disappearing on an adventure. There was no spontaneous, gradual shift in her relatedness. She continued to miss appointments at the same rate, in much the same pattern as characterized her previous therapy. This therapist's attempts to empathize with her view of how her external objects failed her resulted in increased acting out. She used such empathy to justify her "who can blame me" attitude. Interpretations of her self-destructiveness and avoidance of individuation were responded to with increased defiance.

The foregoing clinical picture provides ample justification for the contention, held by many self psychologists, that most borderline patients cannot establish a workable transference, and that they respond to empathy with severe self-fragmentation. The American object relations school would view this case as that of a patient who seeks union to establish the rewarding object relations unit in order to avoid abandonment depression. When the external objects fail to provide union, the withdrawing object relations unit emerges with depression and rage.

The Safety of the Bad Object

This therapist repeatedly stressed to the patient her need to establish the image of the object as rejecting and her self-image as rejected and worthless. I did not argue with her about reality. I empathized that the external objects often did reject her. Her need to dwell on the feelings of rejection was pointed out and gradually demonstrated her tendency to maintain a rejecting image of the other and a rejected, worthless image of herself. When she described a bad experience in reality, I empathized with how she felt but then shifted the focus to what she was doing in her mind to herself with that experience. It was not difficult to show that all of the external objects she discussed reflected one image—that of rejection in relation to her own image as rejected.

It was not long before she began to notice that even if an experience of rejection did not occur in current reality, she would think of past rejections. She began to wonder why she always wanted to think of herself in relation to the other as worthless and rejected. She questioned whether she sometimes even misinterpreted reality in order to conjure up the rejected feeling and sought out external rejecting others. At this point I interpreted that even though she felt miserable when she activated the rejected feeling, she held onto it because she felt safe with that feeling. I suggested that something about feeling accepted was experienced as dangerous and unwelcome. It should not be thought that the patient immediately responded to such comments with insight. Rather, I listened to all that she said and commented from the vantage point of the activation of internal object relations units. I listened to this patient as one would follow the stream of consciousness in a novel by Joyce or Proust, in which reality is always brightened or shaded by the narrator's internal vision and experience. Kohut (1984) has suggested that such novels reflect the fragmented sense of self in severe psychopathology. One does not ignore external reality from such a vantage point; rather, close attention is given to the subtle but constant interplay between internal and external reality.

Ambivalent Symbiosis

Such interpretations gradually moved the transference evolution from the out-of-contact phase to the phase of the ambivalent symbiosis. At one point, I asked the patient about the image she usually held of me in relationship to herself. She responded that she viewed me as caring about her and as the only person in her life who wanted her to grow into independence. I wondered why, then, she did not maintain that image instead of always dwelling on the rejected and rejecting images. She said it was impossible for her to hold on to the image of me or anyone else as caring about her when she could not care about herself. She then reported trying to maintain a positive image of herself and of me but being unable to do so because the negative images and thoughts took over.

The Splitting Off of the Bad-Object Transference

The following clinical data convinced this therapist that the patient was entering a phase of ambivalent symbiosis in the transference. For the first time the patient showed some sign of wanting something other than my continued physical and mental presence. She wanted to know whether I believed that her boyfriend and mother cared for her. As I explored this question with her, she became increasingly anxious to know my opinion. The intensity of her demand was as if she were asking if I liked her. Her certainty that I knew the answer, and the look of rejection that came over her when I did not immediately reassure her, made me feel that she was unconsciously speaking of her and me. If I were to respond in the affirmative she would unconsciously read me to be giving her my unconscious message that I liked her. If I said no, she'd unconsciously think I was rejecting her. This dialogue occurred immediately after she had told me that she had tried and failed to maintain a positive image of the two of us. She had failed because she could not maintain an image of me as caring for her when she could not do so herself. The negative images and thoughts took over. She then asked, through the displacement upon her mother and boyfriend, whether I cared about her. This type of unconscious communication in the therapeutic relationship is characteristic of the emergence of the ambivalent symbiotic phase of the transference–countertransference (Searles 1961).

As she complained about how her mother and boyfriend rejected and mistreated her, it was clear that she wanted something from me. She was no longer simply recounting episodes but instead wanted to know whether I saw her point of view, whether

I was concerned and empathized with her plight. She would for the first time feel reassured and calmed by my empathy. I increasingly had the sense that she was unconsciously reassuring herself that I was not rejecting her. When she complained that her mother and boyfriend never called or visited and that they spent only a couple of hours a week with her, it occurred to me that all of these statements about them could apply to me. Her criticisms that her mother and boyfriend were crazy, exciting, and rejecting objects unconsciously referred to the image of the therapist. When I pointed out that I also did not hang out with or call her and was only available a couple of hours a week, she said that she wouldn't expect more of me. I was a professional; the relationship was limited, and it would not be appropriate for her to expect more. In this manner, she maintained a superficial therapeutic alliance with the therapist as an external object, and she split off the exciting and rejecting aspects of the transference object into her mother and boyfriend. As I pointed out how most of her complaints about her mother and boyfriend could apply to me, she sometimes found herself getting angry between sessions because she could not be with me whenever she wished. When she was drunk, she would now think of me and feel guilty. She did not like this; she felt that I made her feel guilty and was controlling her mind. She would therefore angrily stop herself from thinking of me.

Jealousy of the Internal Object

When I now commented on her internal images, Kim would become angry and complain that I sounded like a computer; was all intellect and had no feelings. She protested that I lacked compassion for her, that I didn't care how everyone mistreated her, that I was more interested in her images than in her. She increasingly felt jealous of my interest in her images and felt that she had to compete with them for my favor. She recalled that as a child she would tell her best friend about imaginary playmates, pretending that they really existed, to make the friend jealous. When she told me of her mother, boyfriend, and friends, she realized that she often tried to make me jealous. She felt as if she were talking of her imaginary playmates and when I responded to them as images, she herself became jealous. She would then ask me questions about the people in my family, as if she wanted to add their images to the ambivalent symbiosis.

Searles (1986) has remarked upon the jealousy of internal objects as a characteristic of the increasing ambivalent symbiosis. As Kim made herself jealous of my interest in her internal objects, she distanced herself from her positive image. Her jealousy was therefore the other side of the coin from her attempts to make me jealous, also a characteristic of antidependent distancing. Kim had often told me that whenever the external object did not reject her but instead expressed undeniable interest and acceptance, she herself grew cold and emotionless. As a child she had often felt that she and her mother continually shifted positions, one in the state of the needy, demanding, insatiable child, and the other cold, emotionless, and distant. Kim now experienced rapid transferential fluctuations of feeling schizoid detachment herself and viewing me as needing closeness or herself as needy and I as schizoid.

Kim complained that she thought of me when she acted out and that she deliberately wanted to take in beer instead of me. She recalled that as a child she had grown to prefer her bottle to her mother. She would joke about preferring "Bud" (Budweiser beer) as her therapist; "Bud" did not expect anything of her, was always there at her command, and helped her to escape her problems. She felt that I thought of myself as Christlike and believed that I wanted her to put my image above all others. She thought to herself, "The hell I will!" and defiantly downed a bottle of beer. She sometimes perceived me as a saint and at other times as a psychotic with delusions of grandeur, like her father.

At this point, about sixteen months into her treatment, she showed a marked change in her pattern of keeping appointments. Now she never missed a session and was visibly upset if she was forced to be late. From this point, she started to cut down on her drinking.

The Exciting Object Transference

The ambivalent symbiosis reached its height beginning with the following incident. I had referred Kim to a physician because of a minor medical problem. She came into our session angry at that physician's nurse. She had attempted to persuade the nurse to allow her to go in ahead of the other patients, because she had an appointment with me afterward and did not want to be late. The nurse had not permitted it but did try to comfort and calm her. Kim stormed out, accusing the nurse of infantilizing her. She complained to me about the nurse and the physician and then grew fearful that I was angry at her for criticizing the referral. She was angry at me for sending her to someone else but then projectively identified her own anger into me and imagined herself as rejected.

That night, still quite fearful that I was angry at her, she had two dreams. In the first, her boyfriend became a homosexual and no longer liked her. In the second dream she received repeated crank calls. I was the caller, but I identified myself as someone else. She recognized my voice and knew it to be me, and she was frightened because this meant that I was psychotic like her father. She had always called me when she was upset, but now she felt terribly alone. She could not call me because I was the one with whom she had the problem.

Her immediate association to the dream was that it was easier to talk to me about her boyfriend going crazy than it was for her to acknowledge her unconscious belief that *I* was crazy. She remembered that she had called me about a year earlier to say that she believed that her boyfriend was making crank calls, pretending that he was someone else, to see if she was home. Then she received some sexually provocative calls when he was angry at her, so she believed that it was he or his friends. Now she could see that the boyfriend and I were one and the same to her. In the dream, she continually thought, "I know he's not someone else; I know he is my therapist." What she thought the dream meant is that she knew that the crazy object image was not the boyfriend, but she pretended it was because if she allowed herself to think that I was crazy, to mistrust my motives, or to feel that I was like her father, then she would be all alone. Whom could she tell? Her mother, her boyfriend, her friends? It was much easier to tell me that she feared that I was crazy and that she had crazy feelings about me if I was disguised in the image of her boyfriend.

Kim's image of me as caring about her was strengthened when I responded to her request to help her find a physician. She therefore activated the all-bad self and object unit by rejecting the referral and viewing me as rejecting her in retaliation. When she saw me as caring about her, she was threatened by her own libidinal needs and by the arousal of the libidinal, self-exciting object transference. She therefore dreamt that the boyfriend, who represented the therapist unconsciously, was not interested in her libidinally. This dream denied the unconscious wish for the therapist to be the exciting object who was interested in her libidinally. The second dream made it apparent that she was splitting off the exciting and rejecting aspects of the transference into the crazy, exciting, rejecting boyfriend.

Following these dreams, she experienced the ambivalent symbiosis directly in the transference. After a weekend, she would come in for a session and say that she felt that I was angry with her and no longer liked her. She would then feel angry herself and reject her image of me. Once she had said "The hell with him" and had gotten drunk. When her reasons for believing that I had rejected her were explored, it became apparent that she had become angry because the weekend meant that she had finished her weekly sessions and could no longer see me. She felt rejected and angry and projectively identified her anger onto me.

Therapist as the Rejecting Object

Kim now perceived me as rejecting her in much the same manner that she had previously felt rejected by her mother and boyfriend. If she called and I was not immediately available to speak to her, she complained that I was always busy, always put her last, and did not care about her. When we did speak by telephone, she invariably felt rejected because at some point I would say that I had to end the conversation. She herself would never end the dialogue and would feel rejected when I had to go, regardless of how long our conversation had been. She believed that I preferred my other patients and that I considered her my craziest patient. She complained that I was too busy, just like her mother, and imagined that I gave her more attention when she was drinking heavily. Now that she was becoming more autonomous and was acting out less often I was becoming busier in my own life and would soon abandon her as everyone else had.

At times she could briefly maintain a positive image of herself and me, but the negative thoughts of herself as rejected by me would soon predominate. She would tell herself that she would no longer care about me. She felt that I had betrayed her by allowing her to depend upon me and by telling her that it was self-destructive to depend upon alcohol. She felt that I had encouraged her to depend upon me but then had left her with only an image to depend upon. She wondered how that was supposed to help her. She needed me—the real external object—to be available whenever she needed me. She would angrily reject the positive image of herself and of me but would then feel depressed and alone and have to reconnect to reconstitute her positive self and object representations. She now experienced rapid fluctuations of the negative and positive self–object representation units in the transference but with the all-negative unit dominant.

The Rejection of the Positive Internal Self and Object Unit

The American object relations school would view Kim's insatiable object need as an attempt to establish the rewarding object relations unit to avoid abandonment depression. The depression and rage she experienced would be viewed as the inevitable outcome of disappointment in the rewarding object. The technical management of the case, from this perspective, would involve the confrontation of the patient with the reality that dependence on the rewarding object must inevitably result in disappointment and frustration. The patient must relinquish the fantasy of the all-good rewarding object and face the abandonment depression.

In my view, the patient activates the all-bad self–object unit to defend against internalization of the positive self and object unit. The insatiable need, the activation of the sadomasochistic, oral, self-exciting object relationship, serves the antidependent defense. By making her need for contact with the external object insatiable, the patient can perceive of herself as rejected regardless of the external object's behavior. Therefore, the patient is always able to think of her needs as being unmet, to think of herself as rejected and worthless and of the object as rejecting. The activation of the all-bad self and object unit results in depression and rage. Insatiable need, the oral self-exciting object relationship, is then activated to counter the depression and rage. In this regard, the all-bad self–object relations unit becomes a vicious cycle constituting both the rejecting and exciting objects.

Self psychology understands that insatiable need can serve to compensate for the depression and rage of the fragmented self. However, self psychology misses the point that insatiable need also serves to maintain the perception of the object as rejecting in antidependent defense. This patient succinctly stated the antidependent position: "If I don't think that you like me, why should I bother to like you?"

When the patient constantly activates the all-bad self and object representation unit in the transference, it is necessary to interpret the antidependent defense. In this way the patient can maintain the positive self and object representation unit and the transference will evolve from the ambivalent to the therapeutic symbiosis. I continually commented upon how Kim focused on all the ways in which I was not available because this was safer than recognizing the ways in which I *was* available. As she increasingly noticed her rejection of internal positive self and object images, she also noted that she often alienated external objects through rejecting and demanding behavior. She realized that if she was not provocative, external objects were not always all bad, and that even her mother, on occasion, had a positive side.

The Awakening of Vulnerability

As she maintained the positive images in the transference, she began to feel vulnerable in relationship to me and in her current life situation. She was astonished that she had taken midnight subway rides and indulged in drunken sprees and joyrides. She felt that she had made herself vulnerable and realized that when the all-bad view of images dominated her, she felt depressed and enraged but also invulnerable. She said that sometimes, when she was out of control, she would experience a sense of power in forcing others to control her. She had been similar to Mahler's practicing child who darts off into danger and forces the mother to give chase and catch her.

She became aware of her inability to take care of herself and began to think about school and work. When such patients are nonfunctional, they often express their antidependent invulnerable position. To admit that one has something to learn, to initially experience the phase of learning and uncertainty that occurs prior to achieving mastery, requires accepting one's vulnerability and lack of omnipotence. By doing nothing, Kim could feel that she had nothing to learn, she could insist on always being right and could avoid the narcissistic injury of having to learn and to depend upon the other for help. It was not difficult to reconstruct the genesis of her denial of vulnerability. Whenever Kim had tried to learn anything, her mother and father were highly critical of her beginning fumblings and imperfections. By attacking her vulnerability in the beginning phase of learning, they also indirectly rejected her strivings for autonomy. Kim could therefore never admit not knowing and could never experience the initial learning process because the internal object rejected this vulnerability. In school she would not permit herself to learn but instead sat apathetically until she quit at the age of 16. She could also not permit herself the vulnerability of learning on a job.

As she entered rapprochement and experienced the wholesale rejection of her vulnerability and autonomy, she fled back to the practicing phase, from which she could at least experience some sense of esteem. In this way she denied the vulnerable self's need for the internal holding object. Instead, she made the object all bad and fled into omnipotence.

The vulnerable self became more connected to the internal holding object through the transference, and she experienced severe separation anxiety. She faced the fact that her life was a mess and that she felt like a vulnerable child. She began to believe that I really was going to help her, that our relationship could affect the direction of the rest of her life. She therefore wondered what would become of her if something were to happen to me. She was experiencing the vulnerability of the rapprochement youngster when he discovers his separateness and his dependence upon the object.

She recalled that as a child she had not experienced separation reactions when she began nursery school for a full day. She remembered other children crying for their mothers and thinking that they were "babies." She felt only elation about starting school. She recalled that the children had not been allowed to play the piano during rest time. She had felt that this rule was unfair, and she repeatedly ran to the piano to play. The teacher became so angry that he pulled Kim's hair. When Kim told her mother of the incident, her mother withdrew her from the school. Kim now wondered whether she had actually been covering up her separation anxiety and vulnerability by acting omnipotent and doing whatever she pleased.

Kim began to feel vulnerable toward me. She had thoughts that I could physically overpower and rape her. Although she did not rationally think of me as a rapist, she would sometimes have a fleeting moment of feeling that I was crazy and could rape her. She did not think of rape only in a physical sense, but also of my somehow mentally raping or overpowering her. She recalled at times thinking of her father as a psychotic rapist. She wondered whether she hadn't defied him out of fear that if she showed her vulnerability, he would rape her physically and mentally.

She had a dream that she had admitted a man to her house who looked like me; the man had been psychotic and had raped her. The fear reflected her anxiety that if she let me into her mind as an internal object, I would overpower and dominate her sense of self.

In addition, the wish for comfort and protection from the internal object promoted the wish to internalize the object through a primitive sexualized and aggressive mode. She therefore thought of internalizing the object in a physical, sexualized sense through a rape fantasy. Her father's psychosis certainly complicated whatever sexualized fantasies she had about him.

As she increasingly accepted her vulnerable need for the internal holding object, she reported feeling self-empathy for the first time in her life. She remembered the lonely and vulnerable child she had been and felt sorry for her. She then criticized herself for feeling sorry for herself. She said that in the past she had always felt victimized and rejected and had tried to make others feel sorry for her so that she could control them, but she had never felt sorry for herself.

Therapeutic Symbiosis

Kim bought a parrot to keep her company. She would joke that the bird was a good listener and provided her with therapy when I was not around. The bird was a transitional object of the therapist, reinforcing the internal positive image. Sometimes the bird represented her vulnerable self; she wanted to be a good mother to the bird and care for it and was very conscious of the fact that the bird's life was in her hands. Sometimes, despite her efforts, she became preoccupied with bad internal self and object images. She would ignore the bird, forgetting its vulnerability and its existence. The bird would become noisy, get into things, and distract her. Kim would become enraged, screaming and chasing the parrot. She would then feel like the "bad mother." She increasingly felt empathy for her mother, realizing the difficulty of devoting oneself to the care of another. When she cared for the bird, she thought of it as a good self–object, always available. She imagined that the bird was grateful and loved her. She felt that she was the good mother and that the bird was a good child, but she simultaneously felt that the bird was a good mother mirroring her for being a good child. When she was bad to the bird, she imagined that it hated and rejected her. She simultaneously felt that she was the bad, rejecting mother to the unworthy child and that the bird was a rejecting, bad mother hating her as the unworthy child. The patient's symbiotic relatedness to the bird reflected the growing therapeutic symbiosis in the transference. Since she could not possibly know what the bird thought, all of her imaginings about its acceptance or rejection of her clearly illustrates how the external self–object serves as a container for the projective identifications of the patient's self and object images.

Her relationships to the bird and to the external therapist reinforced her positive internal images of the therapist object. Gradually, the positive self and object representation unit gained dominance over the negative self and object representation unit. At this point she split off the negative unit to the external, insensitive world and felt protected by the symbiosis. Therefore, although she continued to view the external world as all bad, she was less sensitive to impingement from that world in that this therapist's empathy comforted her. She had, at this point, engaged in the self–object transference. Disruption to the self–object bond came not so much from her side of the therapeutic field as from occasional empathic failures by the therapist. Once when I was tired during a session, my mind wandered from what she had said, and my response revealed that I had misunderstood her. She went into a rage, accusing me of sleeping on the job, of being incompetent and of not caring about her. Her rage was quickly calmed as I abruptly awakened from my therapeutic lethargy and gave her my undivided attention.

As stated previously, this author's view of such self–object or symbiotic transferences subtly differs from the self-psychological one. Kohut (1971) views such failures in the self–object's empathic function as triggering self-fragmentation in reminding the patient of traumatic past failures in empathy. My own point of view stresses that splitting still occurs in the self–object bond, but the positive self and object representation unit is increasingly dominant and reinforced. Disruptions in the therapist's empathy trigger the bad self and object representation unit, which temporarily gains dominance.

Kernberg (1975) and Masterson (1976) consider the symbiotic transference a manifestation of splitting, but their view differs from mine in that they do not recognize the developmental therapeutic significance of the symbiotic transference in strengthening the positive self and object images. Kohut (1971), on the other hand, clearly recognizes the therapeutic developmental value of the symbiotic or self–object transference.

In this patient's treatment, the therapist's occasional nontraumatic failures resulted in the increasing integration of the negative and positive self and object representation units.

Efforts at Individuation

As Kim became less depressed and angry, her vulnerability and strivings for autonomy emerged. Having decided that she must do something to change her life, she managed to earn a high school equivalency diploma. She then pursued college courses and part-time work. In the transference evolution, she increasingly became somewhat disillusioned with the therapist as the mother transference object who discouraged autonomy and encouraged dependence. As she separated in the transference, she brought to the therapist her ambitions and interests for mirroring admiration. Her ambitions, which were originally somewhat grandiose, gradually became realistic.

She informed her addicted boyfriend that he had to stop using cocaine if he wanted to continue to see her. She saw him less as a rejecting object and more as a person with problems that interfered with his capacity for intimacy. His family eventually arranged to have him go for detoxification. Kim remained in contact with him but also started to see other men.

Practicing Omnipotence as a Defense against Mind Control

This case report illustrates how the severe borderline patient in antidependent defense retreats from the vulnerable rapprochement self's need for a holding object to practicing omnipotence, characterized by obliviousness to the transference object and active flight. The major anxiety motivating the antidependent retreat from internalization of the object is the fear that the object will take over and control the mind. The fear of mind control expresses through the internal object relations situation the identical interpersonal concept of merger anxiety. In her fear of mind control, the patient made the object all bad and withdrew. She thereby manifested a paranoid-schizoid position (M. Klein 1946) in her internalized object relations.

At the height of her acting out, she denied her human vulnerability and once said that she wanted to make someone stop her but also that she would not let anyone. Because of the patient's own lack of internal structure and sense of being out of control, she craves an object to take in to provide structure and control but also fears losing her mind and identity to the object. She therefore makes the object all bad to avoid the temptation to internalize a seemingly positive object that could become bad through mind control. And so she rejects the internalization of a positive object through practicing flight and thereby plays out the need for control sadomasochistically in terms of challenging the external object to control her externally and behaviorally. Acting out then becomes a means of shifting the conflict about control from the internal to the external behavioral sphere. The conflict of "Will I or will I not let you in?" shifts to the safer ground of "Can you or can you not control me from the outside?" A patient once expressed this aptly:

I'd like my body to be controlled by someone else. When someone dominates me from the outside, I feel in control of both myself and them. I no longer feel inside of me, but can feel myself outside of my body, as if I joined them in controlling me. I have therefore turned the tables in my mind and feel in control of them and of myself. What I hate is when I feel someone can get in my mind, when I feel they can put thoughts into me, influence my thoughts, or take thoughts out of me. Then I feel they can control my mind.

WILLIAM

William, a 17-year-old male who had been apprehended by the police for car theft, was referred to a psychiatrist by the court. During his first session with the therapist, he argued that he would prefer to see a psychiatrist because as a social worker the therapist knew only about people on welfare. He admired the psychiatrist for smoking a cigar and appearing self-assured. After several weeks, he noted, laughing, that the therapist did not know how to begin sessions and depended upon him to start. The consulting psychiatrist took on the significance of an internal object in William's treatment as he negatively compared me to him.

William came from a middle-class family and had an older brother. His father was currently imprisoned for racketeering but had been at home for the first fourteen years of William's life. His mother was a businesswoman who had sought psychotherapy for depression when he went to prison. She questioned her object choice in marriage and felt that she had injured her sons by encouraging in them the same antisocial character traits she had admired in her husband. She therefore supported her son's treatment.

William had a history of poor academic performance, acting out with peers, and truancy. He presented with bravado and a need to impress others with his power and slickness.

IDEALIZATION OF THE REJECTING OBJECT

William would talk about the powerful males in his community— the chief of police, a wealthy industrialist, and a psychiatrist who was the father of one of his acquaintances. He admired all of these men but viewed them as corrupt. He claimed that the chief of police was "in my father's pocket," the industrialist worked with his father and other mobsters, and the prominent psychiatrist smoked marijuana with his own children. Although William knew of these men mostly from hearsay, he spoke of them as if they were old chums. William invited this therapist to join him in smoking marijuana and when I was unwilling, he said that he planned to inquire if the marijuana-smoking psychiatrist would treat him. He called me a wimp for not giving him permission to smoke marijuana in session; he said that he imagined that I had been a wimpy kid, fearful of getting into trouble. He likened me to a peer in school whom he and his friends scapegoated.

He would demonstrate his powers in karate, kicking and punching, sometimes aiming his blows in my direction to see if I'd flinch. He once saw my car in the parking lot and constantly threatened to steal or damage it.

In our sessions, he identified with the rejecting father image and projectively identified his weak, vulnerable self into me. When he was a child, his father had sadistically teased him for his small stature and helplessness, and had challenged him to "toughen up." He would get him into wrestling holds and belittle him if he gave up quickly. Once, in latency, he was beaten by a gang of boys and returned home bruised and crying. His father berated him for his physical and emotional weakness, boasting of an occasion in his youth when he had beaten off a rival gang single-handedly with a tire iron. William, in contrast, was "too soft" and had been spoiled by his mother.

William described his mother as a perfectionist. When she helped him with homework, she became critical of his mistakes. She expected him to be perfect at once and could not tolerate the fumblings in the learning process. As a result, William stopped trying to learn.

In identifying with the rejecting object, William denied his vulnerable need for a holding object. Because this therapist did not respond to his provocation but instead attempted to understand him, William experienced me as dangerous. In the treatment of the borderline patient, the therapist's empathy and understanding is perceived as a danger, because the therapist presents himself as a potential holding object and thereby excites the dependency and vulnerability of the dependent self.

The internal bad object, based upon the sadistic father, unconsciously fears losing the self component to the potential good object–therapist. Therefore, it attacks the self component for being weak, dependent, and vulnerable in its need for help from a good holding object. In this case, the weak, vulnerable self component is projectively identified into the therapist. The patient therefore attempted to provoke me into becoming the more familiar rejecting object.

On one occasion, William's vulnerable need for me as a holding object emerged. His idealized older brother nearly died of an overdose of heroin, and William came into session quite upset. For the first time, he expressed concern over his brother if he lived and continued to use heroin. He described his brother as a "loser," and worried about the direction of his own life. After this session, he told his mother that I really was a "good guy" and he liked talking to me.

In our next session, his antidependent defense significantly escalated. He bounced around the office in a karate demonstration, challenged me to a sparring match, and struck out at pieces of furniture, stopping just short of hitting them.

The Acting Out of the Bad-Object Transference

In school, William was getting into more trouble. He provoked tougher kids and school authorities just as he had provoked the therapist. He was threatened with expulsion by the school and with violence by his peers.

William was developing an ambivalent symbiosis in the transference. He was simultaneously the sadistic father attacking the masochistic child and the masochistic child provoking the sadistic father to attack. He was conscious of his own identification as sadist and of the therapist as masochist, but he was unconscious of his identification of himself as masochist and of the therapist as sadist. When he could not provoke the therapist to become the sadistic, attacking father, he displaced the sadistic object image into the tougher peers and authorities at school and provoked them to attack him. As he described it, everyone in school wanted to "kick his ass." His efforts to provoke the sadistic father to "kick his ass" reflected an unconscious wish to be anally penetrated by the powerful paternal phallus. He would thereby incorporate the strength and power of the paternal phallus through a sexualized mode.

Because William's acting-out behavior was getting him into serious trouble in school, the therapist interpreted the transference displacement in his acting out. He initially became angry and threatened to punch me for calling him a homosexual. In repeated interpretations, rather than focusing on sexuality, I emphasized his wish to internalize strength and power, and he became increasingly interested in the comments about his need to take in a powerful father in order to feel a strong sense of self. It was also pointed out how he fought off his vulnerable need for the powerful father by rejecting this need in the same fashion that his father had rejected his vulnerability and need for protection and comfort. He therefore could only express the need to take in the powerful father in the "ass-kicking" and fighting mode of his actual father.

At school, whenever he was about to provoke a peer or authority figure, my comments would come to his mind and stop him cold. He complained that I was controlling his mind. He imagined that I had fought in the Vietnam War and knew brainwashing techniques. His image of me became that of a cold, brainwashing killer. He became obsessed with the Vietnam War and would bring books and ask questions about places and battles.

The Transition to Therapeutic Symbiosis

In one session, he began again to demonstrate karate, flying around my office as if he were going to destroy it. He took out matches as if to set fire to papers on the desk. He repeatedly glanced back at me to see if I was readying myself to attack him. I felt no concern whatsoever that he was out of control or that he would wreck my office. He seemed to be testing whether I was, in reality, the sadistic killer. I did not set limits but just calmly observed him. After a time he sat at the desk, lowered his head onto it, and fell asleep. I marked this session as the transitional point in the transference evolution from the ambivalent to the therapeutic symbiosis. His falling asleep demonstrated that he felt secure that I was not the crazy, sadistic paternal object who would kill him in his vulnerability. He let go of the antidependent need to fight me off. He reminded me of a young child falling asleep in the security of his mother's presence.

Unfortunately, William was forced to terminate treatment prematurely when his family unavoidably had to leave the state. However, he did manage to complete high school and was in better control of his acting-out behavior.

In the evolution of the transference, William initially identified with the rejecting father object and attacked his vulnerable need for a holding object by devaluing me. The therapist's empathic response excited the vulnerable and dependent libidinal self's need for a holding object and thereby escalated the negative therapeutic reaction. He brought powerful, corrupt internal objects into the treatment in his idealization of the corrupt chief of police, industrialist, and psychiatrist. They represented the sadistic father figure and were rival internal therapists to ward off his interest in the therapist as a holding object. As he increasingly approached an ambivalent symbiotic transference, he split off his image of the therapist as an exciting, sadistic, crazy object into sadistic peers and authorities. Consciously, he identified himself in the sadistic position and the therapist in the masochistic position. Unconsciously, he attempted to provoke the therapist into behaving as the sadistic object. The displacement of the crazy, sadistic object into the sadistic peers and authorities was under the direction of the internal bad object. His unconscious wish to internalize the therapist object was experienced through the primitive sexualized imagery of anal incorporation of the powerful paternal phallus. Furthermore, the wish was consciously expressed through the medium of fighting and "ass kicking," the comfortable mode of interaction between him and his father. In this way, his unconscious wish to sexually incorporate the father as an exciting object was both defended against and punished by provoking the rejecting father to "kick his ass." With my repeated interpretations, he increasingly became involved in the ambivalent symbiosis and perceived the therapist as the bad, crazy, mind-controlling, sadistic paternal object. He thereby gradually tested out and worked through the bad-object transference and then engaged in the therapeutic symbiosis with the good object.

In self-psychological terms, it could be said that both the idealizing and mirroring needs of the bipolar self had been traumatically rejected. William's vulnerable need to idealize and internalize his father was rejected by his father's sadistic response. His need to win his mother's admiration and mirroring for his individuated achievement was rejected by her perfectionism and intolerance for the fumblings of learning. In this author's view, he internalized the rejection of his own mirroring and idealizing needs. Therefore, before he could activate the idealizing self–object transference, he first had to activate the bad, rejecting, sadistic father transference. Only after he worked through the internal sadistic father's rejection of his vulnerable need for protection and idealization could he permit himself to idealize the good object. The full emergence of the vulnerable self with the idealized object could be seen in his falling asleep in my presence.

The Primitive Sexualized Modes of Incorporation of the Part-Object

Kohut (1971, 1984) points out that when the patient suffers the loss of the external self–object bond, fantasies or acts of sexualized incorporation serve to shore up or compensate for the fragmented sense of self. Fairbairn (1944) states that when the relationship to the good external object is unsatisfactory, the fantasies or acts of sexualized incorporation of the bad (exciting) part-object serve as a substitute satisfaction to compensate for the loss of the external good object. In Fairbairn's theory, the internalization of the bad object initially and invariably occurs through the fantasy of sexualized incorporation of the part-object to compensate for the unsatisfactory relationship with the external good object.

I agree with these authors on the compensatory, shoring-up function of primitive sexualized modes of the incorporation of the part-object, and I also agree with Fairbairn that the initial internalization of the object occurs through sexualized fantasies of incorporating the part-object. However, Fairbairn's view is extended by stating that both the bad object and the good object are initially internalized through fantasies of sexualized incorporation of the part-object. Fairbairn states that libido serves as the signpost to the external good object. He comments that the oral zone is libidinized to serve as a channel to the object. Furthermore, he states that aggression serves separation from the good external and bad internal objects. Blanck and Blanck (1979) state a similar point of view in their developmental theory of libido serving object connection and aggression serving separation (from the object). To extend these views, it can be said that libido serves the internalization of the object and aggression serves separation from the internal object. In this way, object relations theory can be integrated with drive theory.

The sexualized modes of incorporation in cases such as William's serve not only to compensate for an enfeebled sense of self but also to fill the void left by the good internal object. The threatened or actual loss of the external self–object (Kohut 1984) or the good external object (Fairbairn 1944) threatens the patient with the loss of the good *internal* object. The threatened loss of the good internal object threatens the self with fragmentation. The patient therefore regresses to the original primitive mode of sexualized incorporation in order to compensate for the loss of the positive internal self and object representation unit. My view subtly differs from Fairbairn's (1944) in my emphasis on the loss of the internal as opposed to external good object and from Kohut's in my emphasis on the importance of the good internal object in shoring up the enfeebled self.

To elaborate this view, the threatened or actual loss of the external self–object or good object activates the rejecting internal object and rejected self-representation unit and the loss of the positive self and object representation unit. The patient attempts to compensate for the loss of the positive accepted self and holding object unit by sexualized incorporative fantasies that activate the sadomasochistic, libidinal, self-exciting (part) object relationship. As mentioned earlier, the latter internal object relationship gives rise to insatiable need and the inevitable reactivation of the rejecting object–rejected self internal object relationship. In the case of severely disturbed borderline patients who never experience a positive connection to the internal or external good object for an appreciable time, the rejecting object–rejected self representation unit and the sadomasochistic libidinal self-exciting object representation unit rapidly oscillate in a vicious cycle of rejection and excitement, closing off the need for the good internal object. The higher-level borderline or narcissistic patient can, however, sustain a good enough relationship to a positive external and internal good object. When that relationship is disrupted by the good object, the internal rejecting all-bad self and object unit displaces the positive, accepting self and object unit. The sadomasochistic libidinal self-exciting object relationship is activated to compensate for the loss of the internal good self and object images. The insatiable need of the exciting object relationship will give rise to the reemergence of the rejecting self and object internalized object relationship. However, unlike the case of the borderline personality, the vicious cycle of the rejection and excitement in the narcissistic personality can be halted by the reintroduction of the external object's empathy, which reconstitutes the dominance of the positive internal self and object unit.

The American object relations school takes into account only two-thirds of the internalized object relations situation of the borderline patient. Masterson (1976) recognizes the sadomasochistic, libidinal, self-exciting object relationship in his notion of the rewarding object relations unit and the rejecting self and object relations unit in his notion of the withdrawing object relations unit. He views the borderline patient as experiencing only these two part-object relations units and neglects the third part-object relations unit, that of a positive, vulnerable, self-holding object relations symbiotic unit that promotes individuation. American object relations theory can therefore consider only the primitive, sexualized, incorporative modes as rewarding reunion fantasies that defend against the rejecting part-object relations unit and must inevitably fail. The American school is correct but limited because it neglects the third part-object relations unit, the positive symbiotic self and object unit, the lack or loss of which the rewarding or exciting unit serves to compensate for. I will illustrate my theoretical ideas about the sexualized modes of incorporation with a brief case example.

WENDY

This case material was provided by a female therapist whom I have supervised. A female borderline patient, Wendy, had been seeing her for a year. During one session, she hesitantly revealed that she had repeatedly been involved in sexual encounters with men she barely knew. One recent encounter had frightened her because she realized that she had placed herself in a vulnerable position. She met a "shady-looking character" in a bar and they went up to the roof of a building for a sexual encounter. She performed fellatio and had intercourse. She realized that the man could easily have murdered her.

She had had many such brief encounters with men over the years, but it was only during the last month that she had begun to feel vulnerable and attributed this sense of vulnerability to the fact that she had thought of what her therapist might say if she knew. At first she pictured the therapist expressing concern, but then the image became stern and judgmental. She would then become angry at the therapist's image for judging her and say to herself, "The hell with you. I'll do what I want!" At first she avoided telling the therapist of the sexual encounters because she feared her disapproval. Now that she had told her, she was considering leaving treatment. In the course of exploring her perceptions of the therapist, the patient noted that the therapist had always been understanding and sensitive. She recognized that her image of the therapist as judgmental and critical was actually her image of her mother.

The patient was unable to refuse the men who approached her. They were usually unsavory looking and often turned out to be abusive and sadistic. She masochistically surrendered to these men, even when she was not attracted to them. Even in the last incident, when the man had led her to the roof, she did not feel vulnerable or frightened until she thought about it later. When she performed fellatio and the male became sexually aroused, she felt powerful and fantasized of draining him of his strength.

This clinical example illustrates that the oral sadomasochistic libidinal self's relationship to the exciting object serves the antidependent defense; the patient initially perceived men as exciting, rejecting, and powerful. In her masochistic surrender, she orally incorporated the powerful phallus and fantasized that she drained and internalized the strength of the phallus. She felt omnipotent and powerful, absolutely denying her real vulnerability in the situation. In this way she was like Kim, the patient discussed earlier, who would deny her vulnerability and feel omnipotent during midnight subway rides. Cases such as these provide evidence that the masochism of the borderline patient is a method of obtaining omnipotent sadistic control and thereby denying vulnerability and the need for the holding object.

As this patient became increasingly involved with the therapist, she began to feel vulnerable in her acting-out behavior. The emergence of vulnerability was associated to her experience of a positive image of the therapist expressing concern for her well-being and safety. She then immediately had to turn the positive image into a critical, rejecting one so that she could become angry and reject the image of the therapist as all bad. It is this splitting operation of making the internal object all bad that leaves the patient without a positive object image. She must therefore fill the internal void by regressive acts of sexualized incorporation of the part-object.

The sexualized incorporation of the exciting part-object is under the direction of the internal bad object and serves the defense against internalizing the helpful, caring part-object. The sexualized sadomasochistic relationship to the exciting part-object is one in which the patient tries to achieve ruthless, omnipotent power over the object through sadomasochistic fantasies or behavior without any caring, dependence on, or vulnerability toward the object. The fantasy is that the patient can do whatever he will to the object without any concern about it, draining it of power. In this way, the self component remains loyal to the bad object by denying any vulnerability or dependence in a caring relationship toward a positive object. Furthermore, the insatiable need of the oral sadomasochistic self toward the exciting object will inevitably result in disappointment, transforming the exciting object into the rejecting object.

THE SEVERE BORDERLINE PATIENT AS PARANOID-SCHIZOID IN PRACTICING OMNIPOTENCE

The lower-level borderline patient is described by Kernberg (1975) and Masterson (1976) as fearful of merger. I describe the same clinical phenomenon in terms of internalized object relations in saying that the lower-level borderline patient fears that the internal object will control or dominate his mind. The severe borderline patient experiences a paranoid-schizoid position (Klein 1946) in his level of object relations. He makes the object all bad in paranoid fashion, and then flees in schizoid fashion. The flight is marked by action and oblivion to the object relations world.

Mahler (1975) has pointed out that in the practicing subphase, the child experiences the greatest degree of obliviousness to the object. He is more interested in exploring the world and his motoric abilities than in mother. In fact, as Mahler suggests, he will more readily accept substitutes for mother now than at any other phase of development. Therefore, the practicing subphase can be thought of as a normative schizoid position or phase of development. Fairbairn (1940) has related the schizoid position to the wish for and fear of engulfment by the object. Mahler has also remarked upon the relevance of engulfment by the mother to the practicing subphase. Mahler (1975) states:

> We might consider the possibility that the elation of this subphase has to do not only with the exercise of the ego apparatuses, but also with the elated escape from fusion with, from engulfment by, mother. From this point of view we would consider that, just as the infant's peek-a-boo games seem to turn from passive to active, the losing and regaining of the need-gratifying object and then the lost love objects, so too does the toddler's constant running off until he is swooped up by his mother, turn from passive to active the fear of being re-engulfed by mother. This behavior also reassures him that mother will *want* to swoop him up in her arms. [p. 71]

Mahler does not assume that such behavior is primarily intentional but rather that it produces such effects and therefore may be intentionally repeated.

The British object relations school refers to a paranoid-schizoid position and depressive position in normative development (Fairbairn 1944, M. Klein 1946). The paranoid-schizoid position involves a fear of engulfment by the object and defense by schizoid withdrawal. Mahler characterizes the practicing subphase not only by flight from engulfment, but also by oblivion to the object. Therefore, a parallel development can be seen in Mahler's practicing subphase and the British object relations paranoid-schizoid position. I believe that in normative development, the paranoid-schizoid characteristics play a secondary role in the practicing child's love affair with the world. As Mahler points out, the child's practicing behavior is not primarily the result of the fear of the engulfing mother; rather, the practicing produces these effects and can be intentionally repeated. This author believes that the borderline patient is extremely traumatized by the severe rejection of his vulnerability and strivings for autonomy in rapprochement. This would pertain to the severe borderline patient, described earlier as retreating to practicing omnipotence in order to reject the vulnerable need for the holding object. As mentioned earlier, the lower-level borderline's paranoid rejection of the positive aspects of the object world is in compliance with the rejecting internal object that views the external world as all bad and forbids the taking in of positive object experience. The point here is that in the lower-level borderline patient's retreat to practicing, the paranoid-schizoid features of this subphase become predominant in the pathological regression. As Mahler points out, the flight from the engulfing mother can be intentionally repeated later. Klein's paranoid-schizoid position is the pathological version of the practicing subphase as experienced in the regression of the lower-level borderline patient. The severe borderline patient splits the object world into all bad, a paranoid technique, and then takes flight into schizoid withdrawal.

THE HIGHER-LEVEL BORDERLINE PATIENT: THE DEPRESSIVE POSITION AND RAPPROCHEMENT VULNERABILITY

The higher-level or less-disturbed borderline patient stays in contact with the object but attempts to maintain optimal distance through angry distancing. The major anxiety is not fear of merger but fear of object loss. Higher-level borderline patients fear internalizing the positive object because they fear that their aggression will destroy the positive object. In an interpersonal sense, they fear closeness to the object because they fear that the object will disappoint them and abandon them because of their aggression. These patients do not take flight from the object and stay in contact but angrily push the object away to preserve autonomy. Such patients remain in the rapprochement fight instead of retreating to paranoid flight. The case of Kim was characterized by paranoid flight reactions, whereas Justine and William presented rapprochement fight reactions.

The higher-level borderline patient sometimes appears more dependent than the severe borderline patient, who exhibits a pseudoautonomy and obliviousness to the object. Higher-level borderline patients can appear more dependent because they can, to some degree, take in a good object and cling to it because of their aggression and consequent fear of object loss. In a parallel line of development, the rapprochement youngster appears more dependent and clinging than the practicing youngster, who is more oblivious to his vulnerability and separateness and to the object.

The rapprochement subphase is a parallel development to the British object relations' depressive position. Klein (1946) speaks of the infant's need to make reparation to the internal good mother, who has been injured by his aggression. Reparation speaks to reestablishing the relationship with the internal good mother, whereas rapprochement refers to the interpersonal reestablishing of the relationship to the good mother. Klein places the paranoid-schizoid and depressive positions in the first year of life. In integrating her developmental theory with Mahler's phases of separation–individuation, I am placing the Kleinian positions into the chronological timetable of developmental ego psychology.

The severe borderline patient, fearful of merger in the interpersonal realm, experiences paranoid-schizoid anxieties about mind control in the internal object situation. The higher-level borderline patient, fearful of object loss in the interpersonal realm, experiences depressive anxieties about destroying the good object in the internal object situation. Many borderline patients actually exhibit a mixture of paranoid-schizoid and depressive anxieties in relation to the internal object.

The antidependent self rejects the internal positive object in order to avoid paranoid-schizoid or depressive anxieties, or both. The positive internal object is rejected to avoid the vulnerability associated with the fear of mind control and object loss.

The prototype of the normative antidependent self can be understood in terms of Spitz's theory of the third organizer of the psyche. Spitz (1965) describes how the child says "no" in identification with the aggressor in order to assert his autonomy. The angry "no" of the rapprochement youngster is the interpersonal behavioral manifestation of the antidependent self. The "no" is directed to the internal, as well as the external, object. In the case of the future borderline patient, the "no" was not only in the service of realistic limit setting, but also, more malignantly, directed toward vulnerability and autonomy.

Part II

THERAPEUTIC INTERVENTIONS

6

Handling the Negative Therapeutic Reaction in the Treatment of Children

The therapist can serve as a developmental self–object in the treatment of severely disturbed children. Such children are manifesting practicing subphase behavior and a paranoid-schizoid level of object relations. First, a review of some of the literature on the principles of child therapy will compare ego-supportive impulse psychology to self and object relations theory. Then, clinical vignettes will illustrate how the child's disordered, chaotic, destructive behavior serves the bad object's rejection of the holding or self–object transference and how the practice implications of self and object relations theory with these children differs in some ways from classical ego-supportive treatment.

EARLY PRINCIPLES OF CHILD THERAPY

M. Klein (1923) and A. Freud (1946) were among the originators of child therapy, within a classical impulse-psychology perspec-

141

tive (Fairbairn 1944, p. 84). This model suggests that the child suffers from unconscious guilt because of instinctual impulses that are not acceptable to the reality principle or the superego. The symbolic expression of these impulses through the play technique and through verbalization freed the child from the infantile neuroses. The instinctual impulses could find expression in a manner acceptable to the ego, which served as a mediator between id and reality and the superego. A. Freud and M. Klein diverged on questions of technique. A. Freud (1946) developed a preparatory technique based on guidance, education, and support to strengthen the ego and superego in order to ensure that the child did not act on impulses emerging from repression. A. Freud's preparatory technique involved the strengthening of character so that the child was not corrupted by the uncovering of the id or the expression of instinctual derivatives. Klein (1927) disagreed with Freud about the need for a preparatory phase of ego building and instead directly interpreted the id and the transference. Despite their differences in technique, Freud and Klein developed their pioneering techniques within a classical perspective.

Sours (1978) points out that in the course of the history of child therapy, especially in the United States, children were increasingly viewed as having trouble repressing, as opposed to expressing, instinctual impulses. A. Freud's ego-supportive preparatory technique served as a model for an ego-supportive psychotherapeutic approach that increasingly replaced classical psychoanalysis as the treatment of choice. The view of the child patient as suffering from unconscious guilt, repression, and the infantile neurosis was increasingly replaced in the treatment setting by the conduct-disordered or borderline youngster as experiencing problems of impulse control, ego weakness, poor judgment, and superego deficiency. Sours lists the following ego-supportive techniques: suggestion, abreaction, manipulation, clarification, reassurance, and corrective emotional experience with a new object. The emphasis increasingly shifted to viewing such youngsters as experiencing deficits in early object relationships. The parent figure did not provide the child, in early development, with sufficient structure, limits, and support that would build strong ego functions and defenses to serve the ego as a bulwark against the id. In classical ego-supportive treatment, the therapist was viewed as lending a strong auxiliary ego to the patient's weak, chaotic ego. The therapist provided boundaries, limits, and structure in response to disorganized, impulsive behavior. The ego-supportive method remained within a classical perspective in that the focus was still upon instinctual impulses, but with a shift in emphasis from uncovering to suppression or repression of impulses.

EXAMPLES OF THE EGO-SUPPORTIVE TECHNIQUE

In order to illustrate how the clinician working from a classical impulse-psychology model might intervene with ego-supportive techniques, let us consider the typical problem of the child who cheats in a game with the therapist.

If the child is believed to be at the neurotic oedipal level of development, cheating might be met with an interpretive intervention. Cheating would be interpreted to the child in terms of a forbidden oedipal triumph and as unconscious guilt with a wish to be caught and punished.

If the child is viewed as expressing a belief in the omnipotence of instinctual impulse, a predominance of the pleasure over the reality principle, limits might be set on the cheating. The therapist might then empathically encourage the child to verbalize his disappointment, frustration, anger, or sadness over the loss of infantile omnipotent impulse gratification. The therapist would thereby attempt to strengthen the conduct-disordered child's ego functions of impulse control, judgment, and frustration tolerance by directing him away from the realm of action toward that of verbalization.

If the child is predominantly viewed as suffering from a narcissistic disorder and is considered to have fragile self-esteem, the therapist might limit the cheating but provide the child with a handicap or advantage to compensate for the inequality in ability. The therapist thereby limits omnipotence, but also communicates empathy for the child's poor self-worth.

If the child is viewed as severely borderline, and if his ego is so disorganized and unstructured that he is unable to learn the rules of the game and he plays randomly and chaotically, the therapist might allow the child to make up the rules but then attempt to add some consistency and structure to the child's play.

SELF AND OBJECT RELATIONS THEORY

The assumption that the youngster is cheating involves a belief on the therapist's part that the child and the therapist are playing in the realm of instinctual gratification and competition. The therapist believes that the child is trying to omnipotently cheat a reality or morality perspective that child and therapist share. The oedipal competitive dimension becomes the ideal standard that the child cheats, denies, and omnipotently repudiates.

Recent advances in self and object relations theory have raised questions about the reality and morality domain of classical impulse psychology. These theories do not always view omnipotence in terms of unrestricted instinctual gratification and the dominance of the pleasure over the reality principle.

Jacobson (1964) and Mahler (1975) have emphasized the importance and value of a very early period of omnipotent fusion between infant and mother, a symbiotic phase that is only gradually relinquished in a prolonged process of separation–individuation. Kohut (1977) speaks of a sense of omnipotence invested either in self (grandiose self) or in self–object (idealized parental image) that is gradually relinquished through the transmuting internalization of the self–object. Winnicott (1960b) speaks of a true self seeking, through an omnipotent gesture, the acceptance of the object. Despite differences in these self and object relations theories, they all profess that an early phase of some sort of omnipotent fusion between infant and mother, a symbiotic phase in which the mothering object serves as an extension of the child's self, is crucial for the development of separation–individuation and a cohesive sense of self—the true self.

The therapeutic implications of this idea are significant. The therapist, in relating to patients who experience "primitive mental states" (Giovacchini 1986a, pp. 76–99), will attempt to serve as an extension of the patient's self, as a developmental self-object. In self and object relations theory, technique is shifting into the realm of mirroring and idealizing as opposed to provision of direction, education, manipulation, and limits. Searles (1986) describes such primitive transferences in his view of the therapeutic symbiosis and Kohut (1977) in his ideas of the self-object transference.

In the therapy process that I will describe, the child's chaotic activity embodies primitive psychic structures that become mobilized through the self-object transference, promoting higher levels of structuralization and ego functioning. If the therapist attempts to provide active ego-supportive structure, he may inadvertently interfere with the structuralization that can emerge from chaotic activity. From this point of view, the therapist serves as an extension of the child's self instead of imposing his separate self on the patient's self or his strong auxiliary ego on the patient's weak ego by providing external boundaries and structure.

THE NEGATIVE THERAPEUTIC REACTION IN CHILDREN

The children to whom these views may be applied are extremely disturbed in a very specific sense. These children behave as if the ordinary rules and structures in everyday life are an affront to their sense of omnipotence. They are often described as wanting to do whatever they wish whenever they wish. Any instruction in any realm whatsoever is reacted to as a narcissistic injury. Such children are often described as extremely hyperactive, learning disordered, undersocialized, and severely conduct disordered. In their defiance, they often endanger themselves and others. They seem oblivious to others, and they reject help and empathy; the provision of help is also perceived as a narcissistic injury to their sense of omnipotence. These children cannot accept the hesitancies of learning, of not knowing, and they therefore insist that they know all. They resemble a cat chasing its own tail; their frenzied activity is highly chaotic and leads to little visible accomplishment. Efforts to control them are met with temper tantrums. If they are finally restrained or limited, they make no good use of such restraint but instead become apathetic and uninterested.

These youngsters often come from family systems in which the parents are sharply critical of their efforts to learn. The parents are often overbearing or engulfing; they see the child as an extension, or self–object, of themselves rather than permitting the child to relate to them as an extension of the child's self. The child is likely to be harshly rejected or abused if he presents a vulnerable, dependent self to the parental objects for holding or mirroring. The child will also be rejected if he rejects the parents' self–object needs toward him. The parents' engulfing behavior results in the child's becoming overly sensitive to any efforts at control or structure. In an effort to experience some sense of omnipotent control, the child reverts to practicing subphase behavior. He acts as if oblivious to the human external object world. As he runs about, he experiences others as obstacles, or as engulfing, and controlling. At the same time, the child will get into trouble and thereby force the object to chase after him. Mahler (1975) has pointed out that the practicing subphase behavioral pattern can be used by certain youngsters to flee from an engulfing image of the parent. One might add that the child is also in conformity with the unconscious rejecting internal object by fleeing from the possibility of a dependent vulnerable relationship to a potential good object and separation from the internal bad object.

White and Weiner (1986) have related the origins of the grandiose self to Mahler's practicing subphase. The child's newfound ability to crawl and then toddle, the achievement of an upright position, and the attendant feelings of elation and omnipotence, the sense that the world will forever be his oyster, give rise to a sense of healthy grandiosity that consolidates into the grandiose self. This consolidation occurs within the rapprochement subphase, during which the youngster can actively seek out a self–object to mirror his grandiosity. These youngsters revert to practicing subphase grandiosity in order to escape an object world that is sharply critical of their vulnerability. The child can then experience some confidence and esteem from motoric expression while rejecting the vulnerable self's need for a holding or mirroring object.

In the treatment situation, these youngsters often reject empathy, mirroring, and limit setting by the therapist. Any sign of progress or connection with the therapist is immediately undone by a negative therapeutic reaction manifested by increasing acting-out, destructive behavior and rejection or indifference toward the therapist. The following two vignettes illustrate the dynamics of the negative therapeutic reaction and the ways in which the therapist can intervene to mobilize a sustaining self–object transference to create structure from chaos.

ROBERT

Robert was a 9-year-old Hispanic youngster referred for treatment because of severe hyperactive and aggressive behavior. School officials reported that he was out of control, behaved aggressively with other children, and did not follow any of the teacher's instructions. Despite the fact that he attended a small, structured class for emotionally disturbed children, he did not respond to limit setting or nurturing help; according to the principal, he was in need of medication or a structured, authoritative, behavioral-management type of residential program, or both.

Robert responded negatively to help, nurturance, or praise. If he were finally forced to sit still, he became withdrawn and sullen, and just waited for the restraint to be lifted. When his parents or teachers criticized him, he sometimes spoke of wanting to die. He had once made a suicidal gesture by tying a shirt around his neck and saying that he was going to hang himself.

Robert, the only child of divorced parents, lived with his mother and visited his father irregularly. His parents could be severely critical of anything that he tried to do. His mother would ask him to do a chore but then criticize him and take over the task herself. He internalized this rejecting object image of his autonomy as he, himself, rejected whatever he drew or built. He would begin to draw a picture, immediately become dissatisfied with some imperfection, and destroy the picture. Robert stopped trying to learn and instead insisted that he already knew. In this way he avoided the vulnerability associated with learning, and he increasingly assumed an omnipotent position of knowing everything but trying nothing.

Robert's parents often turned to him as a self–object or transitional object (Giovacchini 1986a), treating him as an extension of themselves instead of permitting him to ever experience them as self–objects. Robert's father would never call him, but then he complained that Robert never called him. When the boy appeared in a school play, his father did not come but complained that Robert had invited his mother and not him, although Robert had not extended a special invitation even to his mother. His mother would not hug or demonstrate affection toward her son but complained that he did not kiss her. She would approach him before he left the house for the day and say "Give me a kiss," and he would turn away. Robert experienced his parents' self–object needs toward him as engulfing and attempted to flee from the engulfing object by hyperactivity.

In his initial therapy sessions, Robert did not play with materials in a symbolic, sublimated fashion. Instead he tried to destroy them, pulling the dolls apart, aimlessly throwing them, and distractedly shifting from one activity to the next. Any effort to get to know him in an innocuous way by asking questions about his neighborhood, schools, friends, or interests was ignored. His behavior became increasingly destructive and aggressive.

I generally "hang out" with such children as they become increasingly aggressive and intervene only when they are about to destroy something. For instance, as Robert was pulling a doll apart and a limb was about to be torn from the body, I said in a low tone, "Not so hard." I did not explain that objects in the room are to be played with but not destroyed; nor did I say that he could not break things or hurt himself or me. I have found that such speeches usually exacerbate the severely disturbed child's acting out and result in the therapist's responding with further limits and prohibitions, thereby unwittingly enacting the part of the engulfing object to the child's provocations. I therefore keep such comments to the bare minimum, communicating only the most essential words because I want to limit the child's destruction while still permitting him to bring the stormy behavioral problems into the session.

When Robert would destroy his drawings, I attempted neither to "save" the pictures nor to influence his perceptions of them. The child who destroys all of his work as unworthy has activated the internal rejecting object–rejected self representations, the pictures representing his own rejected self. I have found that if the therapist attempts to align himself prematurely with the child's rejected self, the rejecting behavior will be exacerbated. Robert was rejecting the vulnerable self's need for a good, mirroring object. His rejection of the drawings was the opposite type of behavior from that of the child who draws a picture and hopes for the object's admiration and approval. These are two sides of the same phenomenon. The activation of the rejecting object–rejected self representations served to defend against the activation of the positive, vulnerable, libidinal self and the need for a good, admiring object. In rejecting his own drawings, Robert also rejected his own need for a good object to admire them. This situation is comparable to that of the borderline adult patient who antilibidinally rejects his need for a good object by activating the all-bad internal self and object unit. As Robert threw away his drawings, I intervened by hanging around and not doing anything. This is an intervention because it accepts his activation of the antidependent self and permits him to relate to me in a rejecting, antidependent manner. The therapist often intervenes with borderline children through action and behavior instead of words.

In the first few sessions, no attempt was made to contact Robert except for the initial innocuous introduction. He became increasingly wild and aggressive. At one point, he aimlessly threw a sofa pillow around the room and accidentally hit and broke a picture on the wall. He waited for my reaction, but I wordlessly cleaned up the broken glass. Nothing was said about breaking any more pictures. When he later wildly threw the pillow again in the direction of the picture, I simply said "not so near," glancing in the direction of it. He then made a concerted effort, for the next few throws, to aim away from the pictures. When he threw again in the direction of the picture, I said "Not so near." A few throws later, he again threw in the direction of the picture, and I saw him catch himself as if to say, "Oh, I forgot," though he did not actually say it. I believed that this catching of himself was the first sign that he had internalized me and so I did not say "not so near," thinking that he would hear this comment as engulfing, since he had already said it to himself. I was confirmed in this view by the fact that the next time he threw the pillow, he aimed far away from the pictures.

Robert had serious difficulty with the ego functions of impulse control and judgment. This technique permits the youngster to bring this difficulty into the session. No attempt is made to provide much in the way of limit setting, boundaries, and structure because it is preferable that the child find his own limits to destructive behavior through the process of internalizing the therapist. There is a difficult balance to be achieved here in that the therapist must provide limits in such a way that the child internalizes them instead of rejecting the therapist as engulfing. With children such as Robert, attempts have been made to set limits and provide boundaries and structure by informing the youngster that he cannot throw the sofa pillow aimlessly, by suggesting a game of catch, or by setting up a target or object at which the child can aim. These techniques are ego supportive in the sense that the therapist tries to lend a strong ego to the child's weak ego by actively structuring and directing the child's activity. The therapist introduces reality, boundaries, and structure. I have sometimes found these techniques to be ineffective, however, because the child initially becomes increasingly antilibidinally aggressive and then withdraws if the therapist succeeds in restraining him. The therapist will begin to be internalized if he accepts the child's rejecting relatedness and sets limits only when absolutely necessary. The severe borderline child experiences the therapist's efforts to be helpful as an engulfment.

Robert made his first direct contact with me by throwing the sofa pillow at me. I caught it and waited. He asked me to throw it back and I did. At this point we engaged in our first game of catch. This contact marked a shift in the transference evolution from the out-of-contact phase to that of ambivalent symbiosis.

Robert began to instruct me on how to throw and catch the pillow. I tried to follow his instructions but could never quite do it well enough for him. He began talking to me for the first time. "You didn't do it right. Throw it from the side. No, make it curve. Too straight. That's not right. Watch me. What's the matter with you? Were you watching? Are you a retard? Do it right."

I did not respond verbally to this abuse but followed his instructions as best as I could. His verbal abuse increased, and he would blame me if I threw the pillow to him and he dropped it.

In the transference, he assumed the position of the rejecting object representation and projectively identified into me his inadequate self-representation. Interpersonally, he verbally abused me as his parents abused him. The antilibidinal stance was now becoming fully activated in the transferential situation. He would threaten me with abandonment for my inadequacy, saying "If you don't do it right, I'm not coming back."

He directed me to retrieve the ball, to pick it up from the floor, to move furniture out of the way to clear our field of catch, sometimes referring to me as "slave" and "servant." I followed his instructions silently.

After a time, he replaced the sofa pillow with a ball of clay. The game of catch became quite elaborate. He would do tricks with the ball before throwing it. He'd throw it three times over an outstretched arm, catching it with his other hand, then throw it behind his back from one hand to the next and repeat the throws with the other arm outstretched. He could barely do this juggling act; the ball kept dropping, or he would forget the next step in the sequence. But then he would expect me to do the same trick after watching his fumbling efforts once. If I dropped the ball or did not follow the sequence exactly, he would become enraged and accuse me of being inattentive and stupid, demanding that I return the ball to him so that he could further instruct me. I had to pay close attention to follow the trick, and once I got it right, he would tell me that I was mistaken and add a further step to the trick. He never allowed me to practice anything that I learned, and he set up the situation so that I repeatedly failed. This pattern of interaction went on for one year.

The pattern gradually began to shift. For prolonged periods, Robert would engage me in a game of catch during which we would simply throw the ball as straight as possible to each other. This catch would go on for the entire session, session after session. Sometimes it was very relaxing and I felt that I was in a reverie or a trance. It could be almost hypnotic. At other times it would become monotonous; my mind would wander and I, not fully concentrating, would not catch or throw exactly as Robert wanted. In such instances, he would scream that I was not paying attention, that I must concentrate, and he would make the rules of the game more difficult so that I had to give it my undivided attention. I sometimes still found my mind wandering even though I had made up my mind to give the game my fullest attention. It was as if a form of splitting occurred in which a part of my psyche rebelled against his demand that I fully concentrate on our interaction.

This transference–countertransference relatedness indicated the evolution of a fully activated ambivalent symbiosis. Robert was, on the one hand, the mother demanding the full attention of the child. When he felt that he had lost control of my mind in our interaction, he would become rejecting and abusive in much the same manner that his parents rejected and abused him when his mind wandered outside of their orbit. On the other hand, he was simultaneously the child demanding that his schizoid, detached mother provide him with her full attention.

I met with Robert's mother regularly on a child-guidance basis and I knew her to be extremely absent-minded, "in the clouds," and self-preoccupied. In fact she spontaneously reported that she often felt as if she walked around in a trance and was out of touch with the everyday happenings around her. She was so preoccupied that she often would not hear Robert when he asked her a question. He set up this monotonous game of catch which eventually induced within me the schizoid drifting off of his mother. This interaction repeated the actual ambivalent symbiosis between him and his mother. In their actual ambivalent symbiotic relatedness in Robert's early childhood, she often demanded his full attention and tried to control his every thought. At the same time, when he demanded her attention, she would drift off mentally in schizoid detachment. Her efforts to control his thoughts and attention in turn provoked him into mind wanderings, distraction, and schizoid unrelatedness to flee from her mental engulfment. She had demanded that he concentrate on her, but she wandered off mentally when he tried to get her to concentrate on him. I came to believe that much of his distractibility and hyperactivity reflected his internal efforts to flee from the engulfing object that was demanding his full attention. In school, he was notoriously known for paying no attention to instructions, switching rapidly from one activity to the next, and being in his own world. In our sessions, he attempted to correct the pathological ambivalent symbiosis by omnipotently controlling my attention and demanding that I not mentally wander off into schizoid detachment. At the same time, he re-created an interactional atmosphere (the monotonous game of catch) that would induce my mind to wander in schizoid detachment.

The ambivalent symbiosis was at its peak of intensity when Robert finally ended our game of catch and instructed me to do physical exercise. He commanded that I do army push-ups, which involved clapping one's hands as one pushed oneself up and down. He ordered me to do 50, and I did as many as I could without straining myself. He called me weak and a sissy and then instructed me to do 100 sit-ups. After I rested, with Robert telling me to stop being lazy, I did as many as I could. Robert said that I wasn't so tired and could do more. I rested for a time and did a few more, then rested again while he called me lazy and weak. He then ordered me to do a push-up with one arm. If I had attempted such a push-up I would have fallen flat on my face. However, I got into position to demonstrate that it was not possible. He insisted that I do it and then picked up a pencil and said he would break it if I did not do the push-up. When I did not reply, he said that he would break the pencil by the count of ten. "One, two, three, four," he said and added, ". . . Should I break it? If you don't tell me not to break it, I will . . . five, six, seven. . . . Tell me to break it or not break it . . . seven, eight, nine. . . . You'd better tell me. If you don't say anything, I'll break it. Come on . . . ten. Should I break it? I'm not kidding; say something." He placed the pencil on the desk, unbroken, and said, rather meekly, that he was just kidding, adding, "See, I didn't break it."

I was surprised that he seemed concerned that I recognize that he did not break the pencil. This was the first instance in which my reaction seemed to matter to him. I felt certain that if I told him either to break or to not break the pencil, he would have broken it. This exchange between us demonstrates the need to help the child to find his own limits to his destructive behavior. Our interaction also inaugurated the therapeutic symbiotic phase of the transference evolution.

In our next session, Robert again instructed me to do army push-ups. Again I did as many as I could. He applauded and said that I was terrific. He then told me to do the same number of sit-ups that I had done the last time, instead of the hundred he had previously ordered. I did them, he applauded, and for the first time, he positioned himself to try army push-ups. He then looked at me for my reaction and said, "That wasn't good. Not as many as you did." I said, "You did fine."

In our future interactions, he would sometimes begin to scold me for not doing something right or quickly enough, but then he would become concerned that he had hurt my feelings and add that he did not mean it or that I did all right. In this way, he began to develop a capacity for concern for the object (Winnicott 1963). He became increasingly interested in doing the tricks with the ball of clay himself during our catch play instead of instructing me on how to do them. He would now say, "I didn't do it right—let me practice." I would "hang around" and just watch without commenting on his efforts unless he asked directly. Then I would say, "You did fine." He now seemed able to take in such succinct, positive comments from the object. He began to take pride in how well he and I did exercises, played catch, and so on. On such occasions the all-positive self and object representation unit was in ascendance, and he and I were the best of teams. At other times, when he criticized himself or me, the all-negative self and object representation unit dominated. But the positive object relations unit increasingly gained in ascendance. This phase of therapeutic symbiotic transference, in which we were increasingly the best players in our activities, is equivalent to the symbiotic phase described earlier, in which the adult patient feels that he and the therapist are the best of therapeutic teams.

The change in his behavior during sessions marked a change in his internal object relations. His efforts to do exercises and tricks, with the admission that he did not do them well, and the acceptance of his fumblings in learning meant that the vulnerable true self was emerging in the transference in relation to the holding object. The spontaneous true self was manifest in his feelings and expressions of both disappointment and joy as he practiced tricks and exercises. It was fascinating to watch the transformation as abusive, omnipotent behavior gave way to the natural behavior of a child. He increasingly surrendered the sense of omnipotence for a new-found sense of competence and mastery, with the associated emergence of vulnerability. His acceptance of his own vulnerability and limitations also led to his setting of limits on his own destructive behavior. He now looked to me for admiring mirroring and empathy while at the same time admiring and mirroring my efforts at tricks and exercises and expressing empathy and concern when I failed.

During the treatment I kept in close contact with Robert's school and was informed that he had begun to make an effort to learn and to ask for help. He could also accept limits and discipline from his teachers because he now perceived their efforts as help instead of engulfment.

Robert had undergone psychological testing before I started to treat him, but he was too distractible and uncooperative for the evaluator to arrive at meaningful findings. He was recently tested again and was able to cooperate and complete the evaluation, which indicated that he is intelligent and that he is progressing in learning. I attribute the change in his testing behavior to the fact that he no longer needs to wrestle his attention away from a mind-controlling internal object.

YVETTE

Yvette, a 9-year-old girl, was referred for fighting with peers and having tantrums in reaction to any change in her family or school situation. Yvette had already been to two therapists, and both treatments terminated after several weeks because Yvette sat sullenly and would not respond to the therapists' efforts to engage her in talk or play. The therapists and the mother had agreed that the child was not yet ready for treatment.

Yvette's mother was herself a severely disturbed borderline patient currently in intensive long-term treatment. The mother reported to her therapist that during Yvette's early childhood, the mother had experienced severe separation anxiety and would not allow Yvette out of her sight. Then she would feel trapped and imprisoned with the child and would experience murderous impulses toward her, which she fortunately did not act upon.

Yvette's mother would become verbally abusive toward her whenever she misbehaved. She was overly involved in Yvette's everyday life, and she removed her from activities, friendships, or classes if the child complained of any problem. At the beginning of each school year, Yvette would throw tantrums and cry that she hated her teacher, peers, and school work. The mother's therapist helped her to manage the child's anxiety and not keep her at home. The mother's therapist referred the child to me.

Yvette insisted that she did not want to come for therapy, and she initially sat silently and sullenly and would not look toward me. I made no effort to engage her, and after a few minutes she rose and went out to her mother in the waiting room. She told her mother that she did not like me, and the mother coaxed her to return. She sat silently for a time and then commented that I had an ugly beard. She drew pictures of my ugly beard and showed them to her mother. She continually went in and out of the therapy room during the first session. I never spoke. At the completion of the session, the mother came in and asked whether there was any point in returning with Yvette. I told the mother that the child had done fine and that I would see her the next week.

For the next three sessions, Yvette would first sit silently, and then draw pictures of my ugly beard to show to her mother. She then initiated a new activity by gathering all of the chair and sofa pillows and cushions in the room and burying me where I sat beneath them. She piled them upon me until I was completely buried and could not be seen, and then she brought her mother in to see. For the duration of the session, she buried and unburied me, laughing gleefully, while I remained as still as possible. Yvette's mother protested about her behavior, but I told her it was fine. After the session, I explained to the mother that I wanted Yvette to bring all of her behavioral problems into our session so that I could know where she needed help.

During the next session, Yvette's mother told me that she had discovered Yvette drawing pictures of my ugly beard during the week between our sessions. On these pictures was a running commentary of "I hate Seinfeld. Seinfeld is ugly. Seinfeld's beard is ugly." She also drew one picture in which I breathed fire. Yvette became excited during this session as she buried me beneath everything that could be lifted in the room, cursing and calling me names. At one point she ran out to her mother to report that she was having the best time of her life. I, myself, was quite pleased during our session because I considered her picture drawing during the week as the first indication that she was developing a relationship to an internal image of me that she carried with her after our session, even if that relationship was antidependent. She was relating to me by burying, and therefore destroying, me and then unburying, and therefore re-creating, me. In this way, she both destroyed and then made reparation with the internal object.

At one session, she threw a pillow at me and then said that I was too stupid to throw it back. I understood her statement as a communication that she wanted me to return the throw, so I did. I did not ask her whether she wanted me to throw it or reflect back that she wanted me to. Rather, I understood her name calling as a communication and acted upon it. This action is a nonverbal behavioral intervention through which the therapist serves as an extension of the child. In treating children with borderline disorders, I have found that verbal reflections on what the child is doing or asking tend to place the therapist in too separate a position in relation to the child, at least in the early phases of treatment. Therefore, if I had reflected that "it sounds as if you wanted me to throw the pillow back and as if you're disappointed and angry" or asked "Do you want me to throw it back?" the child would have perceived me as objectifying her and separating myself from her instead of participating as an extension of her.

Children's communications are largely nonverbal, and if the therapist is to serve effectively as an extension to the child, he must behaviorally respond to the nonverbal communication. For instance, during our game of catch with the sofa pillow, Yvette did not verbally direct me to throw it softly or hard. She threw it as hard as she could at me and waited. If I threw it back hard at her, she'd drop it, appear to be upset and disappointed, curse to herself, and throw it back wildly, without aiming. Once I asked her whether I should throw it back softly or hard, and she angrily reacted. "Hard. I'm no sissy." So I threw it hard and she missed it. She threw it back wildly and knocked some books off the shelf. I now threw the pillow very gently to her and she caught it easily but commanded that I throw it hard. I continued to throw it gently even though she called me a sissy for not being able to throw it hard. She became much calmer and began to throw less wildly and with better aim. Her nonverbal communication showed me that she wanted me to throw gently even though she told me to throw hard. As this example illustrates, the therapist must follow the child's direction in order to serve as an extension of the self, not merely the child's verbal directions but even nonverbal communications that might be in oppositon to verbal commands. As Yvette became calmly engaged in playing catch, her antidependent self no longer completely dominated our re-latedness; I had begun to reach and contact her vulnerable self. As she became more competent in our catch game, she would throw wildly if I threw the ball too softly, so I had to begin to throw hard in recognition of her enhanced competence.

Yvette brought a kerchief to our next session and wanted to blindfold me. I permitted her to do so, and she led me around the room and then announced that I was on my own. I was to guess where she was, and she took great pleasure in my inability to do so correctly. At one point she said that she was going to wreck my office and that I could not remove the blindfold. She became quite excited, and it sounded as if a whirlwind was blowing through my office as I heard objects crashing, falling, and tearing. After a time I heard her say "I'm tired" and fall to the floor. With her permission I took off the blindfold and found that the cushions and pillows were removed from the furniture and piled on the floor, chairs were turned over, items on my desk were on the floor, and blank sheets of note paper were torn. However, nothing in the room had been damaged or broken. I was encouraged that Yvette was finding limits to her stormy, destructive behavior. In blind-folding me, Yvette had disarmed the engulfing, intrusive mother in the transference. She had made the object powerless to see or find her. In this way, she asserted her autonomy from the engulf-ing object. She gleefully led me about, singing that I was in her power. She wrecked the room and saw that I trusted her not to become destructive, and I believe that this trust helped her to limit her destructiveness.

In our next few sessions we played a game of hide-and-seek catch; versions of this game are commonly initiated by borderline youngsters during the ambivalent symbiosis. I would cover my eyes, Yvette would hide, and I would try to find her. She would flee once I spotted her, and I would have to catch and tag her. I allowed her to control whether I caught her. For instance, if she cried "stop" as I chased after her, I would stop. I would then not try so hard to catch her until she taunted me, and then I would dart after her. If she did not say "stop" or scream, I would tag her. If I saw that she was getting too upset by my catching her, I would slow down without her overtly directing me to.

Yvette was now in a full-blown ambivalent symbiosis. She maintained a relationship to her internal image of me by drawing pictures between sessions. In some of these pictures I was Seinfeld with the ugly beard and in others I was He-Man saving children from the witch. In some pictures I was a witch with an ugly beard, resembling part man, part woman.

We continued to play various games in which she controlled how close I could come to catching her. As she practiced separating from the engulfing object, she allowed her guard to drop. The more I permitted her to experience a sense of omnipotent control, the more she was able to let go of her antidependent defense and allow her vulnerable self to relate to me as a "holding object."

The ambivalent symbiosis reached its culmination point one session when she brought in a large bag of cookies. She played mommy, I played child, and she fed me. She gave me the cookies, saying, "Aren't they good and yummy? Now eat all of them; they're good for you." After I ate a few, she told me that they were poisoned and would eat my insides out. She had me play at having a tummy ache. She then ordered me to play mommy and feed her the poisonous cookies. She had me play this role exactly as she had played it. First I coaxed her to eat, saying that the cookies were good and yummy, and then after she ate a few, I told her that they were poisonous. She then rolled on the floor, holding her aching tummy. Yvette then called me a "bad" mommy for feeding her poisoned cookies and played at beating me.

Through this play interaction, Yvette recapitulated her early traumatic relationship to her mother. As noted earlier, Yvette's mother overprotected Yvette and would not let her out of her sight, but then felt imprisoned and trapped by their closeness and had murderous impulses toward Yvette. The child reenacted that pathological symbiosis by having me offer her good nurturance which later proved to be poison.

I allowed Yvette to play out this ambivalent symbiotic sequence for as long as she needed to. After a time, she began to feed me good cookies and call me a "good child" and herself a "good mommy." She then had me play the good mommy, feeding the good child the good cookies. After we ate, she directed us both to lie on the floor and then said, "Good night, Mommy," and we played at sleeping. In this way, Yvette began to experience the therapeutic symbiosis in the transference.

In subsequent sessions, Yvette would sit in my chair and have me wheel her through the room singing lullabies. She would then have us shift roles as she rocked me in the carriage chair. The sessions now shifted their emotional tone from stormy and active to comforting and soothing. Whereas before we had chased each other around the room, we now comforted, soothed, and nurtured each other. In the pictures she drew at home, I was no longer He-Man or the man with the ugly beard, but rather a Christ-like figure caring for small animals and children.

Yvette brought in her pet lizard and asked me to help her take care of it. She said that the lizard looked mean but was really gentle, quiet, and unable to move quickly. Her behavior also changed in school and at home in that she became more compliant and responsive, and actively sought comforting and help from peers and teachers.

After the stage of therapeutic symbiosis, she began to show evidence of separating and individuating in the transference. She again initiated games, but now she wanted me to "really try." She told me to throw the ball the way that I wanted to throw it, and I did so. She no longer wanted to teach me. When we played hide-

and-seek catch, I was to try to catch her. She was no longer defiant but did respond if I set limits on occasion. We continued to eat cookies, but we no longer fed each other; we ate independently. On occasion Yvette might revert to the mother–child feeding game if she was upset, but then she would want to discontinue the "baby game." Her autonomous and competitive functioning carried over in school, as she tried to do well and brought her achievements into sessions for me to admire. I now no longer acted as an extension of her, but related to her as a separate object.

7

Intervention with the Out-of-Contact Patient

This chapter illustrates interventions with patients who remain emotionally out of contact in the transference. These patients experience a structural deficit in positive self and object representations and are therefore dominated by negative self and object representations. The absence of positive external object relations results in a deficit of internal positive self and object representations that could serve as receptors for internalizing the positive aspects of the therapeutic relationship. These patients do not experience a sense of deprivation or the lack of a good object. They literally do not know what they are missing.

THE STRUCTURAL DEFICIT

Intervention can address the structural deficit by first showing these patients that they are lacking in a positive self and object representation unit. The therapist initiates this process by empathically demonstrating through the clinical material that the patient is not able to expect help from the external therapist or to internalize potentially positive aspects of the therapeutic relationship.

The severely disturbed borderline patient's well-known sensitivity to environmental impingement is the result of the dominance of the negative self and object representation unit, which transforms a difficult problem into an utterly hopeless one. The patient's incapacity to use the therapist's potential help becomes the medium through which the therapist demonstrates the patient's deficit in receptive positive self and object representations. It is important that the patient not experience the therapist's interventions as accusatory in the sense of blaming him for not making use of the therapy.

The following case discussion will focus on the clinical management of the borderline patient's severe rejecting behavior in the transferential relationship. The patient suffered from extreme environmental hardships. It can be demonstrated that the therapist can respond to the patient to facilitate the internalization of the therapist as a helping object. These interventions are particularly relevant during the out-of-contact and symbiotic phases of the transference evolution. The issue of countertransference is also important.

DIANE

Diane is a 29-year-old Hispanic woman seeking help for her latency-age son, who was having academic and behavioral problems in school. She had also been reported to the child welfare authorities for child abuse and neglect before coming for help. I have been treating Diane for five years.

Diane grew up in a large family supported by public assistance. She and her siblings were severely abused by an embittered mother. Once, after Diane and her mother had quarreled, her mother beat her with a metal rod until she was covered with blood. Such incidents resulted in the temporary removal of Diane and her siblings from the home by child welfare authorities on several occasions. Diane's father, an alcoholic, deserted the family during Diane's childhood.

Diane made a serious suicide attempt in adolescence and left home permanently at the age of 16. She began to live with a man, became pregnant, and left him when he asked her to marry him. She said that she wanted no part of an emotional commitment.

Since that time, Diane has lived with her son and has worked sporadically at various jobs. She generally sought temporary positions where she could make her own hours and work independently. Unable to get along with supervisors or co-workers, she would quit or get fired. She moved around a great deal and was evicted on occasion for not paying the rent.

Diane preferred to see only married men so that they would not expect a commitment. If a man became serious about their relationship, she would leave. She said that she sought relationships in which both she and the man clearly understood that they used each other for sex and fun. During the time of treatment she was seeing two men who were both married. I often wondered how she managed to survive the precariousness of her existence. She says that everyone asks her that. She sees herself as a survivor and explains that throughout her adolescence, she went to the toughest and poorest schools in the Bronx, New York, and she had fought constantly to survive. She was so violent, disruptive, and out of control that she was eventually placed in a junior high school for delinquent youth. Because of her reputation for violence, the other girls eventually left her alone. She was one of a few Puerto Ricans among mostly black youth, and to make matters worse, she was white-skinned and pretty. She did not belong to a street gang and wanted only to be left alone.

The Problem of the Patient Acting Rather than Reflecting

Diane began treatment on a once-weekly basis. She had been to the clinic once about a year earlier, and after a few sessions she came in high on marijuana. She reported that the worker had lectured her, so she walked out and did not return.

There was a hyperactivity about Diane. She would sit on the edge of her seat, as if she were ready to pounce, shifting about uncomfortably and continually looking at her watch. She did not stay for the full 45-minute session but left after "saying her piece."

Often, the session lasted for only 20 minutes. She would discuss events of the week—a fight with her current supervisor, a problem with her son, or a quarrel with her lover. She was extremely action oriented and described all situations in terms of the actions and behavior of the participants, without any reflection or insight into underlying feelings or motivations. She described a fight with a female supervisor:

> She stormed into the office. It was full of people but she stood over me like the Incredible Hulk. She's a huge woman, large like a mountain. With her hands on her hips, towering over me, she shouted "Diane?" I just looked up at her and she raved at me like a mad woman, screaming that she can't stand me anymore and who do I think I am and that I can't continue like this anymore. The next thing I knew, I was on my feet too. We were screaming back and forth. I thought she was going to hit me. I thought I'd hit her. I walked out. I put on my coat, said "Drop dead, you pig" and walked right out. If I return tomorrow and she says one word, I'll hit her. I almost hit her today. She's a big lady. I'm large, but she's a mountain. She's a Black Muslim. She hates Puerto Ricans. She might kill me. I'll stick her with my knife first.

A Lack of Communication between Patient and Therapist

During these initial sessions, it was impossible to get a sense of what was causing Diane's interpersonal problems. Diane could not reflect on why this supervisor hated her, on whether she had any part in the problem. If I asked what she thought was happening between herself and the supervisor, she would present another action-filled story. After the telling, she would be ready to leave. She wanted no feedback from me. It seemed that my role was to serve as a witness to the story. Given that her work and housing situations were unstable and that she tended to become depressed and hopeless between jobs, I felt a responsibility to confront her with the self-destructive consequences of her actions. If I attempted, while empathizing with her feelings, to point out the destructive consequences of her actions, she just stared at me as if I were a creature from another planet. When I said something to the effect that she spites only herself when she walks off a job because she is angry, she looked at me as if I were a fool. She could not verbalize her disagreements or lack of understanding, no matter how much I attempted to elicit such discussion. Instead, she communicated through movements or facial expressions. I often had the distinct impression that she did not understand a word I said.

When a problem arose in her life, such as unemployment or the threat of eviction, she was even less eager to relate to me. She often did not come in or call to cancel. When she did appear and I opened the issue for discussion, she would say that it was a waste of time to talk about the situation, that she must act and *do* something about it. She would begin to look at her watch, as if the only problem she faced was sitting here and talking to me and that this oppressive discussion was the only thing in her life getting in the way of her acting to solve her problem. No sooner did I think this when she would rise to leave. Interventions such as "You are right. You do have to act to solve your problems, but sometimes sitting down and first figuring out the problem, getting some distance on it, can help you act more effectively" were met with a blank stare. I would ask whether she agreed or had other thoughts about it, and she would shrug and roll her eyes as if to say, "I wish he'd shut up already so I can get out of here and do something useful." If I told her what I believed she was thinking, she would say, "Yes, I have a lot to do. I have to get going now."

Empathy was no more effective than problem solving, confrontation, or pointing out reality. For instance, as Diane described the hardships and struggles in her life, how supervisors, landlords, or lovers oppressed her, she would look at me if I expressed understanding as if to say, "So what if you understand? What good does that do for me?" If I made an empathic statement about how she feels that everyone is trying to control her, to stop her from achieving her goals, she looked as if she could not wait for me to be quiet so that she could either continue to talk or leave. When I commented on how the abuse and oppression she was experiencing in her current life was similar to that which she had suffered from earliest childhood, she looked at me as if to say, "So what else is new?" If I interpreted that oppression and instability were all that she had ever known, so that she might be afraid of actively trying to change her way of life, to take control instead of passively suffering and fleeing from her troubles, she looked at me as if to say, "What is he talking about?" When I remained silent and just allowed her to talk, she would glance repeatedly at her watch as if to say, "Why am I wasting my time talking to myself?" and then leave.

I do not mean to suggest that every week, in frustration and exasperation, I tried a different approach. Rather, I tried these interventions over a four-year period and found all ineffectual. Yet she continued to come, though irregularly. We did have one area of mutual understanding—that it was bad for her to beat up her child. Therefore, when she was angry at him, she no longer hit him but instead broke things or threw things around in her house. Once she was in a rage at him for watching television and not doing his homework. She refrained from beating his brains out and instead kicked in the television screen. Another time, she punched her fist through a window and needed to go to the hospital for treatment. When I encouraged her to verbalize instead of acting on her angry feelings, she replied that she felt better when she threw something, broke something, or hit something. She said that she verbalized her angry feelings as well, but action made her feel better. Much of her communication to me was through facial expressions. On those rare occasions when she felt pleased with something I said, she would look directly at me and laugh. When she was angry, she would snarl. When she thought what I said was stupid, she would roll her eyes as if to say, "What is wrong with him?" At other times, she would stare at me blankly, as if I were communicating in a strange language.

The Countertransference

As I listened to Diane over the first four years of treatment, I noted two opposing tendencies in myself. Sometimes I attempted to understand her world view. I tried, in other words, to get into her mind. At other times, I wanted her to learn about reality and morality, to impose a higher developmental level and structure, to put her into my mind, so to speak. She had a favorite expression she regularly used when someone irritated her to the point at which she decided to put him out of her life. She would say, "I'm not going to entertain this nonsense anymore." On occasions, I found myself repeating this phrase in my own mind when I was irritated about something. At other times, I would be in an unpleasant situation and I would think of what Diane would have done in the same circumstance. I would picture her doing anything she pleased without worrying about the consequences of reality or morality, and I would feel envy and admire her. In this way, I began to carry an image of her in my mind, and she started to become an internal object to me. I increasingly wondered whether some of my reality–morality interventions were not the result of envy of her ability to dare to do whatever she pleased. I now perceived the situations she discussed through her eyes instead of from my own view. I became intrigued with how she experienced and felt about everything. This was not only an objective, scientific interest, although that too played a part, but also an intensely personal one in the sense that I felt that there were some important things that I could learn from her. This internal shift also marked a change in the actual treatment process.

For the first four years Diane was inconsistent about keeping appointments. She would come for several weeks and then disappear for a time without calling. We might run into one another in the neighborhood. She would stop and say, "I've been intending to call you." I would hear from her shortly afterward. At first, when she disappeared, I would call her to find out what had happened. She would say that she had forgotten to make an appointment. After a while, I gave up on calling her. In this way, our relationship was detached. I at first rationalized permitting her space by thinking that she needed distance because of her fear of engulfment, but now I wondered about my own fear of symbiosis. I also had the feeling that she was headed toward a disaster, that she was a volcano ready to explode, and I wasn't interested in being close by when it happened. She had always indicated that she felt that people who pursued her were stupid, and I had a sense that she derived some pleasure in making people "stupid." I now wondered if her internal rejecting object did not keep others, including me, at bay, by making them feel stupid if they tried to become involved in an emotionally meaningful relationship with her.

A second problem occurred to me. Her constant crises were always the focus of our sessions. It felt absurd to focus on our relationship when she had such pressing reality problems, so we would discuss these problems week after week, but nothing ever seemed to change. She would resolve one crisis or problem only to encounter another one. I felt that we were going around in circles, that her reality problems stood between us, and also that she did not have a significant enough internal relationship with me to use my help. Furthermore, such respected and knowledgeable theorists as Winnicott and Guntrip cautioned against bringing about a therapeutic regression or intense transference experience with patients in unstable environmental situations. Yet I felt that this patient needed such an intense transferential experience in order to begin to cope with and change her environmental situation. I decided to begin to address all of these issues with her.

Tracking the Absence of an Internal Object

The point of entry was her habit of missing appointments and disappearing at irregular intervals. I did not approach this problem from the perspective of resistance or limit setting. Rather, I became intrigued with how she experienced, or did not experience, our relationship during these absences. I thought of myself as a professional helping person, and intellectually at least, she accepted this designation of my role. She realized that she was in something called psychotherapy with me, and she came in and discussed problems in the role of a patient. On an emotional level, however, at least during certain periods, she did not seem to expect any help. I said this to her and added that when she disappeared, she did not have a picture in her head of me as being able to help her. I guessed that she did not expect help at these times.

She explained that during times of severe stress, such as when she was unemployed, short of money, or in danger of eviction, "the thought of you does not enter my head. I completely forget that you, that even this office, exists."

I said, "Then you are all alone with the problem."

She replied, "I've been alone all my life. I've always solved my problems alone."

I said, "Sometimes that has worked. But sometimes the problems seem too great for you to handle all by yourself. They seem insurmountable, overwhelming, and since you feel all alone, you feel totally hopeless and helpless to manage them, so you give up and become depressed, and in giving up, there is then no chance to change anything."

I asked her what happened to her relationship to me in her mind between our sessions. She looked at me as if I were crazy and said that she never thought of it. I asked whether she ever thought of me or the therapy when she was faced with a problem. When she felt depressed or angry, did she ever reflect on what we had discussed? "Never," she replied.

I said, "It's like I disappear for you when you leave."

She replied, "Yes, and I'm like that with everyone and everything. I forget that my own son exists. People get angry at me because I forget appointments or don't call them. I don't do it on purpose; it just happens. It's always been like that. So you know, I never even thought about it before." Laughing, she added, "It's not normal, is it?"

I replied, "It's good that we've begun to think about it. Do you know that it causes you a problem?"

For the first time since I had been treating her, she was listening curiously to what I was saying. She actually said, "What?"

I replied, "When you forget about everyone in your life, you are always all alone inside."

She replied, "Sometimes I feel very isolated. Not lonely. I don't want other people's company. I like being alone. But sometimes I feel that there is no place for me, like I'm an outcast. I never fit in anywhere. I didn't fit in with my family. I didn't fit in with other kids, and I can't fit in on a job. I always feel misplaced."

Now when she failed to come for appointments, I called her five minutes into the session. I told her that I was doing so in order to help her remember me and our relationship. I would call, and she would say that she had forgotten. Then she would run to the clinic, which was a few blocks from her apartment. She now said, "I'm crazy. Don't feel that you have to say I'm not. I'm not sensitive at all. I've actually known I was crazy, but I never knew exactly how. Now I'm starting to see. Not everyone forgets people like I do. But I don't know what to do about it. It just happens automatically."

Building the Positive Self and Object Representation Unit

Over the next three months there were some subtle indications that Diane began to internalize me. The first sign occurred when she called me at the *exact moment* our session was to begin and said, "Do we have an appointment today? I'm not sure." She began to show some beginning capacity to expect help by saying that she wanted to see me first thing in the morning, before starting her job hunt or going to work on a temporary job, to get herself going. She noticed that the workers in the clinic were drinking coffee, so she asked me if she could have some "to clear her head" during our early appointments. On the one hand, it might be thought that she did not expect much feeding from me, so she wanted to feed herself concretely in order to avoid her oral rage at the depriving bad object. From this view, the coffee could serve to split off the negative transference. On one level, I believe that this interpretation is accurate, but as I pointed out earlier in the theoretical discussion, I think that splitting can serve internalization for a time by allowing the patient to begin to internalize an all-good object. By asking for coffee, she was beginning to take something in from me and internalize a positive image of the object as feeding her. She initially gulped down the coffee as if she were dying of thirst. The atmosphere of our sessions changed radically. She stopped sitting on the edge of her seat and glancing at her watch. She pulled over another chair, placed her feet on it, and semireclined. I did the same.

She alternated between remembering and forgetting our appointments. I noticed that whenever we had a particularly "good" session and I felt close to her, she would forget the following one. I did not interpret her rejection of closeness or involvement yet but remained focused on her inability to remember our relationship. She became increasingly able to see that she did not keep in her mind positive experiences with others. The first evidence of some self-awareness on her part was her increasing realization of her inability to remember. She began to wonder herself about why she had this "lack," as she called it. I made a very general statement that "when a person has not had many positive experiences with other people, they grow up not being able to recognize or take in such experience. It is as if they don't know or recognize help or care when they see it. It is like something from another planet." I made it clear that this was not her fault, that she could not take in or hold onto something she had never had. I also posed a problem to her: "Therapy is supposed to be about providing something intangible, that you can't see. If you are out of a job or in danger of eviction or broke, I don't pull a job, apartment, or money out of a hat. I might inform you about where you can get what you need and even help you find a community resource, but I myself don't provide you with material help. Instead, therapy is about providing emotional help and you taking in that help, and you and I studying our relationship. But this is all very vague and mystical-sounding to you, I know. You have not had the life experience to even know what such help is, so our first step together is to learn about that."

She responded, "I don't have the faintest idea about what emotional help or emotional connection or relationships mean. I know of people who go to therapists and say they feel much better, supported, and helped in their lives. I don't know about emotion in that way. I just can't do it."

Exploring the Past and the Beginning of Self-Empathy

Diane now began to spontaneously discuss childhood memories. I was very encouraged because she wanted to understand why she did not have any understanding of emotional help. She recalled that as a young child she had saved all her pennies to fix her shoes when they wore out. She could not ask her parents to fix her worn shoes. Not only would they refuse, but they would blame her for not taking care of them and severely beat her. She now told me about the time when her mother calculatedly attacked her with the metal rod.

As she recalled numerous incidents of abuse and neglect, she said that she had never thought of these horrendous experiences as strange, unusual, or in any way abnormal. Her thoughts had only carried her to the conclusion that she was a bad kid and her parents hated her for it, so she in turn hated them. But she also thought that this was just the way it was and always would be, and she decided that she would rather go it alone than be bothered with people. To be close to someone could only mean what she had already experienced. She now could see that she had no basis upon which to understand the idea that I could care about her or want to help her. As she said, "I cannot remember an image of you caring about me because I know nothing about being cared about or caring about others. I don't know of those emotions. It's all foreign to me." She could not remember any occasions of making up with her parents after a fight or of them caring about any of her activities. She did not remember them permitting dependence. She did recall that if she spoke her own opinion about a family problem, she was beaten. As she recalled these incidents, she felt flooded with rage and wanted to put a knife through her mother. She said that at a very early age, she decided that she would just hate everyone around her and go it alone and take care of herself.

For the first time since I had known her, she became decidedly discontent with her life situation. She said that she had no direction, that she was just running around in endless circles and going nowhere. Before, when she would become hopeless and depressed when she was out of work, she would grit her teeth, tell herself that she had to get tough, and find some temporary answer to her problem. She said, "I never before questioned my whole life— only some temporary uncomfortable aspect of it." She increasingly began to want more for herself, a steady place to live, a steady job that she liked, but she had no idea how to begin to effect it. She became enraged at her parents for their ignorance and inability to provide her with what she needed, emotionally and materially, to direct herself. She said, "I'm beginning to feel that I've spent my entire life just existing, seeing only the surface, acting blindly just to survive. It's like I'm becoming aware and everything is collapsing." She began to feel increasingly vulnerable about her lack of direction, about the mess her life was in.

One day she noticed a book that her son had brought home from school. It was Richard Wright's autobiography *Black Boy*. She became engrossed. She explained that it was about a black family exploited and abused in the white-majority society of the deep South. The author described how his parents vented their frustrations and powerlessness by viciously abusing him. In a sense, the family abused him to protect him. It was dangerous for a black boy to grow up with ambitions, competitiveness, and a striving for success and autonomy. Numerous stories were told at home of blacks who were lynched by hostile and envious whites for "not knowing their place." The parents would viciously beat him if he asserted his own opinion, disrespected his elders, and disregarded his place. If he behaved with confidence, it was beaten out of him. In this way, they tried to prepare him for a hostile, dangerous world. Diane found her own experience of abuse in childhood to be remarkably similar to what Wright described. She now became enraged at her current situation and her lack of opportunities. Yet she felt a certain empathy for her parents, who were victims as well. Her life felt like a disaster. She became frightened about what would become of her. Both the vulnerable and autonomous self began to emerge in the transference to me as a holding object.

Until this point, in the out-of-contact phase, I had not interpreted the lack of an internal good object in terms of the active rejection of the good object and identification with the rejecting object. Instead, I initially focused on empathically making Diane aware of the lack of a good internal object experience and the deficit in actual positive object experience to account for it. In this way I helped her to be aware of the lack of a good object, internally and externally, in her past and present life. As I helped her to gradually become aware of this internal and external deficit, she started to connect to me as a positive object.

With this type of treatment, I always initially intervene by empathically addressing the deficit and the patient's understandable inability to internalize the therapeutic relationship. This approach enables the patient to begin to make symbiotic contact with the therapist. However, the patient then begins to reject the therapist as a positive object in much the same way that the original object rejected his need for a good object. The transference has therefore evolved from the out-of-contact phase to the ambivalent symbiotic phase. During this phase the patient manifests increasingly stormy and rejecting behavior, and the therapist must address both the deficit and internal bad-object situation, which serve together in a vicious cycle to close out the positive object.

The Ambivalent Symbiosis

The shift to the ambivalent symbiosis was marked by Diane's no longer completely forgetting our appointments but instead calling a day or an hour early to ask whether this was our appointment time. In thinking that the scheduled appointment was earlier than it actually was, she communicated her need for contact, but in forgetting the actual time, she communicated the rejection of the contact. Such simultaneous approach–avoidance characterized ambivalent symbiosis. I also noted a shift in her coffee-drinking behavior: When she appeared to be in contact by laughing with me or listening and understanding me, she would drink all of it; when she looked at me with disgust, rolled her eyes, or tuned me out, she hardly touched it.

To fully explain the ambivalent symbiosis, I must first elaborate upon Diane's environmental crisis. The transference evolution and the environmental situation were inseparable and I cannot speak of one without the other. Diane had been living in an apartment where her tenant's rights were legally questionable.

This was complicated by the fact that she hadn't paid her rent for a long time. The landlord took her to court at a time when she was going through the initial phase of the ambivalent symbiotic transference. Since she could not win the case because she could not pay the back rent in the event of a favorable judgment, she agreed to an out-of-court settlement to be out of the apartment by late June. This meant that she had from January to late June to find a job to earn enough money to move into a new apartment. The housing shortage in New York made finding an apartment difficult. She would need at least one month's rent money for a security deposit, the rent money, and possibly a real-estate broker's fee, plus moving expenses. In addition, she was now forced to pay some old debts. I realized that her precarious life-style was gradually catching up with her. However, she also had a hand in bringing the crisis to a head because she could have dragged out the court battle, but she decided that she no longer wanted to live so precariously but wanted a more settled situation. During the coming months, she experienced her environmental crisis as a do-or-die situation. On the one side she faced "disaster, homelessness, and suicide"; on the other side she faced "a new beginning, a new life," a rebirth experience. She herself thought of it alternately in these terms. As she said, the volcano would erupt in June, and she was preparing herself for it.

The Transference and the Creation of Crisis

Searles (1986) has commented on the extreme sense of suspense, on the part of both the patient and the therapist, that often arises in intensive therapy with the borderline patient. Many writers, including Guntrip (1969), Searles (1986), and Winnicott (1963), have described the regressive, symbiotic transference as a psychic rebirth. In bringing her environmental crisis to a head, Diane forced herself to consider some issues that she had never before seriously considered: the need to have a steady, salaried job; the need to conform to rules, regulations, and expectations; the need to reevaluate her current relationships with her lovers; the need to think about a permanent place to live; and the need to face her vulnerability and the lack of direction in her life. Early in the treatment, I had actively tried to confront her with all of these issues, but to no avail. However, the evolution of the transference had now resulted in the patient's creating a crisis that would force her to face all of these concerns.

When Diane came in for a session following the out-of-court settlement, she said that something had happened that had made her "become human." She could no longer tolerate her transient, uncertain life situation. She wanted a stable life. She was going to look for a permanent, steady job that would allow her to live "like a human being."

For our next session, just four days later, she left a message on my answering machine: "I just found a temporary job. I'll be making my own hours. I'll be working late. No time to see you. I'll call when I have time."

Reacting to the Crisis: No Time for Therapy

It was as if we had never had the dialogue about the "permanent, steady job." I viewed her behavior as transferential in terms of her closing me off as a helper and in terms of what she was beginning to face through our relationship. I left numerous phone messages asking her to call me, but she was too busy to respond. Finally she came in to see me one night after work. She said that she felt like an automaton. She was working day and night, driving herself *forward to meet her June eviction deadline*, and she had no time to see me. She could not afford to stop. "When things get rough, I get going. I don't have time for this now."

"How long will this job last?"

"A few weeks."

"What will you do then?"

"I'll cross that bridge when I come to it. I don't want to think now. I have no time. I have to survive; that's all I know. When I have to survive, that's all I know. When I have to survive, I become a tough bitch. That's what I have to be. I'm not thinking of anything but survival."

I tried to remind her of our previous discussions. I could see that she wasn't listening. I commented upon this. She said she was just too exhausted and she had to go. She would call me.

Handling Fragmentation and Hopelessness

When the temporary job ended, Diane came in again. She was depressed. She had paid off the old debts with what she had earned, but she still didn't have a penny toward moving. She now saw that taking the temporary job had been a stupid decision. Now she had to look for a real job. Back to the drawing board.

She went on interviews over the next two weeks—two, three, four interviews a day. Employers and agency interviewers questioned her about her spotty, checkered work history: "Why did you quit so many jobs?" "Why weren't you working for this period? What were you doing at that time?" She felt like a criminal undergoing an interrogation. In sessions, she revealed much ego fragmentation. She would be calm, hopeful, reassured one day, and the next time she would be hopeless, depressed, and wanting to die. Another time, she'd be carefree and joke about the absurdity of her situation. Often she would shift from one state to another repeatedly in the same session.

Whenever she became hopeless and depressed, I insisted that the situation was not hopeless. I said that it was depressing but it was not hopeless unless she gave it up as hopeless. I said that during the hopeless time, she was all alone in her head again; she had lost her relationship with me and was again a small child all alone, carrying too great a burden. She would reply that she was not giving up but that she felt depressed and angry. She then suddenly realized that she had had other work experience in the past that she hadn't been considering, and when she looked in this new direction she was offered a job on her first interview. Her recollection of this past experience followed one of our sessions directly during which I had commented on how she was alone inside of herself again. She now became highly ambivalent about taking this job. The thought of working from 9:00 until 5:00, of sitting in an office all day, of having to take orders; it felt overburdening, imprisoning. She nearly did not take the job. Right before she started one of the temporary agencies called her about a cocktail waitress job. She struggled with that idea but decided that she must take the regular job even though the thought depressed her considerably. She started to work. I felt sure she would quit in the first week; she sounded so depressed. She said that she had to *force* herself to go in every day. "You have no idea how terrible it is. I feel smothered. All these people in one office. I don't know how long I can take it. I feel like running out."

Denying Humanity

She said that she would not quit. To straighten out her life, she had to endure it, no matter what. She complained that co-workers tried to socialize with her, talked about their personal lives, tried to show her pictures of their families, asking her to join the group for lunch. She wanted no part of it. Someone showed her family pictures and she replied, "I'm not interested in your family. I'm just here to do this job." She told them that she did not want to join them for lunch, ever. When she came in every morning, they'd all smile, pleasant, robotlike smiles, "Good morning, good morning, good morning." She imitated them for me and said that she looked away and didn't acknowledge them. She said that she was doing all she could manage by going into the office every day, and she just wanted to be left alone. She had no intention of acting friendly. She had no intention of going that far in joining the human race. Often, when she told me of the everyday office life, she did so in a very humorous way, and at times I found myself joining in the laughter and understanding how she felt. At other times, I would try to caution her about jeopardizing her job or to interpret her distance from the close, smothering family in terms of her experience in her own family. She said that she understood all that and it was true, but she had no intention of changing her behavior. When I commented on her rejection of the other workers, she said, "Damn right I'm rejecting them."

Within a month, she was fired. The boss said, "You're a good worker but you don't fit in." She came to see me on the day she was fired and she appeared to be very happy. She said she had hated it there, but she denied wanting or provoking them to fire her.

Activation of the Negative Object Relations Unit to Defend against the Positive Object Relations Unit

It was now late April and Diane was becoming panicky. She was living on the money she had saved from her last temporary job. When she had spent nearly the last of it, I referred her to a social service agency, where she received some limited funds. She now came into sessions enraged at her twelve-year-old son. It seemed that as she was feeling powerless and helpless in her own life, she was increasingly picking on and controlling him. He, in turn, was also experiencing much stress and fear both because of his unstable environment and her erratic moods. She would recite everything that was bad about him. He answered her back. She said that he needed a good fist in his face. I argued with her about this pointing out that they were both living under the same stress, that what he needed now was her understanding, not a fist. She replied, "You think I should comfort the poor boy? He's not doing any school work and I should just comfort him? He answers me back and I should comfort him? All he understands is macho. Well, I'm macho mother. I'll punch him in the face."

I said, "You're not able to do anything now, no matter how hard you try. You're mad at him for doing nothing. You feel that both of you are failures, and for the moment, you can't direct your own life, so you focus on directing him and seeing you and him as all bad."

She agreed that she did feel he was a reflection of her, her report card, so to speak. She then said that when he answered her back, something crazy was triggered in her head. If she didn't beat him down she would feel weak. I commented that her own mother had acted the same way to her and for the same reason. Diane now remembered that several years ago her mother had visited, and Diane had felt that her son had to be perfect in her mother's presence. She continually picked on him, and he started to answer her back. Her mother said, "Do you take that from him? I'd never allow a kid to talk to me that way." Diane punched her son in the eye. She could now see that it was the internal abusive object calling her inadequate as a mother. Before she left the session, she appeared much softer and more empathic toward her son; she said that she knew that his attitude would change if she treated him in a more human fashion. For a couple of weeks, we had repeated sessions in which she'd start out by ridiculing herself or her son for their failures. I would immediately comment that she was abusing herself or her image of her son as her mother had abused her, and I reminded her that whenever she did so, she would begin to feel hopeless. I would wonder aloud why she abused herself instead of reminding herself of how she felt understood by me. I reminded her of how she once saved every penny because she couldn't ask her parents for help and knew they would abuse her. I commented that she also needed help and understanding now, but instead of turning to herself or her remembrance of our relationship for that, she blamed and rejected herself instead. I asked, "Do you feel that I reject or abuse you?" When she said no, I said, "Then why do you blame yourself and hate yourself instead of remembering the way you feel I understand you?"

She replied, "That's what I'm used to. It's easier. When I get in a really bad state, I can't remember. You just don't enter into the picture. The picture is just all bad, and I become my mother and me."

I told her that it was important to try to have our relationship enter the picture at such times. She said that she couldn't yet. I asked whether she ever thought of calling, especially when she began to feel angry with her son or when she was in a "bad" state herself. She said no, she hadn't thought of it, but she would try to remember the next time. It was just that she became so negative that even the *thought* of anything positive did not occur to her. It was outside the realm of possibility on those "all-bad" occasions. But she would try.

She would leave each of these sessions feeling calmer and not entirely hopeless and negative. She also continued to look for a job, scheduling one to three interviews daily. Although she was extremely frustrated and angry, I felt optimistic because she continued to say that she was not giving up or becoming hopeless. In addition, most of the tirades against her son were occurring in my office and not with him. In fact, when she left, she made an active effort to treat him empathically and even encouraged him to tell her how he was feeling. Likewise, although she told me how angry and disappointed she felt, she nevertheless continued to go on interviews and hold herself together. I had the sense that she was increasingly seeing me as a containing object into whom she could discharge all of her pent-up negative feelings so that she could then go out into the world and continue to function.

Identification with the Bad Object and Rejection of the Therapist as a Good Object

One morning in April, Diane came into my office, sat down, and shouted, "I can't take it anymore!" She took off her sunglasses and threw them against my wall, barely missing the window. Then she threw and broke a plastic ashtray, screaming, "I can't take it anymore!" She continued, "There's just too much stress in my life. I don't want to be here today." I said, "Don't leave. Stay. Let's . . ." She stormed out, slamming the door behind her.

Later I called her. She said, in a sarcastic tone, "I'm sorry I wrecked your office."

She then told me that she had packed her son's bags to send him to Puerto Rico, that she was giving up. After asking me to hold the line while she spoke to her son for a moment, she told me that she had sent him out to sell his cat since he could not take it with him.

I said, in a slightly raised voice, "You always say that our sessions help, that you come in stressed and then leave calmed. So why did you storm out today? Why did you reject my help just when you need it the most? You came in feeling totally stressed out. But instead of trying to take in my help, you threw me out of your mind in throwing everything around. I remember you told me that this is what your mother always did. You would need something from her and she'd start going crazy and throwing things. Your situation is terrible. So you need me for help and you reject that need by throwing things around, just as your mother threw things around when you needed her."

She replied, "I couldn't help it. Today has been one of the worst days of my entire life. I felt this bad only one other time in

my life, when I was a teenager and tried to kill myself after a fight
with my mother. I'm not going to do that now. I'm worried about
my son. This is too abrupt. I just came home from you and told
him that I'm sending him away. He doesn't know what's going
on. I'm going out to find him. He went to sell his cat. I want to
find him first. He loves his cat."

Internalizing the Therapeutic Relationship

In our next session, Diane was calm and reflecting. She said that she
would never again allow herself to lose control. The other day had
been the worst of her life. She had been out of control, on the edge.
She just became totally hopeless. My statements had somehow
brought her back into control. She realized that she had come to
my office to reject me as a helper. She just was not used to having
someone else in her mind. She had been trying what I said, not to
feel isolated, to feel and remember my presence as a helper. She was
working on it. It felt strange, and uncomfortable. She was not
accustomed to this reality. She needed time to get used to it. When
she remembered our relationship, she would no longer feel hopeless. She could think straight. When she felt isolated and forgot me,
she would feel hopeless, as if she were heading for a disaster. She
felt like a building that had been erected on a weak foundation;
sooner or later the foundation would have to collapse. She felt
isolated, directionless. She felt that she had no place in society, no
contact point with it. A lot of it, she said, was outlook. When she
was not hopeless, she was able to mobilize and plan ahead. When
she felt all alone inside and isolated, she felt out of contact with
everything and believed that there was no future for her.

I replied, "For you to carve out a place in society, as you say, you
need to continue trying to carve out a place within yourself for a
relationship with me." I phrased these comments about internalization in her own language. What I was saying, in essence, was that if
she could maintain a positive self and object representation unit, she
would become more connected to the external object world.

Diane continued to go on interviews and began to tell me of the
people in her life. She told me that she had an older girlfriend and

considered her a best friend. They would go out dancing, picking up men, or getting high. Diane began to tell the friend about her problems. Shortly thereafter, the friend began to make herself scarce. The friend said she had no time to talk, and she stopped returning Diane's calls.

Diane told her wealthy married lover of her situation. He told her that if she would become his mistress exclusively, her problems would be solved. He offered to buy her a co-op apartment. She said that she didn't want to be his possession or his property, so she turned him down. Every time he took her out, he told her about how his business was expanding and about how well his daughters were doing, how he paid for their schooling and housing and how successful they were. She began to feel hurt by his remarks. She had never before felt sensitive to what people said, but now she had begun to feel that he was trying to hurt her by insensitively discussing his wealth while Diane was faced with the threat of homelessness.

She was also dissatisfied with her other lover. They had always gone out and had fun, but had never told each other anything about their personal lives. She now felt that she couldn't just pretend that everything was all right and continue to have a "grand old time." If she tried to tell him about her difficulties, he would say, "Let's forget it and have fun." Sometimes she could not simply forget, and she would appear visibly depressed. He said that she was changing for the worse: she was becoming too emotional. She had to put her problems behind her and have fun. He offered her some cocaine to help. She increasingly felt that the people in her life were emotionally shallow automatons. She said that she was now looking beneath her own and other people's surfaces and could no longer accept her life and relationships as they were.

Diane began to realize that she would have to join the human race more fully when she found a job. She was making an increasing effort to be pleasant and enthusiastic during interviews. She said that when she found a job, she would act "human." She would say good morning to people. When someone showed her the family pictures, she would look and smile. If she was invited to lunch, she would go . . . on occasion.

Sometimes she would lose hope. I would comment on how she was losing our relationship. She said she was beginning to feel connected to me even when we were not together, but it sometimes felt like an intrusion, like someone was moving in with her and she was losing her freedom. She was not accustomed to this. She said, "You can't imagine how strange this relationship feels to me."

When she started to feel isolated and hopeless . . . that the situation was too much to manage, I would say something like "The abuse you suffered throughout your life was too much to bear, so you built a wall around yourself. The only way you've ever known to protect yourself was to go it alone and not let anyone in emotionally. You took care of yourself the only way you knew how, but it's become too much for you. You were like a little child trying to be grown up, but then the burden you carried became too great and you were in danger of collapsing. You could never commit yourself to anyone or anything. It would be too much like giving yourself over to your abusive, controlling family. Now I'm asking you to do something very scary, something that is the opposite of the way you've always coped. I'm asking you to commit yourself emotionally to this therapy, and I'm not at all surprised how difficult this is for you. Yet I believe that it is necessary if you are to find some direction in your life. In fact, I think the therapy is the most important thing in your life now to help you deal with this situation that you struggle with." To my surprise, she replied that she knew that it was, and that she was trying to commit herself. I would on occasion ask if it bothered her to have me repeatedly bring up the therapeutic relationship on top of all the problems that she faced in her life. She replied that it did not bother her, that she needed to be reminded because she could not remind herself.

At times, after a particularly frustrating day of interviews, she would feel like quitting, getting on a plane, and never returning. I was encouraged that as bad as the situation was, she was no longer talking of suicide but rather of just taking a trip. I couldn't blame her for wanting to escape, but I always insisted that the situation was depressing but not hopeless, and that the hopeless feeling was related solely to her rejection of the internal positive object relationship and to her feeling all alone or dominated by the internal abusive object. Once, when she felt particularly helpless, weak, and powerless, I reminded her of the "tough bitch" part of herself and said that the weak and powerless self that now felt in complete control was not the "whole story" about her. I recalled how she had told me that she had had to be a tough bitch all of her life in order to survive. I had tried to help her find other parts to herself, but there were some occasions when the tough bitch side of her was needed, and this was one of those times. She responded that she just felt like getting away because she was tired; she knew that she had to continue to fight.

She gradually came to keep all of her appointments without ever forgetting, and she increasingly brought her negative self and object unit into the session for me to "contain." I now had the sense that when she previously avoided our sessions, it was to protect herself and me from the all-negative self and object representation unit. Forming a connection with me as a positive object heightened the internal rejecting object situation, so she had avoided it all by staying away.

Recently I saw some evidence that Diane is beginning to understand what the therapy process is about and is internalizing me as a helping object. Her son's portable radio, which was in his bookbag, was stolen. He asked his mother to buy him another radio, and she said that she couldn't afford one now. He asked whether he should sell his cat to purchase another one. She asked which gave him more comfort, the cat or the radio. He sold his cat and immediately regretted it. He asked Diane to get the cat back for him. She said that he would have to retrieve it himself, but she would accompany him to give him support. She said that she would not do the talking for him; he would have to ask for the cat back himself, but she would be there with him.

It seemed to me that Diane understood that she should not make the decision for her son, but that she should instead get him to think actively about the decision. She also understood his need for emotional support so that he wouldn't have to go it alone. Her behavior toward her son was very much like my treatment of her; the only difference was that she provided him with her actual presence for support, while I encouraged her to internalize my presence.

In early May, she came upon another idea to raise money. A former lover had given her a gift of a very expensive piece of furniture. She said that it looked very much out of place in her apartment, and since she no longer felt a need for it she would rather sell it. She sold it for $1,000, which increased the possibility that she could find an apartment by late June. She then found a job and has begun to work and is trying hard to get along with co-workers and supervisors. She is no longer panicked by the dead-line for finding an apartment; she feels that it will be a new beginning. At the same time, as she tries to fit into society, she reminds me that "The majority of people in this world suck."

8

Interpreting the Tie
to the Bad Internal Object

This chapter will focus upon those patients who enter treatment in
a primarily ambivalent, symbiotic mode of relatedness which is
acted out by the projection of the internal bad object into the
patient's everyday external relationships. This type of patient
presents a common clinical problem. The therapist is experienced
as a good *external* object serving as a "coach" to help the patient
deal with the external person who is driving him crazy. In this
way, the patient remains out of emotional contact with the therapist in that the therapist does not become a significant ambivalently symbiotic *internal* object. The ideal relationship to the therapist can closely resemble a therapeutic symbiosis, but the
therapist does not become more than an *external* symbiotic object.
Therefore, the symbiosis remains primarily a folie à deux as
opposed to a therapeutic symbiosis.

Vignettes will illustrate how the therapist intervenes to demonstrate the "internal" nature of the bad object by empathically

189

acknowledging the suitability of the external object as a fitting container for the internal bad object. Techniques will be introduced to illustrate how the therapist identifies and tracks the internal dialogue with the bad object and reconstructs the historical basis of the tie to the bad object. As the patient becomes aware of his tie to the bad object, it becomes activated in the transference.

MARILYN

Marilyn was a 46-year-old white married patient with older adolescent and young adult children. She came to treatment stating that her 28-year marriage was falling apart and that she and her husband had recently attempted marital therapy but to no avail. She reported that she had always had personality difficulties that her husband could no longer tolerate. She had become demanding and clinging, and overly sensitive to rejection and criticism. Her husband protested that he needed space and distance, and that if she did not stop taking out her problems on him, he would leave.

History

Marilyn's mother died when Marilyn was 4 years old. Her mother had suffered a serious stroke two years before her death and was often bedridden. She finally collapsed and died in Marilyn's presence. The patient grew up being cared for by her father, grandmother, and an aunt. The grandmother was the most consistent of the caretakers, but she died when Marilyn was 10. The father was a selfish, distant man described as more interested in finding a wife to take care of him than in taking care of his daughter. The father remarried the following year and Marilyn at first idolized and adored her glamorous stepmother. Once they began to live together, however, the stepmother proved to suffer from severe mood swings and would verbally and physically abuse her. The patient nevertheless tried to please her new mother by behaving independently and compliantly. During Marilyn's adolescence, her stepmother was tyrannically domineering, and Marilyn finally began to protest. The stepmother beat her even though the girl had grown larger and stronger. The patient finally struck back, and from that time the two lived under the same roof but ignored each other. Her father then told her to meet a man, get married, and leave.

Shortly afterward, she met and married her husband after several months of courtship. At first, she felt he had saved her; she did not need anyone so long as she had him, and she did not have any problems so long as he cared for her. She described her early relationship to him in "ideal, blissful" terms but added that he was unemotional, never seeming to experience any genuine feelings, although he would do anything for her. Very early on, she became extremely jealous of his close relationship to his sisters and mother. She would withdraw into her room and sulk whenever he had any contact with them, and he would have to reach out and comfort her. These interrelationships became complicated by the fact that both she and one of the sisters went to work in the husband's business. She lived in constant dread that he would abandon her and would panic at any evidence that he was emotionally moving away, preferred other activities to her company, or appeared unhappy. She would then become enraged, accuse him of not really caring for her or loving her, and then cling to him for reassurance, crying that she could not live without him.

Marilyn's husband had grown up with an engulfing mother, with whom he alternately complied and rebelled. He seemed to recapitulate this relationship with his wife as he first acceded to her needs and thereby avoided living in his own orbit. Later he began to insist upon his own space. When he began to show resentment and to distance himself, Marilyn went into a classical analysis for nine years. It seems that her chief motivation in seeking treatment was to find another arena in which to discharge her anger and fear so that she would not jeopardize her marriage by exhibiting the difficult behavior that her husband could not tolerate. The analyst encouraged her to express all of her fears, rage, and disappointment during treatment instead of to her husband, and she was amenable. The analyst focused attention on oedipal conflicts. He pointed out the similarity between her husband's emotional shallowness and distance and her father's selfishness and aloofness. He interpreted that her rivalry with her sisters-in-law referred back to her wish to replace her mother/stepmother and to win her father over. After a time, the analyst stopped interpreting the rivalry for the father and focused upon her conflict between dependency and autonomy. The analyst continually interpreted that she clung to her husband because she feared independence and that she was overly sensitive to rejection because she feared a disruption of their union, which she tried to believe was perfect. She experienced all of these interpretations as intellectual and said that they did not help her to resolve her basic emotional insecurity and dread of abandonment. She terminated analysis during a "good period" with her husband. They agreed that she intellectually understood her problems but needed practice in putting her insights into action by becoming more independent.

When the "good period" with her husband ended, Marilyn did not return to the analyst but instead saw a behaviorally oriented therapist. Her husband went into treatment and was now insisting on pursuing some of his own interests and activities and not revolving his life around her. She panicked when he enrolled in a night course and an athletic club, and was certain that these steps would mean that he would abandon her. When she threatened to kill herself, he responded angrily that he would no longer let her blackmail him. At this point she went into behavioral therapy to try to put her insights into action.

She described the behavioral therapist as a warm, kindly man and said that his supportive attitude was, in itself, therapeutic. He would suggest various ways that she could become more independent, such as enrolling in a night class and pursuing recreational activities. Always good at taking directions, Marilyn followed through every suggestion, but none of her activities changed her basic feelings of helplessness or her dread of abandonment. For a time her husband was pleased with her efforts and was more supportive of her. But when an older son became seriously ill, the strain was too much for their fragile marital relationship, and in her insecurity, she became even more controlling of her husband while he withdrew further. When their son recovered, Marilyn's husband informed her that he was seriously considering leaving. She panicked and begged him to try marital therapy. He agreed and they saw a marital therapist for a few months. The therapist concluded that Marilyn was too dependent and her husband was too distant, and he assigned them tasks in which she would behave more independently and he would try harder to relate. They managed these tasks for several weeks, but then Marilyn again began to experience the dread that her husband would inevitably leave her and interpreted all of his behavior in this way. She felt herself falling into more dread and anger than she had experienced before and at this point contacted me for treatment.

Marilyn came for a consultation ambivalent about whether she would continue treatment with me because the trip to my office was about a 40-mile drive. As she told me of her fear that her husband would abandon her, however, she decided that she had to try to come. In our first sessions, I had the impression that she had a strong need to be the center of her husband's life, but in her intense neediness, she pushed him away. He, in turn, seemed to have a need for an engulfing object against which he would then rebel.

In the initial sessions, I asked her to tell me her story and her current problem. I listened silently, gathering to myself many examples of how she essentially viewed her husband sometimes as an all-good, providing, available, mothering object and at other times as an all-bad, rejecting, abandoning, mothering object. The borderline patient's interpersonal relationships are complicated by the projective identification of the internal rejecting object situation into the external relationship. This view does not imply that the external other does not actually behave in a rejecting fashion. One might say that the borderline patient has a need for an external rejecting other, but I emphasize that this need serves the reinforcement and maintenance of the internal rejecting object. When a borderline patient obsesses in session about an external other, I consider this "other" as representing an internal object that the patient is bringing into the treatment. On the one hand the patient wants the therapist to "cure" the internal rejecting object, while on the other hand the patient places that object between himself and the therapist so that the internal bad object does not become activated in the ambivalent symbiotic transference (Searles 1986).

In this situation, I first attempted to illustrate to the patient how the external object represents an internal object, and to demonstrate how she defensively and actively maintains her relationship to the bad internal object. Once she became emotionally aware of the internal status of the bad object, she began to experience the bad object situation in the transference.

Interpreting the Projective Identification

As Marilyn described how her husband had taken care of her at the beginning of their marriage and how his love protected her from feeling overwhelmed by day-to-day living, I commented that his availability and care made her feel that all was right with herself and the world, just as a young child feels protected in the world when he experiences his mother as available, protective, and good. I said, "When you felt protected and cared for by him, you felt as if you were an accepted, worthy, and loved child, and he was the accepting, comforting, loving mother."

Marilyn described her terror and panic that her husband might leave her, noting that if he was in a bad mood or had had a bad day at work, she felt certain that he was unhappy with her and that it would be only a matter of time before he left. I commented that her feelings of terror and panic were the same feelings that a young child would have if he feared that his mother might abandon him. I said that when this terror and panic overwhelmed her, it was as if she was an unworthy, unwanted, discarded child and he was an abandoning, rejecting, uncaring mother. I repeatedly made such interventions to begin to demonstrate the all-good and all-bad self and object relations unit. I never denied her perception that her husband sometimes behaved in a distancing, rejecting, or insensitive fashion, but I focused on how she experienced his behavior as a rejected child would at the hands of a rejecting parent, and I emphasized that this experience compounded her difficulty in dealing with him.

Once she could see that she related to her husband as either a loving, all-good or a rejecting, all-bad parent, I attempted to make her aware of the internal nature of her object relations. I told her that I was interested not only in how she dealt with her husband in reality, but also in how she dealt with him in her mind. I pointed out that we carry in our minds images of ourselves and other people and that we sometimes even carry on internal dialogues with the other, which can give rise to a variety of strong feelings. Marilyn then replied that she often had imaginary fights with her husband and other people in her mind. I asked her to describe one of these imaginary fights.

She explained that she would accuse her husband of being overly involved with his sisters, his mother, or some other person, and then tell him that he was a fool for not realizing how selfish, manipulative, or cold the other person was. She would then imagine that he would become angry, tell her that she was crazy and hopeless, and say that he could not spend every moment of his waking hours focused on her. He would tell her that if she didn't give him space and cease her irrational jealousy, he would leave her. She would then become terrified and tell him that she could not live without him, and he would take pity upon her and reassure her. She would initially feel relieved but would then become frightened and angry that he only pitied her but did not love her. She would accuse him of not loving her, of loving everyone else more, and then he would become enraged and say he could not put up with her any longer. The internal dialogue thus became an endless, vicious cycle.

Marilyn stated that these internal dialogues replicated her interpersonal relationship with her husband. When "running through" such an internal dialogue, she would experience overwhelming terror, rage, relief, depression, love, and hate in rapid succession. As she imagined her husband responding to her, she would feel as if he were doing so right at that moment, in reality. I said that it was as if her image of him took on a life of its own; she responded that that was exactly correct. She added that she tended to have such fantasies whenever she was alone for a prolonged period, and I commented that on such occasions she did not have to feel alone because she kept herself company with the internal version of her husband.

In exploring the internal dialogues of such patients during this initial phase of the treatment, I do not try to learn much about the actual behavior of the significant others. For instance, when Marilyn alluded to her husband's overinvolvement with his sisters and his lack of attention to her, I might explore the matter briefly, but I would not focus a great deal of attention upon the external reality. Patients such as Marilyn tend to give very convincing examples of how the "other" is victimizing or mistreating them when the all-bad internalized object unit is dominant; in the very next session, however, they will often report that they greatly exaggerated the other's badness in their earlier fit of wrath. Marilyn, for example, would say that her husband actually wanted only a "normal relationship" with his relatives, but she was unable to allow it because of her insane jealousy. But then, when she again became angry, she would say that she had been making excuses for her husband and denying his real overinvolvement with his relatives; actually, she would say, he was worse than she had ever described.

Each of Marilyn's pictures of her husband was supported by convincing evidence and examples. Such patients often present the "truth," but they describe the situation in a highly selective manner, such that only the all-good or all-bad picture is presented and evidence to the contrary is ignored. The therapist cannot arrive at anything like a realistic picture of the other, because what is being presented is an all-good or all-bad internal object that is colored or reinforced by selected examples of all-good or all-bad behavior on the part of the external object. Therefore, in this initial phase of treatment, I will focus almost exclusively on the internal object situation. As patients gradually become aware that they are projectively identifying an internal object into the external object, they will begin to distinguish the two and present a more realistic picture of the external object. I therefore focus interventions almost exclusively toward the internal object situation.

I began to do this with Marilyn by repeating aloud her internal dialogue in a way that demonstrated the internal nature of the object. I said, "Let me see if I have this right. In your internal dialogue, you first express your anger and jealousy at your husband. Then *you have him*, or your image of him, get angry at you and threaten to leave you. Next, you are terrified and beg him not to leave, and then *you have him* pity you, and you then feel rejected that he pities you and doesn't love you, so you tell him so, and then *you have him* threaten to leave you."

Such patients nearly always notice that I retell the fantasy or internal dialogue with them as an active agent directing the rejecting object. When Marilyn asked me about this, I replied that it was *her* story, and *she* had the husband mistreat her. I immediately qualified that I was not saying that she consciously or purposefully wanted her husband in reality to mistreat her or that she enjoyed or experienced masochistic pleasure in such treatment. I added, however, that she must be getting something out of this very unpleasant fantasy and that I was wondering what it might be. She replied that the fantasy just replicates what actually goes on in the relationship. I assured her that I believed that this was so, but then I wondered why she would repeatedly tell herself such an unpleasant daydream. It was her daydream, so she could do as she pleased with it. Sometimes, I said, when people have bad experiences, they daydream about a positive outcome. "I'm wondering why you maintain the negative outcome and make yourself feel the same bad way that the actual negative experience makes you feel. Not only do you sometimes experience rejection at the hands of your husband in reality, but then you go on to daydream about being rejected by him. It is as if you are always turning on a rejected image of yourself and a rejecting image of him."

Marilyn then admitted that these images of rejection often severely depress her. Sometimes she had these images in her mind before anything negative had occurred, and her husband would just take one look at her face, see trouble, and want to get away. She would then become enraged and accuse him of avoiding her, and the actual fight would begin.

I asked her to tell me more about this. Marilyn explained that every Sunday morning, she awakens and automatically begins to think of everything her husband has ever done "wrong" to her. She relives all of these experiences as if they had happened yesterday, even though many had occurred years ago. She might recall something her husband did that angered her a day or so ago; it might not have seemed like any big deal at the time. Or she might even anticipate something that he *might* do. Then she would get angry and imagine herself telling him off and then picture him rejecting her. She would then become enraged as she was flooded by memories of every wrong he had ever committed. I commented that the all-bad, rejected image of herself and the rejecting image of him had taken over in her mind, and she would be divorced from any positive mental images or experiences they had ever had. She confirmed that positive images and experiences were the furthest thing from her mind. By the time he would awaken, she would be in a rage. She would even be angry at him for sleeping when she had so much to say to him. I commented that his sleeping reinforced the rejecting image of him; she experienced his sleep as a rejection. She said to herself, "Why don't you wake up already, you bastard?"

When he awakened, he would see the angry look on her face and try to avoid her, anticipating trouble. She commented that when she would get into these states, it would show all over her face, and her husband could immediately see that they were in for trouble. I had not yet seen the "angry face" but would have the opportunity in the near future when the bad internal object became activated in the transference.

Marilyn inevitably fell into this all-bad mental state every Sunday morning. This was the one day in the week that they could spend in a leisurely, enjoyable way, but it always ended in a terrible fight or they avoided each other in order not to fight. I then interpreted that she might activate the rejecting image of her husband in order to create distance between them. The very fact that they had the opportunity to spend the day together and be close might give rise to her anger. I added that her husband played a part in this interaction as well, but it did seem that she activated and held on to the rejecting images in order to create distance.

She felt that my comments were diametrically opposed to what she had always been told about herself in previous therapies and how she had always thought of herself. She had always thought of herself as extremely dependent, as wanting closeness, and as clinging to her husband. Both her previous therapists had said that she sought the perfect union and then became enraged if she couldn't achieve it. This view made sense to her because she had always thought of herself this way. She had never thought of herself as a person who wanted distance.

I did not yet interpret that her strong dependency needs give rise to merger anxiety and result in her creating distance through conjuring up rage and the rejecting image of the other. Such interpretations should await the full activation of the bad internal object situation in the transference. I merely commented that she does seek dependency, as her other therapists had said, but that she also seeks distance. She replied that she could not believe that a person as dependent as she was would want distance, but she would think about it.

During our next sessions, she reported improvement in her relationship with her husband. She would wake up on Sundays and the anger would begin, and she would recall what I had told her. She would say to herself that the all-bad images of rejection were taking over. She felt as if she were looking for reasons to be angry and to create distance, even though this realization continued to conflict with her dependent, needy self-image. She now reported spending relatively pleasant Sundays with her husband, and she noted that he seemed to be less distant as she stopped treating him as all-bad and rejecting. For several sessions she actively tried to figure out when he was really behaving with insensitivity and distancing himself and when she was projecting the internal rejecting object image into him. As she sorted this out, she found that when he did actually remove himself, she could begin to assert herself in a controlled, less infantile fashion. She also began to understand his need for distance not as an abandonment of her as a worthless child, but as the result of his own need to continue to declare his independence from the engulfing mother image that he projected into her. Thus our sessions for a time consisted of our analysis of the internal object situation—as projected into her husband. As she began to distinguish him from the internal object, she also used him as a transitional object (Searles 1986) in the therapy. She and I made contact through the medium of her husband; he was our focus of discourse while at the same time his presence served as a barrier between us, preventing the activation of the all-bad object transference until she was ready. Therefore, the out-of-contact phase of the transference was characterized by using the husband as an internal object serving both contact and distance functions.

As she distinguished the internal rejecting object from the external object, she increasingly began to explore the origin of the internal rejecting object. I helped her to do so by suggesting that she try to remember when, in her childhood, she had felt a similar dread of abandonment and rejection. What came to her mind was the death of her mother. She recalled that for at least two years prior to the death, she was in terror that her mother was ill and that something might happen to her. Her mother had become ill when Marilyn was 2 years old. She gradually recalled instances when she couldn't be with her bedridden mother, and she realized that she had felt that same sense of rejection and rage that she felt in relation to her husband. As we discussed the threatened and actual loss of her mother, Marilyn began to relive those feelings of terror, vulnerability, abandonment, and loss. She recalled how the death of her mother had left her in the hands of family members who she did not feel cared about her. She relived the feeling of vulnerability and recalled how she had had to deny her terror because the family did not want her to bother them.

Interpreting the Transference

At this point, the need for the good mother and the vulnerable self emerged directly in the ambivalent symbiotic transference. Immediately following the session in which Marilyn recalled the denial of her vulnerability at being left in the hands of her uncaring family, she came into our session complaining about the long trip, and saying that it had been a serious mistake to start with a new therapist and uncover all of her childhood, given that I was so far away from where she lived. For the first time I saw the angry facial expression that she had described as frightening her husband and prompting him to think that there was going to be trouble ahead. She complained that she could easily have an accident driving in the crazy Manhattan traffic; she might be mugged, her car might be broken into, or she might be poisoned by the air pollution. She said that my office seemed stuffy, hot, and closed in. Could we somehow use another office? She doubted that she could remain in this one.

She reported that after leaving my office last week, she had felt terrified and vulnerable, just as she had as a child after her mother died. She had been reliving those feelings all week. She almost did not make it to me today. Pretty soon she wouldn't be able to leave her house. The world seemed terrible, dangerous, and frightening. I had opened up a Pandora's box last week. She was driving her family crazy. At first the therapy had helped her to get along better at home. But this week she had taken out all her frustrations on her family, especially her husband. They just couldn't do anything right, no matter how they tried. She kept feeling that they didn't really care about her. Even when they tried to help, they couldn't do anything right, but she feared that they would abandon her because of her extreme dependency. She felt that she needed me more than before, but I was so far away, and this thought made her not want to come.

I interpreted that I was no further away than I had been all along, but that I seemed further away because she placed me at a greater distance in her mind. In other words, she had distanced herself from me mentally and emotionally, so I seemed far away physically. I acknowledged that it was a long trip from her home to my office, but that when she had felt better about our relationship in her mind, she had felt that the trip was pleasant. She had liked spending the day in the city, and she had felt autonomous making the trip. Now that she felt all bad about our relationship, the trip and the city seemed all bad and she had forgotten the positive features. In this way, I began to interpret the all-positive and all-negative self and object relations units as they were activated in the transference.

She acknowledged the connection between her negative feelings about the trip and the city and our relationship. She then again began to discuss how terrible her family life was, how they were stuck with one another. She attributed her difficult behavior with her family to the therapy's uncovering her vulnerability about the death of her mother. She said that after our last session she had realized, for the first time, how enraged she had been with her family after her mother's death. She immediately had to deny her anger at them because "you can't bite the hand that feeds you." Following her mother's death, her family had abruptly moved her from a crib to a tremendous bed in which she had felt lost, and she started to have to walk to and from school by herself every day. She was at first enraged that they didn't protect or care about her; she felt extremely vulnerable, walking to and from school, terrified that she was so small and the world seemed so dangerous. But then she had swallowed her fear, just as she had swallowed her rage, and had told herself that she had to be a big girl.

I interpreted that when her mother died she was enraged at her for leaving and at her family because they were taking the place of her mother, but did not protect or care about her. She had to swallow her rage at her mother and at them, but that rage had to go somewhere, so she saw and felt it in the surrounding world, into which she was suddenly thrown, and which appeared so menacing both because she was small and vulnerable and because she saw her own rage in it. In this way, I interpreted the projective identification of her own anger into the dangerous external world without using the terminology. Further along in our discussion, I commented that she was feeling both dissatisfied with her current family and fearful that they would abandon her because she was reliving her feelings about her original family after her mother's death with her current family. She admitted that her feelings that her family did not care about her were irrational in view of the effort they had been making to help all week. I commented that our discussions of how the internal abandoning image of the other related to the loss of her mother had reawakened within her the need for the good mother as she experienced it following her mother's death. She therefore wanted to be reunited with her good mother and not with the "uncaring family" of her early childhood. I added that the wish for the good mother had been transferred into me, that since I was helping her to understand, she was seeing me as the good mother and was experiencing a greater dependency upon me. All week she had felt that I was extremely far away, that she would never get to me, just as during her childhood she had wanted her mother but could never again be reunited with her. She was experiencing me as very far away, just as her mother had been after she died, and she was dissatisfied with the family with whom I had left her. I added that she was also placing me very far away in her mind because her heightened need for me as a good mother threatened her in some way. I explained that she therefore reacted to her heightened dependency needs by distancing me in her mind in order to protect herself.

This case illustrates the way in which the therapist can interpret and "isolate" the internal self and object representations that are complicating and distorting the patient's interpersonal relationships. Furthermore, it illustrates how the patient begins to transfer the rejecting internal object situation from everyday external interpersonal relationships into the transference, and how the therapist might facilitate this process. I repeatedly and directly interpreted the internal bad-object situation. In the last interview, Marilyn became visibly calmer and felt more "put together" as she took in these comments. With borderline patients whose all-good and all-bad internal self and object images complicate their interpersonal relationships, direct interpretation is usually effective.

MYRNA

The psychodynamics at work with severely disturbed patients play out with less disturbed, higher functioning borderline and narcissistic patients.

Myrna is a 40-year-old single mother of an adolescent daughter. Her husband left the family several years ago and is no longer in contact with them. The 17-year-old daughter, Peggy, currently lives away from home at a private high school, but returns on weekends.

Myrna functions well at her job as a public-school teacher. She has held the job for 15 years, and she gets along well with colleagues and is respected and valued. She lives by herself and keeps a tidy, tastefully furnished apartment. She takes care of herself competently, and because on the surface things seem to be going well, she says that no one could ever imagine the problems she has.

In treatment, she initially related to me in the same appropriate, rational fashion that she described in relating to others. She has been seeing a man for eight years, and the relationship is not going anywhere, but she can't seem to end it. While dating her all these years, this man, Joe, is still searching for the right woman. Every Saturday night, Joe dates another woman whom he had met through a computer-dating club. None of these women prove to be "right." Myrna complains that she would sometimes like to see Joe on a Saturday night, but he says that she is too demanding of his time and attention, that she is not the right woman for him nor is he the right man for her, and that he has no intention of ever changing. If she doesn't like it, she should leave him.

Myrna is aware that the relationship is limited. She says that it is crazy; she is masochistic to be involved in it. She provides further examples of how crazy their relationship is. Joe takes her to a restaurant. He becomes irritable when she chooses an expensive dish, so she offers to pay for her own food so that she can be free to order what she likes. He becomes resentful when she pays. Either way, she cannot enjoy her dinner and loses out on one of her favorite pastimes, eating out.

"Well if what you describe is so," I asked, "and the relationship is so bad for you, why don't you leave him? What keeps you in it?"

"The times when we're close, I like it. I like cuddling up to him. His body smells so good. He is into his body. It's nearly an obsession. He lifts weights everyday. He's very fastidious about his appearance. He always wears cologne and smells of fresh soap. Sometimes I become jealous: He cares more for his body than for me. Narcissus. I don't really care for sex. It doesn't excite me. He's not a great lover either. He's really only interested in satisfying himself. But I like the closeness and holding. But that's no reason to stay with him. It certainly doesn't outweigh the suffering. If I leave him, I'll have no one. I'm afraid to be all alone. But several times, when I was angry at him for seeing other women every Saturday, I went out with other men. Some treated me very nicely, at least better than Joe treats me. In fact, before I started to see Joe, I was going with another man, Marvin. He treated me as if I were really special. When I look back on it now, he really cared about me. Joe and I have nothing in common. He's a racist. He puts down everything I believe in. We don't share the same values. Marvin was much more like me. But it seemed that the longer I saw him, and the more he acted as if he cared for me, the more flaws I saw in him. I started to see Joe while I was with Marvin. Instead of telling me to get lost, Marvin pursued me. I thought he was weak. Once I remember he told me, 'Why do you prefer him to me? Everything you say about him leads me to believe he's bad for you. I'm much better for you. I don't understand.' In a sense, Marvin was right. I didn't have all of these highs and lows with him."

"Tell me about the highs and lows," I said.

"I always feel like Joe is dangling a carrot in front of me," she replied. "He won't call and I won't see him for a while. Then I'll get angry and finally be about to give up. Then he puts out some kind of feeler. Some show of interest. I get all excited. I feel like he cares for me finally. But as soon as I bite, he's no longer interested. I'm high for a while believing he cares, but then I always drop down into the emotional dumps. Sometimes I believe he purposely plays with me. Maybe he's sadistic. He seems to want me in his life but not too much."

The first several months of treatment are comprised of "Joe" sessions. Myrna describes in minute detail all of the weekly ups and downs with Joe. On occasion her daughter or female friends enter the picture. During such infrequent occurrences, they are described in "Joe" terms. Her daughter doesn't telephone as promised or would rather spend the weekend with friends than at home with Myrna. She gives so much to Peggy, but her daughter is unappreciative, uncaring, calls her smothering. Or friends make themselves scarce when Myrna wants to go out to dinner or spend an evening out when Joe isn't around. Myrna has a day off from work. Joe is unavailable. Myrna calls her brother, who has made plans for the day. Myrna is enraged that he doesn't invite her, that her daughter doesn't want to return home for the day, that her friends have other plans. She goes into a tirade, criticizing her brother, daughter, and friends for ignoring her. These criticisms only thinly veil that she is really angry because their own lives keep them from being available on her days without Joe.

Listening to Myrna over these months, I get the sense that the "other," which includes predominantly Joe but also sometimes her daugher, brother, and friends, accuses her of being smothering, demanding, and entitled and is distant, rejecting, and uncaring toward her. Her voice reaches a certain emotional pitch as she describes all of them as preoccupied.

"Peggy has no sense of money," Myrna reports. "She buys clothes with whatever she earned from her part-time job. I never did that. I saved all the money I earned for school. This weekend she's going to the shore with her friends. She could be working here. I don't know what kind of job she has. Her boss lets her work whenever she wishes. Instead of saving her money for school or working here this weekend to earn more money, she will spend all of it with her friends. The kids she is with at school are rich. I don't believe they are a good influence on her. All she does is think about herself, her friends, and having a good time."

The weekend Myrna refers to will be one without Joe. He is going hunting. She wants Peggy to return from school to keep her company, but she does not come right out and say this. Instead she complains of Peggy's self-preoccupation, irresponsibility, and choice of friends. She had tried to say as much to her, but Peggy accused her of being too demanding. Peggy, who knows about the "Joe agenda," asked Myrna, "What's the matter—Joe isn't coming over this weekend? You want me home to cry on my shoulder. You always ask *me* to take care of *you*. I'm not doing it anymore."

Identifying the Characteristics of the Bad Object

The practical issues of Peggy's sense of responsibility and attitude about work are important, and I will return to them later in another context. For now, a certain motif can be identified in Myrna's mode of relating to the other, comprising Joe, Peggy, and her brother and friends.

Myrna complains that the "other" puts itself and others before her. Joe puts his body and girlfriends before her. Peggy puts her clothes, fun, and peers before her. Her brother puts his Sunday newspaper and his wife and children before her. Her neighbors and friends put relaxing and watching television before her. Myrna does not phrase these complaints directly, however; instead, she criticizes the other's way of life, the implication being that all of these others put themselves and others before her. Furthermore, she relates to these persons in a manner that results in their calling her demanding, entitled, and smothering, and they all make themselves increasingly unavailable. Myrna is therefore dominated psychically by an internal bad-object situation in which she views the internal bad object as rejecting and self-preoccupied, and she becomes demanding, entitled, and smothering toward that internal object. The man she selects very much fits the description of the internal object. He is not transformed into a likeness of the internal object by her behavior, but rather is a suitable external object to contain the projection of her internal object. Her projective identifications do not cause him to become different from who he is; rather, they reinforce what he already is.

It will be recalled that Myrna generally functions well. Therefore, not all of her interpersonal relationships are colored by this internal object situation, nor is her overall relationship to her environment dominated by it (as Diane's was). Only her closest, most significant relationships become emotionally stormy due to her internal object situation. Furthermore, the significant external object selected closely resembles the internal object. Therefore, there is much less distortion and loss of reality testing among higher-level borderline patients. At the same time, the projection of an internal bad object into a troubled interpersonal relationship can easily be missed by the therapist since the external object so closely resembles the internal object.

Focusing upon the Internal Status of the Object Relationship

I intervene with such patients by relating almost exclusively to the internal object situation. If the patient is behaving in such a self-destructive way as to endanger his life, I will, of course, confront the self-destructive aspects of the behavior. With most of these higher-level patients, however, the self-destructive quality is more in how they feel than in how they behave. Therefore, I remain neutral about what they do with the external relationship and address all of my remarks to the internal object relationship. In a sense, I do not take the external relationship so seriously. By this attitude, I convey to the patient that the external bad object is not fully real but rather is a reflection of his internal situation.

When Myrna asked me fairly soon if she should leave Joe, I shrugged and said that she could leave him or stay. When she would ask my opinion after telling me that she had acted self-destructively by running to him after she had insisted that she was going to leave him, I would say that it didn't matter much. She would then say, "But he'll think I'm weak, or he'll think he really has me now." I'd say, "So?" Before long, she would begin to say, "I know that you think what I actually do with Joe or what he thinks about me doesn't matter much. You think all of this is really about something else . . ."

How does the therapist get to the "something else" with such patients and illustrate what that something else is? This method of intervention is quite easy compared to the techniques I described earlier with the severely disturbed patient and is usually very effective in enabling the patient to relate to significant objects as real instead of by their internal status. Only after I intervene with the internal object do I address dealing with the real object.

I initially set up a preliminary framework to address the internal object situation. When Myrna tells me of her complaints about Joe, I ask her what she gets out of the relationship. She tells me how she loves cuddling up to him, the holding; she doesn't really enjoy sex, but it's something she gives so that she will not be abandoned by a man. I therefore discuss with her how she seeks a certain mothering or nurturing from the relationship in that cuddling, holding, being taken care of, and fearing abandonment are feelings that a child often experiences in the mother–child relationship. This makes sense to her and logically leads to some discussion about her relationship to her own mother.

Myrna reports that her mother was a very narcissistic woman. Her father, an alcoholic, did not relate to the children, and left the home for prolonged periods. The patient had an older brother.

She describes her mother as beautiful and glamorous, interested only in her appearance and in seeking attention from men. Myrna suffered from a certain "benign neglect." She emphasizes that her mother did not abuse her, verbally or physically. However, when she brought home an excellent report card, her mother would say, "That's nice," as if her mind was a million miles away. She does not believe that her mother was threatened by her achievements, but rather that she was indifferent.

She describes herself as an "overly good child." She would help her mother by complimenting her appearance, doing household chores, shopping. Years later she asked her mother why she did not seem more concerned or attentive to Myrna's school performance or outside activities, and her mother said, "I never had to worry about you. You always did excellently."

Myrna adds that her mother was not all bad. After Myrna had helped her in some way, her mother would allow her to cuddle up to her and she would smell her mother's scented skin or brush her lovely hair. Myrna's mother had a very likeable, appealing personality, and when Myrna grew older, she loved talking to her. Many of her friends envied her relationship with her mother because she was more like a sister or a friend than a mother and was quite permissive during Myrna's adolescence.

The one thing she recalled being angry at her mother for was that her mother was much more involved and interested in Myrna's brother and that her mother was always going out with men and leaving Myrna and her brother home alone. Myrna's mother's solicitous and ingratiating behavior toward men made Myrna angry; she felt that her mother cared more for these men than for her. Although she sometimes felt jealous of her brother because of his closeness to their mother, she also experienced him as actively supportive of and caring toward her and continued to have a close relationship with him in adult life. He would often invite her to spend holidays and vacations at his home and would talk to her on the phone for prolonged periods when she was upset.

During our sessions, as she told me of her anger at Joe for his self-absorption, I would remind her of what she had told me of her mother's self-absorption. My comment helped her to recall how much attention her mother had paid to her own body and to grooming, how she was always freshly scented and how Myrna loved being close to her. Myrna connected her mother's preoccupation with her body to Joe's preoccupation with his. At this point I interpreted that she sometimes felt jealous about her mother's preoccupation with her body instead of with Myrna, but she repressed that jealousy; it was now emerging in her anger at Joe for his self-love.

When she would come in and complain to me that Joe was leaving her alone on Saturday nights to go out with other women, I reminded her of how her mother had left her alone to go out with men. I then interpreted that she remains attached to a mother who puts herself and her lovers before Myrna.

I emphasized that the issue is not simply that Joe reminds her of the mother from her past, but rather that she has always been attached to that mother from her past in her mind and that the attachment has been transferred to Joe. Instead of talking about Joe, I commented frequently on her attachment to or love and hate for an *image* of a mother who rejects her by putting herself and others before Myrna.

Myrna would then ask whether it is because her mother treated her in this way that she allows Joe to mistreat her by seeing other women. I replied that this is only part of it, that her strong feelings toward others always involve her seeing them as placing themselves and others before her. I added that Joe just fits this description. I now focused on how she thinks of Joe as rejecting her and obsesses about this image even when he is not present, and I emphasized that this image is not really him, but her mother. The actual Joe simply reinforces the image that she always carries in her mind of her mother rejecting her. Whenever she would broach the subject of Joe, I would talk to her about her mother. If she said, "I'm upset because Joe didn't call," I would say, "You're thinking of yourself as not being cared about by your mother."

Myrna bought a book on masochism and assertiveness. For several weeks, all she talked about was the book. I had the sense that she was putting the book between me and her, and using it as a substitute for me as a therapist, but I did not interpret this. She was practicing assertiveness with Joe and would sometimes come in feeling elated because she had stood up to him or refrained from calling him when he mistreated her. When I explored this further, however, she admitted that she felt so elated because she may have made an impression upon him, that he might respect her for her assertiveness and she might win him in this way. I commented that she was now trying to be assertive in order to win over her mother. She then said, "So even when I distance myself or demand to be treated better, it's still about my inner relationship to my mother." Sometimes she would say, "So you think he cares for me?"

I would reply, "Who knows? What is the difference if he does or doesn't? He's just Joe. You're wondering if your mother cares for you."

Sometimes she would be upset that she hadn't followed through on her assertiveness. Joe had come to her house for a few hours. Then he said that he wanted to leave. Instead of telling him that she was angry, she would cry and plead with him to stay. He left. She now felt that she was weak, that he would see her as such. I explained that, in her early relationship to her mother, she did not protest or cry about being left because she feared that her mother would be completely fed up and abandon her. Now when she pleaded with "Mother Joe" not to leave, she feared that he would abandon her. Again, I reminded her that we were speaking only of "Mother Joe." At around this time she said that the assertiveness business was useless in this situation because it was only another way to win over Mother Joe.

When she would bring up her fear of being abandoned by Joe, I would say "So what if he leaves? What difference does it make in your life? You're only terrified because it's your mother leaving you and you're a helpless infant. You continue to live those early fears in your mind. What difference does it make in reality if Joe leaves or stays? If he stays, you'll continue to have him to go out with on occasion for better or worse. If he leaves, you'll lose that."

She said, "All I ever do is suffer about him anyway. How often do I speak of something positive? I see what you're saying. In reality, I don't lose much if he leaves. I lose this grief. I'd probably be better off. The way I'm so terrified, it's like something much more major, like it would be a disaster if he leaves."

For several weeks, she and Joe had a couple of stormy fights and she clung to him when he wanted to go home; then she let him go a number of times. She stated in session that she really gets nothing from the relationship, that it's "a headache." She fears breaking it off because she doesn't want to be alone. But if he isn't going to change, what's the use of it?

Joe and Myrna met and agreed that it would be better to end their relationship, that they "weren't going anywhere" and just gave each other grief. They broke up, and she called him a couple of times after and went to see him but found that nothing had changed. She then stopped calling and seeing him.

Myrna became quite distressed about being alone. It became quite apparent that she was psychically dominated by a bad internal object situation, and it became easier to address this situation through direct interventions. As Joe gradually faded in her thoughts, Myrna became increasingly upset about her daughter and brother. She stated that she could not tolerate being alone. Since she was no longer seeing Joe, she expected her brother to invite her to his house or her daughter to call. Her brother generally accommodated her. However, on one holiday he and his family had planned to visit friends. Her daughter had also made other plans. Myrna sat home for much of the day thinking of how her brother betrayed her by placing his family first and her daughter did not care about her. When Peggy did call, she burdened her with how terrible she felt about breaking off with Joe and how much she needed her daughter's support. This pushed Peggy further away.

Peggy was in her last year in high school and was expected to begin college the following fall. Myrna was quite anxious about whether Peggy would graduate, since she was only marginally passing. Myrna would want to know every detail about school, but Peggy responded by becoming more reserved. Myrna saw her daughter's poor grades as a personal rejection of her, as a sign that Peggy did not appreciate or care about her mother. Myrna would sometimes come in or call me, quite hysterical.

"I had a raging fight with Peggy this morning. She's not coming home this weekend. Her grades are terrible, but she's off with her friends. She could be home; she could study. I told her that I would make it quiet and nice. I said that we could go out for dinner. She just told me to cut it out. She said she's not coming home to take care of me. I told her never to come home. She can fail this year and never go to college. She doesn't care about anything. When I went to school, I stayed home, I studied. I would never go out all weekend with friends if I might fail."

"I can appreciate your concern about her grades," I responded. "But wouldn't you prefer that she come home even if her grades were fine? It isn't really just about her grades."

"You sound just like her. You're saying the same thing she said, but in a less abrasive way. Yes, I know it's true. I want her home because I don't want to be alone. There's no Joe anymore. Am I asking too much wanting her at home? My brother didn't invite me either. He went with his family visiting. Couldn't he have invited me? When I called him Sunday morning, he sounded abrupt. He'd rather read his paper. I'm all alone. No one cares if I live or die. What kind of family do I have? I'm thinking of calling Joe. Should I call Joe?"

"If you're in the mood to spend the day with Joe," I replied, "call him."

"I know. You don't think it matters if I call or not. 'Joe's not the issue.' But look how terrible my life is. I'm all alone. I don't have a family. No one cares if I live or die. Maybe I'll never have anyone."

"I don't quite see things that way," I said.

"Well, how do you see them?" she asked.

"All you're talking about is spending a day alone. Solitary confinement can drive a person crazy. You know, if you were locked in a room all by yourself, day after day, no human contact, just someone bringing food and water, yes, you'd go psycho. You are now reacting to spending a day alone as if you are in solitary confinement. Do you see that what's making it so bad is what is going on in your mind about it? Do you see that?"

"What do you mean?" she asked.

"Well, you're seeing it in a very certain way," I explained. "You're thinking of your daughter and your brother putting themselves and others before you. Remember how we talked about how you always looked at everything with Joe that way. How Mother Joe put himself and his women before you. Now your daughter and your brother are putting themselves and others before you. You are thinking that Peggy puts her fun and her friends first. Your brother puts his newspaper and his family first. So you are thinking of yourself again, just as you did with Mother Joe, as last on the list. You are thinking of yourself as unwanted and of your brother and Peggy as putting you last. You've got that same image of yourself as rejected and the others as rejecting you, driving you crazy. Only the actors have changed. Instead of Joe, it's your daughter and your brother. Now I'm not saying that they're not selfish. I don't really know. They might be as bad as you say. Who knows? But the consequence is that you have to spend a day on your own. That doesn't seem like such a big deal to me. I think what troubles you is not that you have to spend a day alone, but that you feel abandoned by your mother again."

"I see what you're saying. It's just like with Joe. Let me see if I have it right. You're saying that it's not really what they are doing to me. That doesn't mean they're right. But it's really what I'm doing to myself. I see that. I'm acting like I'm being tortured the way I'm carrying on. It's actually quite comfortable here. I have my stereo, my books. There's a lot of reading I want to do. I could even go out. Tomorrow I go back to work. I see what you're saying. I'm doing this all to myself. Joe, my brother, Peggy, it's all the same. They're all my mother. Mother's Day again. My brother hasn't been so bad. When he said I shouldn't come, he said that I could come there next weekend, that they'd love to have me. He acted concerned. But I just kept on telling him that I have no family, that he doesn't care. I acted like a crazy woman. I pushed him away. He eventually became angry. He said he wants to read his paper. He said that because he was mad. I would never behave this way in front of a stranger. I know it would look crazy. I'm all right now."

The internal bad object situation is now shifting from Joe to her daughter, brother, and friends. It would be a mistake to empathize with her about her loneliness and her feelings that no one cares about her. This would only intensify her feelings that she is being victimized and support her projection of the internal bad object. Instead I say that spending a day on her own is not torture, that the people in her life might be bad or might not be, but the issue is the projection of a bad internal object.

Myrna often comes in now and complains about Peggy. She brought home a bad report card, didn't call when she promised to, spends money foolishly, prefers to see her friends. Peggy accuses her mother of being smothering and demanding. Peggy has replaced Joe as the bad internal object in our sessions. The themes about her are exactly the same as they were with Joe. I interpret that she is seeking mothering from Peggy. She wants Peggy to bring home a good report card *for her*. She wants Peggy to come home *for her*, to call *for her*. She is always thinking of what she is not getting from Peggy. I say, "The issue is not just your real relationship to Peggy, but how you want to think all the time of what she's not giving you. You torture yourself with how Peggy is neglecting you just as you tortured yourself with how Joe neglected you. All day you keep in your mind an image of your mother as neglecting you."

Gradually Myrna stopped criticizing Peggy about school work, money, time. As Peggy neared graduation, her own anxieties grew. For a time, there was a possibility that she might not graduate. Myrna would ask, "Should I leave her alone even if she might fail?"

I'd reply, "Yes, it's her responsibility."

With difficulty, Myrna would step back from Peggy. As Myrna stepped back, Peggy's own problems became more prominent. Although she was in danger of failing, she wanted her mother to pay the entire bill for the most expensive college that accepted her. She would accuse Myrna of not wanting her to succeed, of holding her back. Peggy had some money of her own, and Myrna wanted them to share the expense of a more reasonably priced college. Peggy accused her of not wanting her to be independent or successful. Peggy would also project her own bad internal object situation onto her mother. For instance, she would call Myrna and say that she was feeling terrible, but as soon as her mother asked what was wrong, Peggy would scream, "You're being intrusive!" Or she would call and say that she was depressed and didn't know what to do with herself for the weekend, that she feared she would get into trouble. When her mother invited her to come home, Peggy would shout, "You just want me to come and take care of you."

Myrna was now expressing some confusion about how to handle the "real" Peggy. "When I got it clear in my head that Joe was my internal mother," she said, "I decided that I wasn't getting anything much from the real Joe, so I got rid of him. I'm getting tired of being abused. I don't want to allow people to mistreat me anymore. I really don't have a need for Peggy to come home and take care of me. I'm learning to be happy on my own. I'm having a full life. If she went away to college next week and only visited on vacations, that would be fine. I don't want her at home when she's unpleasant. But this is different from Joe. I don't want to abandon my child. What should I do?"

I encouraged Myrna to stand up to Peggy. The next time Peggy made her out to be an all-bad mother and picked a fight, I encouraged Myrna to insist that she's not so bad, that she's not perfect but she's done a lot of things right. She's put Peggy through school, has always had a home for her, took care of her although she was a struggling single parent, and gave her love the best way she could. Myrna did as I suggested, meaning what she said and feeling strongly about it, and she reports that since that occasion, Peggy is significantly more appreciative and non-abusive. She graduated from high school and was accepted at college. Myrna is currently dating men who she finds are not much better than Joe, but she is much quicker to let them go.

An indication that the bad internal object situation might now begin to emerge in the transference can be seen in the following occurrence. Myrna came to my office the other day and rang the buzzer but didn't press hard enough for the bell to ring. Instead of ringing again, she just stood there and imagined that I had forgotten the session. She became angry that she was so unimportant to me that I could forget about her. I spotted her outside the window and let her in. When she told me her fantasy that I had forgotten her, I asked her, "So why do you want to think of me as forgetting and rejecting you?"

The therapist's interventions gradually result in the patient recognizing the internal status of the bad object. At this point, the patient activates an interpretable bad object transference. The next chapter will elaborate upon the bad object transference and interpretations of complications that ensue.

9

Interpreting the
Bad Object Transference

The patient's tie to an external bad object, especially if it commences or becomes intense in the course of treatment, could reflect the splitting off or displacement of a bad object (or ambivalently symbiotic) transference. The clinical problem is similar to that depicted in the preceding chapter, except that the patients in that chapter, Marilyn and Myrna, initiated treatment after they were already involved in an ambivalent symbiotic relationship with an external object, whereas the patients to be described in this chapter manifest the ambivalent symbiosis with an external object during the course of the treatment. These patients are actually developing an ambivalent symbiotic transference, but they split the transference off into external objects in their everyday lives. They experience the external objects in their lives as persecutory, exciting, and enmeshing. The therapist remains a good, idealized external object to comfort, soothe, understand, or rescue them from their bad external object world. The bad object transference can be expressed in a secondary, indirect fashion as these patients become angry or apathetic toward the therapist, who cannot protect them from their persecutory bad objects. The following cases will demonstrate that the patient's specific complaints about the therapist's inability to help often unknowingly express clues of the underlying bad object transference and its historical genesis.

LORRAINE

The patient, a single woman in her mid-30s, was seen by a female therapist for about a year. The therapist stated that the case was a relatively easy one. Lorraine ran her own business and maintained her own apartment. She presented herself as an independent type and noted that she was sometimes drawn into taking care of others at her own expense. She presented two relationships that were the "nemeses" of her life. The first was with her mother, an alcoholic who lived alone and often called upon the patient for help. Lorraine, who was the oldest child in her family, had always responded when her mother needed help. Her father had left the family when Lorraine was about 3 years old. She grew up missing a father and always wishing either that he would return or that her mother would remarry. Her mother claimed that the father's desertion had driven her to drink, but Lorraine sometimes thought that her mother's drinking might have driven the father to leave. The mother had depended upon the patient to help raise her younger siblings. She conscientiously cared for her siblings and served as a confidante to mother. In turn, the mother would tell the patient that she was the best child in the whole world and that she could never get along without her.

In her late adolescence, the patient met a man named Felix whom she described as the second nemesis of her life. She immediately fell overwhelmingly in love with this adventurous, handsome, personable man. He told her that he needed her desperately to straighten out his life. Felix was unemployed and used drugs. For the first time, her mother was unable to control her. Her mother pleaded with her not to "run off with that bum." She begged her to take her family, especially her siblings, into consideration. Lorraine felt that her mother was right, that she should not run off against her wishes, but she could not fight her love for Felix. He found a job, swore off drugs, and told

Lorraine that he was ready to start a new life with her. They married, Felix quit his job and went back to drugs, and for a long time Lorraine supported him and his drug abuse. She gradually began to feel fed up and to believe that Felix had married her to be taken care of and not because he loved her. After many fights and repeated threats on his part to leave, she finally told him to get out and never return.

The patient eventually started her own business and found that she could live without Felix. Nevertheless, Felix and her mother continued to plague her. Often her mother would ask her to visit because she had some scheme in mind. She would want something from one of her children and the patient was elected to persuade the sibling to do whatever it was that the mother wanted. Lorraine felt exploited and controlled, but she could not tolerate her mother's anger or disapproval. She also felt a certain sense of well-being and security when her mother rewarded her by saying "You are the only one I can depend upon. What would I ever do without you?"

The patient had not entirely rid herself of Felix. He would often come around in trouble, and she would bail him out. Sometimes he needed a place to sleep. She did not allow him to return permanently, but she remained available.

In the course of her treatment, it became apparent that Lorraine was still very much emotionally involved with Felix and with her mother. She would report that she spent much of her time ruminating over how unlovable she was and thinking that her mother and Felix were interested only in what they could get from her. She became aware that she was comforted when they spoke of needing her because this meant that they wouldn't abandon her. She felt that her only choices were either to be the good, special, dependable savior child admired for her goodness or to be the unwanted, unloved child, abandoned for her worthlessness. These choices resulted in two split-off sets of internalized object relations—the good child defending against the unwanted, unloved, worthless child.

In therapy, the patient at first presented a grandiose self; she emphasized what a good, loving, caring person she was to everyone. The therapist did not immediately challenge this identity because it was the only source of the patient's self-esteem. She felt good about herself only when she helped someone else. In accepting Lorraine's goodness for being helpful, the therapist became, in the transference, the mother who valued her for these traits. The patient boasted about what she did for her mother, for Felix, and for an employee in trouble or a friend in need. She repeatedly expressed the value that "it is good to go out of your way for others," and the therapist nodded and accepted her comments. Underlying this remark was the unspoken communication that no one goes out of his way for her. Gradually, as she told of incidents in which she had helped others, she began to express her resentment. As her complaints increased, the therapist introduced the idea that "it's good for you to be helpful to others, and it's good for you to care, but when it's at your expense, it gets you into trouble."

Lorraine told how her mother and Felix took advantage of her, explaining that both talked of how good it was to be helpful but that they always seemed to be on the helped, instead of the helping, side of the equation. The therapist commented on some of the similarities between the alcoholic mother and the drug-addicted Felix. The patient began to see that both represented an object that she feared would abandon her if she did not help it.

Lorraine was able to make good use of the therapy. She would think about the therapist's remarks between sessions and draw on a comforting image of the therapist when she feared that the bad object might abandon her. She told the therapist that she was the only person who had ever helped her selflessly. She and the therapist were alike in that they both helped others and wanted nothing in return, whereas her mother and Felix were hypocrites who spoke of help only so that they could be on the receiving end.

The issue of the bad object transference emerged after the therapist told Lorraine of her impending vacation. The patient responded by talking about her frustration with and resentment of Felix and her mother. The therapist noted that the two external bad objects' treatment of the patient had not actually worsened; rather, the patient seemed increasingly sensitive to their customary treatment. The therapist commented that the patient might be directing her anger about the therapist's vacation onto Felix and her mother. The patient disagreed. She said that she was not angry about the therapist's vacation, that that would be irrational. Everybody takes a vacation, including the patient, and anyway, she was not that dependent on the therapist.

In the subsequent sessions before the vacation, Lorraine complained about Felix and her mother. She began to wonder whether therapy was helping. She had felt better for a time over the past year, but how could this have lasted when Felix and her mother were such rats in reality? The therapist could not change them. What she really needed was to meet new people, good people. She needed to meet a man. How could the therapist help her to meet a good man? She had not wanted to say anything, but she has been thinking about this for a while. She needed to meet men, and the therapy was not helping her to do that. Laughing, she emphasized that she was not blaming the therapist. After all, she didn't expect the therapist to introduce her to men. But maybe she should stop coming because her real problem is that she needs a man, and the therapist could not help her with that.

The last comment about how the therapist cannot help her to meet a man is the mark of the underlying bad object transference. Lorraine's predominant mode of relatedness to her mother on the conscious level in her childhood was that both she and her mother were good in that they valued helpfulness and caring. On occasion, she also thought of her mother as bad for having deprived her of a father; maybe her mother had even deliberately driven the father out so that she would only have mother to relate to. The child must therefore be close to the mother and serve the mother's needs, and no man would ever come between them. If the child does not serve the mother's needs, then she would no longer be the special savior child, but rather would become an unworthy, unloved child that mother would abandon.

The patient has thus far expressed to the mother therapist that she is the savior child. The therapist, like the mother, accepts and values her as the savior child. The therapist then begins to help the patient not sacrifice herself to save the actual mother and Felix. The patient consciously says, We are just alike; we are the only ones who value selfless help. Mother and Felix are hypocrites.

However, the patient may unconsciously understand the therapist's interpretations to mean, Stop devoting yourself to your
mother and Felix, and devote yourself *exclusively* to me: "Thou
shalt place no other mothers before me."

The patient's statement that the therapist is not helping her to
find a man refers to her mother's having deprived her of the father.
At this moment in the transference, Felix and the actual mother
represent the father whom the mother therapist is getting rid of.
Lorraine complains that the therapist has taken away her bad
objects but does not provide her with a new father. The patient
says, "I can see now that Felix and my mother exploit me. I no
longer want to help them at my own expense. I can see that they
give me nothing in return. I'm disgusted with them now. But how
can this therapy help? You cannot introduce me to new people.
What I really need is a man. You can't help me find a man." The
issue of finding a man, which seems to have come out of nowhere,
is actually an association to the loss of the mother and Felix.
Lorraine is reliving with the therapist the early cry to her mother
to "Get me a new father." The patient complains that the therapist
cannot help. Her statement of the therapist's ineffectuality and
impotence is a coverup for her unconscious belief that the bad
mother is depriving her of the father because the mother wants to
get rid of the father as a buffer between them. She threatens to
leave therapy because she perceives the bad mother as threatening
her with merger, and with abandonment if she refuses to merge.
The impending vacation, a symbolic threat of abandonment,
triggers the bad object transference.

I am not implying that the therapist should not have made the
interpretations that she made. The interpretations and comments
about the role played by Felix and the mother in the patient's
psyche were accurate and led to a reliving of the bad-mother
transference, though in a disguised form. The therapist needs to
recognize the emergence of the transference and to directly interpret that the patient is threatened by both merger and abandonment and perceives the therapist as a bad mother getting rid of the
father (Felix and the actual mother) and depriving her of a new
father, causing Lorraine to want to flee. It is not enough for the

therapist to simply interpret the patient's anger at Felix and her mother as a displacement of anger at the therapist.

The next case illustrates similar dynamics with a much more disturbed patient. Afterward, the two cases will be compared.

WANDA

Wanda is a rather wealthy, married female. The therapist, who has seen the patient for only three months, believes that the patient is deteriorating. For the first few sessions, the patient expressed a rather unrealistic idealization in the transference. She described her current life situation, and the therapist simply listened. Wanda enthusiastically said, "I love coming here. You understand everything. I feel I can talk to you about anything. Could I come more frequently?"

The therapist replied that they should maintain the once-a-week schedule until they could decide on what frequency of sessions would be helpful. At times the patient remarked on the therapist's clothing. She would say, "Oh, you dress just like me. We have the same taste. That skirt must have been very expensive."

After the first few sessions, Wanda embarked on a crash liquid diet. She attributed her efforts to diet to the benefits of the treatment, even though the therapist had not offered encouragement and had taken an exploratory stance. The patient, who was not significantly over-weight, seemed manic about the diet.

In subsequent sessions, Wanda became distraught about her life situation. She complained that her husband earned only a little over a $100,000 a year; therefore, she had married a failure. She devalued the flowers he gave her, saying that he was cheap and should have bought jewelry. She saw the other people and situations in her life as all bad. She felt like going off to California to start a new life.

The therapist was confused. Only months before, the patient had described her life in glowing, ecstatic terms. She had the most wonderful husband in the world, a man who earned a terrific living, who regularly brought her flowers. "What woman has a husband like that?" she had asked. She loved her work. Now her job was "worthy of a mental midget" and she hated every last one of her co-workers. Her life was hopeless. How could therapy help? The therapist could not change her husband, her job, or her life. She was sick of talking; what good did it do? She was fed up. Maybe she should stop coming.

In listening to the patient describe her terrible life, the therapist had completely forgotten about the diet, and the patient hadn't mentioned it. Then something that Wanda said about food reminded the therapist. She learned that the patient was still on the diet. Many of the activities that enabled the patient to maintain her manic defenses related to social activities that centered around food. In the past couple of weeks, she had had to curtail those activities because of the diet. The diet had been the precipitant to much of her current sense of deprivation.

The therapist missed the rapidly developing bad object transference that had resulted in the patient's acting-out behavior. In a sense, Wanda was correct in attributing the diet to the "benefits" of the therapy. Because of the regressed, primitive level of her dependency needs, she perceived the therapist's understanding and acceptance as intensely exciting. She reacted to the therapist as an exciting breast that she couldn't get enough of. For example, she immediately wanted to see the therapist more frequently and reacted with manic enthusiasm to the therapist's understanding and acceptance.

M. Klein (1957) has noted that intense oral dependency in the transference can give rise to envy and hatred of the breast that contains everything on the earth that one needs. I am translating Klein's view to refer not only to oral instinctual need but also to the need for empathy and emotional care. The therapist's empathy and acceptance gave rise to the patient's excited dependency and envy on a very primitive level. The clinical evidence of envy can first be seen in the patient's remarks about the therapist's clothing and about how she and the therapist dress alike. Immediately following this remark, the patient began her crash diet and then complained that no one in her life gave her enough. The diet unconsciously referred to the therapist as an exciting object. Wanda was not going to take in any more of the therapist's empathic breast because it excited too much dependency and envy. Her refusal of solid food referred to an unconscious equation of solid food, breast, and empathy. She then immediately complained that no one in her life gave her anything good. These complaints referred to her state of empathic starvation: She was no longer taking in the therapist's empathy. The complaints were also triggered by her envy of the therapist. If others would only give her more, then she would not need to depend upon and envy the therapist. In turn, she could devalue the therapist and her help by saying, in effect, how can your empathy help me when I'm so deprived of the material things in life? In essence, her insatiable need for nonhuman exciting objects was a mental construction serving her as a defense against her need for human empathy.

The therapist should have immediately and directly interpreted the crash diet as a reaction to her excited need for the therapist. The therapist should also have empathized with her need to maintain her autonomy and not totally surrender to excited dependency. In addition, the therapist should have interpreted her sense of deprivation with everyone in her life as self-induced starvation from the therapist's empathy and also as envy in feeling that the therapist has everything and she has nothing.

Case Comparison

The first patient, Lorraine maintained a good object transference much longer than Wanda, a more severely disturbed patient. In the first case, it took over a year for the bad object transference to emerge. In the second case, the bad object transference appeared after only a few sessions. However, both cases projectively identify the bad object transference into the external objects of their everyday lives. Lorraine possesses a stronger positive self and object unit, which protects her from the bad internal object situation.

An important clinical distinction is the way in which the bad object transference emerges in these two cases. In the case of

Lorraine, the therapist does something in reality that is bad from the patient's perspective; she goes away on vacation. In the case of Wanda, the bad object transference is activated spontaneously, not from a real event such as a planned vacation, but rather from the threat of the relationship itself. The therapist as a hoped-for good object stimulated the patient's insatiable object need and oral envy. She defended against deprivation by going on the diet, which created a psychic state of oral dependence, enabling her to split off the exciting transference object into the external objects in her life. In starving herself, she created a situation in which she felt deprived and irritable with everyone instead of with the therapist.

Lorraine is protected from the bad object situation by a narcissistic positive self and object representation, which she constitutes as the good savior child admired by the depressed mother for her helping qualities. With some other cases, the narcissistic positive self and object representation unit consists of a special child with special gifts receiving unconditional praise from an admiring object. These positive self and object representation units are pathological in the sense of being split off from the other sectors of the personality and serving to defend against the emergence of other aggressively cathected self and object representation units. However, as I pointed out in Chapters 3 and 4, they also have adaptive functions for the patient. For instance, Lorraine is able to care for others (even if it is at her own expense) and is not left totally at the mercy of the bad object situation. The patient's positive self and object representation unit is readily reinforced by the therapist's empathic mirroring of the grandiose self (Kohut 1971). With such narcissistic patients, the therapist has the dual task of reinforcing the positive self and object representation unit through empathy and later interpreting the split-off, defensive aspect so that it can be integrated into the personality.

Wanda, who is severely borderline, does not possess a consolidated pathological grandiose self that consistently protects her from the bad object situation through a prolonged narcissistic transference (Kernberg 1975). Instead, the activation of a mirroring transference is precipitously and spontaneously aborted by the bad object situation. With the severe borderline patient, the therapist must actually build the positive self and object representations (and not merely reinforce them) while interpreting the massive, acute bad object transference activations.

HELEN

This patient, a single woman in her early 20s, worked as a commercial artist and lived with a female roommate. She was separated from her husband and planning on divorce. She was being seen by a male therapist whom I supervised.

Helen began treatment after separating from her husband and reported to the therapist that the separation was the result of her husband's alcohol and drug abuse. They had been married for several years, and throughout that time she had tried to persuade her husband to go to Alcoholics Anonymous, a drug program, or marital therapy, but he had adamantly refused, denying his substance abuse. After a while, Helen saw no hope of her husband's changing and decided that she must leave him. She told the therapist her story and was pleased that he seemed to believe her and to support her decision to separate.

She stated, "My mother and my brother both tell me that I exaggerate my husband's problems and that I should accept him as he is. My father tried to sexually abuse me when I was a teenager, and when I told my mother, she didn't believe me and accused me of making up stories." The therapist empathized with the patient's experience of her mother as not taking her seriously in response to both her father's sexual abuse and her husband's substance abuse. The patient replied, "You are the first person ever to take me seriously. I like you a lot. I wish I could meet a man like you."

Over the course of a year's treatment, the patient would come into sessions and report various incidents in which the men in her life did not respect her and either subtly or overtly viewed her as an inferior female, or in which her mother or brother did not take her seriously, or her colleagues or roommate tried to take advan-

tage of her. The therapist repeatedly empathized with her perceptions and helped her to assert herself and not permit others to
manipulate her. She, in turn, would praise the therapist as the only
person in her life who had ever understood her.

Gradually, certain minor problems began to arise that troubled
the therapist. The patient would, on occasion, come for a session
and report that she had nothing to say. She would become visibly
uncomfortable and ask whether she still needed to come so frequently. The therapist wondered whether her positive feelings
toward him made her uncomfortable. The patient would talk for a
time about how different he was, and she would verbalize affectionate and sexual feelings toward him. The therapist became
increasingly uncomfortable with the fact that she appeared to view
everybody in her life, with the exception of himself, as all bad and
as injuring her in some way. Yet she presented a good case that
many of these persons did, in fact, treat her badly. The therapist
then raised the issue of whether she was not in some way drawn to
persons who treat her badly. She readily acknowledged that she
appeared to be drawn to men who were similar to her father. Her
father abused alcohol, disrespected and exploited women, and was
highly narcissistic. She seemed to be drawn to similar men even
though she quickly became disappointed in them. But these insights made little difference in her relatedness in the treatment
sessions. She increasingly had nothing to say and thought about
dropping out.

When the therapist presented this case to me, I wondered
whether the patient's stated view that the therapist was different
from anyone she had ever met was the entire story. Could it be
that the bad object aspect of the transference was being split off
into those in her environment and thereby compounding or adding to her view of them as all bad? I suggested that the therapist
should not immediately interpret this to the patient, but that he
should keep it in mind when he saw her.

The therapist planned to take a short vacation. In the beginning
of the next session, he explored the patient's feelings about this.
She said that she felt a bit angry but also that she considered her
anger unreasonable; after all, he had a right to take a vacation, and

he was not doing so to reject her personally. She then changed the subject to the bus ride on the way to the session.

"This guy got on the bus. He and his friend sat directly across from me. I couldn't believe what he was saying. In the loudest voice, he was saying the most terrible things about women. He was discussing all of the things he did to some woman and teaching his friend how to treat a woman to get whatever you want. He said all of this without any regard for who heard him. In fact, he kept looking directly across at me to see my reaction. I gave him a dirty look. I can't believe how people are."

The therapist responded by empathizing with her feelings. She then discussed how her father, her husband, and the men she dates all view women in a similar fashion, how most men were like that, with the exception of the therapist.

The fact that she began to discuss the man on the bus directly after the discussion of the therapist's vacation could suggest an unconscious association between the therapist and the man on the bus. I asked the therapist what the patient had said that the man on the bus specifically did to the woman in the scene that he had depicted to his friend. He said that the patient had not volunteered the specifics, and he had not inquired. I wondered why. The therapist said that the thought had occurred to him, but he had felt "funny" asking her what the man on the bus had described doing to this unknown woman. I asked what he had felt funny about, and he said that he had imagined that the patient might wonder about his motives for wanting to know the specifics. She might feel offended that he would ask and that he would expect her to repeat what might have been a very vulgar depiction of the treatment of a woman. The therapist said that he feared that she might view him as "bad," like the man on the bus, if he wanted to know about these sexual exploits. I then suggested to the therapist that he might be inhibited in this way in defending against her viewing him as a bad object.

In their next session, as the patient continued to discuss the men in her life, he asked her what the common characteristic was that such men felt about women. She said that women are dispensable to them. He then asked her whether she felt that way about him, that women, and she in particular, were dispensable to him in that he was now planning to leave her for a time to go off on vacation. She agreed that the word *dispensable* was apt for how she felt. She said that his going away made her dispensed with, but at the same time she did not feel that she could reasonably protest. He wondered whether she was not using her "reasonableness" to protect their relationship. She said that she feared becoming unreasonable toward him. She was afraid that if she became demanding, dependent, or angry, he would find her "a headache" and get "pissed off," as all the other persons in her life did. She then said that she was much more reasonable with him than with other people. She felt that she must act "like a grownup." When she became angry or experienced unreasonable expectations, she reminded herself that theirs was a professional relationship and that she should behave in a mature manner. She could not tolerate it if she became demanding or enraged and he rejected her as everyone else in her life did.

This case illustrates how the "therapeutic alliance" in such cases can sometimes be a resistance to the activation of the bad object transference. The patient subsequently revealed that in the silent, uncomfortable sessions in which she had nothing to say to the therapist and thought of leaving treatment, she had fleeting negative thoughts about him. She would sometimes say to herself, "I don't really know anything about him. I don't really know how he feels about women, how he treats women in his own life, what his political beliefs are. Yes, he says the right things here all the time, but he's trained and paid by me to understand and respond sensitively. That's how he acts professionally, but who knows what he's really like?"

Her questions about what the therapist was really like refer to her view of him as a bad object. She revealed that she believed that if she expressed what she was really like, then the personal instead of the professional "him" would react. The personal "him" that she imagined was impatient, rejecting, and intolerant. She later explained that when she was a child, if she made demands on her father or expressed anger over his mistreatment of her, he would become impatient, rejecting, and intolerant. She attributed these characteristics to the "personal" side of the therapist and then behaved so that this bad side of him would not emerge in their interaction.

This patient therefore had two relationships to the therapist. On the surface, the therapist was a good, understanding, empathic object, the only person ever to understand her in a world, past and present, peopled with bad objects. This idealizing transference was neither a mere illusion nor solely a defense, but in fact reflected one side of reality. To this patient, who was sexually abused by her father and mistreated by nearly all others throughout her life, the therapist's professional stance and empathy provided an important experience of being understood, valued, and considered worthwhile. At the same time, on another level, she related to the therapist as the bad, sadistic, exciting, and rejecting object/father.

The idealizing good object transference should not be interpreted as a mere defense against the split-off bad object transference. As Fairbairn (1943) states, the therapist must be a good-enough object in reality for the patient to risk the release of the bad internal object situation in the transference. The increasingly frequent uncomfortable sessions in which the patient had nothing to say were an indication that it was time to interpret the defensive *aspect* of the idealizing transference and the split-off bad object situation.

THE CLASSICAL OEDIPAL CONFLICT AND THE BAD OBJECT

John has applied for treatment because of a tendency to sabotage himself in love relationships and in his work life. He has just completed college, and he fears that he will "screw himself up" on his first job. John has been involved for the last several years in a steady relationship with a woman. He is concerned about his impulses to sleep with other women. In the past, he has fouled up "good relationships" by sleeping with others and then telling his steady girlfriend out of guilt.

John quickly demonstrates his self-sabotaging tendencies. He oversleeps and fails to report to work. Not long afterward, he oversleeps for his therapy session. John states, "See, this is what I mean. I'm showing you what I do. I get something that will be good for me, that could help me, and I screw it up. Then at work, I find myself flirting with any woman who lets me. I'm thinking of how to seduce her. I'm not doing my work. I'm spending more and more of my time in the offices of my attractive female co-workers. I only seek out the attractive ones. I never make friends with a woman who doesn't turn me on. I don't even talk to them. I never do any work. I'm always thinking of how to seduce Karen, and this is the way I'll screw up my job and my relationship with Patti. I tell you, I do this kind of thing all of the time. I can see it coming."

John has a relationship with Patti, whom he loves, but he can't seem to allow himself the happiness of a steady relationship.

John is of Irish descent and is the first member of his working-class family to receive a college education. His father left the family when John was 5 years old and his mother was pregnant with his younger brother. John's father was an alcoholic with poor work habits who ran around with other women. His mother became exasperated when his father repeatedly stayed out all night while she was pregnant with her second child, and she finally threw him out and refused a reconciliation. His father's life "went down the drain," and he became "a good-for-nothing bum."

John feels that he is the "apple of his mother's eye." His younger brother was a habitual drug user with poor work habits. John's mother is proud that he's managed to make something out of his life. When he brought her a plaque he had won for outstanding scholarly achievement, she hung it on her wall. But John also feels it is a bit strange that he "surrendered the plaque" to his mother instead of keeping it himself. After all, he adds, he earned the plaque; why give it to her? John now wonders whether his resentment about surrendering the plaque "goes deeper." He states that he has always felt that he achieved everything for his mother. He would bring her all of his good report cards and achievements from school, and she would say, when he did well,

"You did that for Mommy. See how much Johnny loves Mommy? You're my little man."

John has always felt disturbed about his "little man" relationship to his mother. She never dated and never remarried. She referred to John as her little man, her little lover, and her little boyfriend. She said that she didn't need a man; she needed only her children. John helped her to take care of his younger brother, Shaun. It was as if the mother and John were the parents to Shaun. Therefore, one aspect of John's relationship to his mother was his role as her little man, lover, boyfriend, and husband who brought her home his trophies and acted as a co-parent to his brother. John felt quite special to and admired by his mother as both her hero and her helper. She had dreams of success for him and would often tell him that when he became an important man, he could take care of her. The idea of being his mother's man, hero, and helper excited and threatened John with incest.

However, this was only one side of John's relationship to his mother. Often he would come very close to fulfilling some plan or hope she had for him but then somehow sabotage his chances at the last minute. His mother would then say that she knows how brilliant he is and how well he could do, but that he is lazy and no good like his father. I do not mean to suggest that the predominant characteristic of John's relationship to his mother was one of his failing her; this dynamic characterized the younger brother's relationship to his mother. For the most part, John was his mother's successful, special child. Often enough, however, John would disappoint her just as he was on the verge of fulfilling one of her dreams for him. For instance, before embarking upon his current career, he had pursued training in another area, but he had stopped working and then dropped out right before completion. Now that John had finished his studies, he was frightened of failing again.

In becoming a "lazy bum" just as he was about to triumph, John was bringing his father back into his internal scene. He would call himself a lazy bum who would never be anybody, and his mother would join in and say that he was exactly like his father. The identification with his father served as a buffer between the special, successful son and the admiring mother. The special son-loving mother were in essence interrupted by the unworthy father and denigating mother. Internally, John ridiculed himself just as his mother criticized his father, and he therefore sustained his internal relationship to his father. At the same time, in identifying with the abandoning father as a bum and then condemning that side of himself, he enacted the psychodynamics described by Freud (1917) in "Mourning and Melancholia." In denigrating himself as identified with his father, he kept alive his own relationship to a father who had abandoned him. He also sustained within himself the relationship between his mother and father, and he placed the internal parental relationship between the special, successful John and his loving mother.

In bringing his trophies to his mother, John was a special object to her, a precious phallus that she had always desired. While John's mother denigrated his father, she looked up to other idealized, powerful males. She described her own father as a powerful, successful, self-made man. She wondered how she had found a man like her husband, weak and passive, exactly the opposite of her father. Before she met her husband, she had gone with another man, "the love of her life," whom she always compared to her husband. She claimed never to have stopped loving this remarkable, powerful, former lover. Her ideal son represented the powerful, bountiful, successful former lover/father. John therefore often felt that he was the only love of his mother's life, that she admired him more than she did his father, and that if he could only fulfill his mother's dreams for his success, the two of them would be emotionally married and live happily ever after. The incest taboo that John experienced at such direct oedipal wishes caused him to raise the specter of his father in identification between him and his mother. In sessions, the internalized split-off object relations units would become alternately manifested as he presented long monologues about his achievements at work and in winning the admiration of the various women in his life, only to interrupt himself with self-recriminations for messing up at work or wanting to seduce women other than Patti.

The foregoing comments describe John's internalized object relations from an oedipal point of view. However, these relations also enacted a significant preoedipal theme. John felt that he had surrendered his autonomous achievements to his mother. He felt that she lived only for him, and there was much truth to this. Therefore, if he had kept his achievements solely for himself, his mother would have felt threatened and abandoned. John could therefore be autonomous only if he surrendered the prizes of the other-than-mother world to his mother. But then he would begin to feel that she had castrated him or robbed him of his triumphs, and he would become enraged at her. John felt that his mother had robbed him of his autonomy and therefore his "screwing up" behavior was also his way of exacting revenge.

The transference was manifested in the following dream. As an adolescent, John had idolized the rock'n'roll star Bruce Springsteen. In the dream, he meets his idol, but the star is in decline. Bruce has a long, shaggy beard, he is very overweight, and his clothes are ragged. John feels sorry for Bruce and feels that he may not be aware of the terrible shape he's in. John decides not to tell him and to pretend to continue to look up to him. Then he awakens.

His first association is that Bruce does not have a beard, but I, the therapist, do. He can think of no further associations, so I ask him what brought about Bruce's decline in the dream. He immediately associates to Bruce's marital problems. He imagines that Bruce has left his wife and has gone into a decline. He is really unsure about whether Bruce is still living with his wife, but he imagines that the break-up of the marital relationship leading to Bruce's decline is significant. I ask whether that situation reminds him of anything in his own life, and he suddenly recalls the breaking up of his parents' marriage and how his father became a bum. He then thinks about how the dream signifies that he was going to hide from the father the fact that the father was losing the oedipal competition and was instead going to pretend to go on idealizing his father. Up to this point, the patient had idealized me as a "star therapist" and denied his competitive wishes to make me into a bum, but the bad object transference finally emerged in the oedipal drama.

10

Intervention
during Symbiosis

DORA: THE CLASSIC HYSTERICAL PATIENT

Dora was 18 years old when she began her treatment with Freud. Freud (1905) describes his patient as an attractive and intelligent young woman, in the first bloom of youth, but depressed and dissatisfied with both herself and her family and suffering from "a petite hysterie" (p. 31). Her symptoms include a chronic cough and hoarseness, episodic aphonia (loss of voice), asthma, and migraine headaches. She also experiences depression and hysterical unsociability. As Freud points out, Dora's symptoms suggest a relatively mildly disturbed patient. She is a nineteenth-century patient expressing forbidden fantasies through the language of physical symptoms. Freud works at decoding this secret language.

Dora is brought to treatment by her father. One day, she threw her parents into a state of alarm when they found that she had written a letter in which she stated that she could no longer endure life. Despite her protestations, her father insisted that she seek treatment.

The family included Dora, a brother a year-and-a-half older than Dora, and her two parents. Her father, an intelligent man in his late forties was a successful manufacturer who tended to be domineering. Because Dora had always been attached to him, she often took offense at his peculiarities. Dora's affection for her father had grown as a result of the many severe illnesses he had suffered since Dora's sixth year. He had been ill with tuberculosis, and the family moved to another climate for the sake of his health. His lung problems improved considerably, but the family remained in this spot for ten years or so as a precaution. Freud calls this spot *B*, and it plays an important role in the story of Dora. Dora's sympathies were always with her father. It was from the father's side of the family, Freud states, that Dora had derived both her natural gifts and her predisposition to illness.

Freud never met Dora's mother. From the accounts given by Dora and her father, Freud was led to imagine the mother as an uncultured woman and above all a foolish one, who had concentrated all interests on domestic affairs, especially since her husband's illness and the estrangement to which it led. She had no understanding of her children's interests and was preoccupied with housecleaning, which made it impossible to use or enjoy the home.

Freud states that the relationship between daughter and mother had been unfriendly for years. Dora criticized her mother mercilessly and withdrew from her influence.

Dora's brother had been her model during her early years, but in later years the brother and sister became estranged. He tried to keep out of the family disputes, but when forced to take sides he supported his mother. Freud comments that the usual sexual attraction had drawn mother and son on the one side and father and daughter on the other.

Dora began to develop neurotic symptoms at the age of 8. After a short mountain expedition, she developed asthma, which was attributed to overexertion. In the course of a six-month rest period, the condition gradually improved and was diagnosed as a nervous condition.

Dora went through the usual infectious diseases of childhood without any permanent effects. When she was about 12, she began to suffer from migraines, associated with a chronic, nervous cough. The cough persisted until Dora was 16, and each episode lasted three to five weeks or longer. The most troublesome symptom was the loss of her voice, which persisted throughout the first half of each attack.

Dora had been taken for treatment prior to seeing Freud. She had undergone the usual methods of therapy, including hydrotherapy and the local application of electricity, but they had been ineffective. Freud comments on Dora's contempt for and ridicule of doctors, a point to which I will return during the discussion of her treatment with Freud.

Freud stresses that in understanding the psychological processes of hysteria, the intrapsychic, social, and familial circumstances of the patient must be taken into account. He states that in the case of Dora, much of the information gathered that shows the points of contact between the circumstances of the patient's life and the illness are learned from Dora's father. Freud states that family members cannot be considered completely reliable in presenting information because they often have a need to protect themselves and their participation in the patient's problems. However, because of gaps due to repression, Freud himself often cannot present a full picture of the problem. Therefore, the clinical picture unfolds during the treatment process as the therapist unravels the meaning of the symptoms.

Freud learned, mostly from Dora's father, that he and his family, while at a health resort had developed an intimate friendship with a married couple, Herr and Frau K. Frau K. had nursed Dora's father during his long illness. Herr K. had always been kind to Dora. They often went for long walks together, and he presented her with gifts. No one had thought that there was any harm in that. Dora had taken devoted care of Herr and Frau K.'s two little children.

When Dora was 16 years old, she and Herr K. were walking around a lake, and Herr K. made sexual advances toward her. Dora went to her father and demanded that they immediately leave, but she did not give him a reason for the demand. Days later, Dora told her mother of the incident with Herr K., depending on her mother to pass the information on to her father. When the father called Herr K. to account, Herr K. threw suspicion on Dora, saying that he had learned from Frau K. that Dora took no interest in anything but sexual matters and read erotic books. Herr K. claimed that Dora was overexcited by her erotic reading and therefore had imagined the scene by the lake.

Following this incident, Dora's symptoms became worse, so her father took her for her first consultation with Freud. The father, who had suffered from symptoms of paralysis and a mental disturbance related to a venereal disease contracted before his marriage, was treated successfully by Freud four years earlier. The father had been referred to Freud by Herr K. Freud diagnosed Dora as having a "nervous cough," a neurotic disorder, and recommended psychological treatment. His proposal was not accepted at the time, since the episode passed spontaneously.

Dora and her family then went to live in a small town near her father's factory. They remained there for nearly a year and then went to live in Vienna. The father insisted that Dora return to Freud for treatment following the discovery of the suicide note and a worsening of her symptoms.

Dora's Psychodynamics and the Bad Object

Dora is surrounded by external objects that are, in reality, "bad." Her father sends her for treatment so that she will stop making a fuss by insisting that he break off his friendship with Frau K. Frau K. had befriended her in order to gain greater access to her father. Herr K. had been attempting to seduce her since her early adolescence. Dora's own governess is interested in her only because she wants to win over Dora's father, with whom she, like Frau K., is in love. Dora's mother is described as shallow, unable to relate to her children's interests or concerns.

Freud never suggests that Dora is distorting her external reality. He describes her as a keen observer, correct in what she concludes about her father's character and accurate in describing reality. He describes her argument as sound but adds that the patient uses thoughts of this kind to mask others in order to escape consciousness and criticism. He points to the obsessive, pressured, relentless quality of Dora's complaints that her father gave her to Herr K. and refused to break off relations with Frau K. Freud states that such incontestable but pressured thoughts often carry a supervalence of unconscious meaning that determines their intensity.

I would introduce an object relations perspective here by stating that Dora's realistic external objects are suitable and fitting containers for the internal objects projected into them. The intensity and pressure in her presentation of the external object world suggest that such objects are carrying a supervalence of affect related to the projection of internal objects.

Freud's description of Dora as a "petite hysterie" coincides with my own view that mildly disturbed patients often show less distortion than do severely disturbed patients in their depiction of reality. Reality testing in such patients is basically intact, so that they choose external objects that are generally suitable and fitting containers of internal objects. As a result, it is more difficult for the therapist to detect the projection of the internal object into the external reality. Freud's method of seeing the supervalence of affect in reality material as a sign of unconscious meaning is the same method that I have described in a number of vignettes to determine projection of bad internal objects. In discussing Dora's obsessive thoughts about her father's relationship to Herr K., Freud states:

> A train of thought such as this may be described as exaggerated, or better reinforced or *supervalent*. . . . It shows its pathological character, in spite of its apparently reasonable content, by the single peculiarity that no amount of conscious and voluntary effort of thought on the patient's part is able to dissipate or remove it. [pp. 66–67]

Freud concludes that the supervalent or exaggerated train of thoughts are reinforced by the unconscious. This statement is especially relevant to detecting an internal object situation complicating the patient's relations to the external object world.

Freud suggested that many of Dora's reproaches toward another, although true, also pertained to herself. For instance, just as her father overlooked Herr K.'s efforts to seduce Dora, so did Dora overlook her father's love affair with Frau K. In this way, Dora could have Herr K. and father could have Frau K. Much of Freud's analysis of Dora is centered upon his uncovering Dora's erotic love for Herr K. underlying her rejection of him. A closer look at this situation will reveal the nature of the internal bad object situation for Dora.

When we first meet this patient, we learn that she is in a rejecting mode of object relating. Freud describes how she has rejected her previous physicians and the help they had offered her. I will return to this point later in the discussion of the transference–countertransference situation in this treatment. Dora is also rejecting of many of Freud's interpretations and all of the persons in her life: her father, Herr K., her former governess, Frau K., and her mother. Therefore an internal rejecting object situation is dominating her conscious psychic life. In this way, Dora is similar to many of the patients I have described in my own vignettes. Freud's analysis of Dora begins to reveal the function of this rejecting mode of object relations. In unraveling Dora's predominant symptom, her coughing and hoarseness, Freud uncovers a fellatio fantasy. Dora is fantasizing orally incorporating and then rejecting the phallus symbolized in the sensations of her throat tickling and closing on her. We learn that Dora's father is impotent and that his love affair with Frau K. must involve oral intercourse, a fact of which Dora is unconsciously aware and enacts through her symptom. Freud emphasizes the oedipal level of object relations in Dora's wish to have erotic possession of father and rid herself of the rival mother (symbolized by Frau K.). But Dora's fantasy toward her father is a preoedipal one, that of oral incorporation. Therefore, at this point we can see that Dora's internal rejecting object situation is directed against her need for the exciting part-object phallus.

Freud reveals that Dora was a thumb sucker. He states, "This young woman had never broken herself of the habit of sucking. She retained a memory of her childhood, dating back, according to her, to the first half of her second year, in which she saw herself sucking at her mother's breast. . . ."

Freud then describes the oral area as a primary erotogenic zone. The intense activity of the oral area in early childhood will result in a "somatic compliance" of the erotogenic zone. He says that when the male organ becomes known as a sexual object, there may be an increase in the excitation of the oral erotogenic zone. Freud continues:

> It then needs very little creative power to substitute the sexual object of the moment (the penis) for the original object (the nipple). . . . So we see that this . . . phantasy of sucking at a penis has the most innocent origin. It is a new version of what may be described as a prehistoric impression of sucking at the mother's or nurse's breast. . . . [pp. 64–65]

Underlying Dora's rejection of the exciting phallus is her rejection of the exciting breast, for which the phallus is a substitute. Freud focuses more on the somatic compliance of the erotogenic zone than on the issue of object relations. The breast is mentioned, but there is no discussion of Dora's early relationship with the female figures in her life, such as her mother or her nurse.

This brings to mind the case report of the Wolf Man, in which there is no discussion of the childhood relationship to the mother. At this point in theory development, the emphasis was on the oedipal level of object relations. Preoedipal drives became known, but there was as yet no focus on preoedipal object relations and their effect on drive development or later oedipal object relations. Nevertheless, Freud, in this case, did come close to the issue of the preoedipal relationship to the mothering object. He states that Dora's jealousy of her father's relationship with Frau K. referred not only to her rivalry with Frau K. to win her father's love, but also to her rivalry with her father for Frau K.'s love. Freud even goes so far as to suggest that Dora's love for Frau K. is unconsciously deeper and more significant than her love for Herr K. and for her father. He states that Dora was quite intimate with Frau K., spoke of her adorable, beautiful white body as one would speak of a lover, and became disillusioned with Frau K. only when she sided with Herr K. in accusing Dora of imagining the incident by the lake. Even then, however, Dora's remarks about Frau K. were never expressed with the same harshness or hatred as were reflected in her remarks about Herr K. and her father. Freud therefore states that Dora's jealous remarks about her father and Frau K. are more strongly but unconsciously influenced by her love for Frau K. than by her love for her father.

Freud speaks of Dora's love for Frau K. from the vantage point of the negative oedipal complex. He makes no connection between Dora's love for Frau K. and her attachment to the preoedipal phallus. I would suggest that both Dora's love for Frau K. and her attachment to the exciting preoedipal breast imply that Dora is still unconsciously attached to the symbiotic, exciting mother object.

Another clinical fact that speaks to Dora's attachment to the symbiotic object is that Freud repeatedly shows that the symptom (the cough) arises whenever she is temporarily separated from the external love object (first father, then Herr K.). Therefore we can think of her symptom as an effort to incorporate the lost external object.

Freud states that Dora has rejected her mother since early adolescence, speaks in a completely negative manner about her, and utterly rejects her influence. The mother is presented by Dora and her father as fanatically devoted only to housecleaning, with no enthusiasm for the children's interests. We learn that from an early age, Dora turned to the father for love and care. Dora's complete rejection of the mother speaks to an adolescent effort to individuate from her. Dora's adoration for Frau K.'s body and her unconscious need to incorporate the phallus/breast speaks to her continued need for the symbiotic mother, which she fights. Another fact speaking to her conflict about the early symbiotic mother is Freud's remark that Dora eats little and is very fussy about food.

In Freud's interpretation of Dora's dreams, he uncovers her love for Herr K. Interestingly, he states that Dora revived her old oedipal love for her father in order to push aside her current love for Herr K. Therefore, in the current situation, Dora is repressing and displacing her love for Herr K. by focusing, in sessions, on her love for her father and on her sense of his betrayal of her. The oedipal situation presented to Freud is Dora's love for her father, her wish to replace Frau K. and her rage at her father for continuing his relationship with Frau K. Yet Freud detects that Dora's revived love for her father is motivated by a wish to push aside her love for Frau K. and Herr K. Freud repeatedly states that such current scenarios are renditions of old memory traces. Therefore, I believe it is justified to assume that Dora's reviving her father's love in order to push aside a former love is reflective of a long-ago memory trace in which she used her love for her father to push aside the love for the symbiotic mother. Just as her love for her father in the current situation subsumed her love for Herr K., so her former oedipal love for her father subsumed her love for the early mother. Therefore, in the current situation, both Frau and Herr K. represent the early exciting, symbiotic mother that Dora must escape.

Dora's initial attachment to Frau and Herr K. enabled her to try to separate from the early maternal and paternal representations. She idealized this couple as adolescents make use of "teen idols" to separate from symbiotic and incestuous introjects. However, the acting-out of the adults around her prompted Dora to draw upon old pathological object relations to separate from bad objects instead of providing her with a second opportunity for separation–individuation. She both identified with the external objects around her and had to regress to the oedipal drama to effect some separation from the reawakened exciting, symbiotic object.

The Transference–Countertransference Situation

When Dora begins treatment with Freud, she is in a process of rejecting the adults in her life. Freud reveals that Dora had a treatment history prior to seeing him that included hydrotherapy and electric treatment, none of which helped. According to Freud, Dora would laugh at the efforts of doctors and rejected their help. She had resisted all previous treatments and only agreed to see Freud due to her father's authority (p. 30).

Freud is explicitly aware of Dora's rejection of therapists, and he realizes that this will have implications for her relationship with him. Much of their interaction seems to center on Freud's attempting to feed her interpretations, with Dora responding by spitting them out. On occasion, one gets the sense of an interaction of force feeding. Dora is enacting the transference situation of rejecting the symbiotic, exciting object. She is as reluctant to take in Freud's remarks as she is to take in food. Freud, on the other hand, is repeatedly telling her that she is not really disgusted by Herr K.; rather, she is in love with him. Freud, in this way, aggressively tries to persuade Dora to take in her love for Herr K. Freud becomes the exciting feeding object, offering Dora his sexually explicit menu. Dora is the child, spitting it all out, rejecting Freud and her love for Herr K.

It is possible that Freud occasionally overidentifies with Herr K. For instance, he remarks ". . . I was beginning to realize that Herr K. himself had not regarded his proposal to Dora as a mere frivolous attempt at seduction. I looked upon her having told her parents of the episode as an action which she had taken when she was already under the influence of a morbid craving for revenge" (p. 115). In this statement, Freud appears to be empathizing with Herr K. for being victimized by Dora's thirst for revenge. The facts of the case do not support Freud's view that Herr K. was so serious in his proposal. We later learn that days before Herr K. proposed to Dora, she had learned from the governess in his employ that he had proposed to her and that they had engaged in a love affair, after which he left her. It was the fact that Herr K. used the same words in proposing to Dora that he had used in approaching the governess that prompted Dora to strike him. It seems to me that in the projective identifications that permeate the treatment process, Freud is seeing Dora as a rejecting object and is feeling that he and Herr K. are in much the same boat. Therefore, he sometimes sounds almost empathic toward Herr K. and Dora's father as objects of her rejection.

The major problem in the treatment, according to Freud, is that he did not address the transference on time. I would agree with him. At one point, he astutely detects that Dora has the same feelings toward him that she has toward Herr K. and is planning to flee from him as an exciting love object. He states as much, but Dora does not pick up on the interpretation, and they continue to discuss the Ks and Dora's father. Freud does not place himself directly in the line of her rejecting tendencies. Instead, Herr K. is passed back and forth between them: "You love him." "I love him not." This is not a case in which Freud offered up food for thought which Dora repeatedly rejected. In spitting out the Freudian entree, Dora was practicing at individuating from the symbiotic object, and up to a point, this interaction was therapeutic. Nor should Freud have been less explicit about the sexual fantasies underlying her symptoms. Rather, Freud should have allowed Dora to play at rejecting him more directly. When she rejected his interpretation of her attachment and fear of him, it would have been therapeutically effective for Freud to have asked Dora to elaborate on her conscious reasons for her lack of attachment to him. As she elaborated on all that was wrong with Freud and on why she was not in love with him, she would have increasingly established contact with him. She might have told him that he was not as smart as he thinks he is, that his interpretations reflect his own "dirty state of mind" and not hers, that he is trying to seduce or stimulate her with his frank sexual discussions but that she is not attracted to him, that in fact she is disgusted. In turn, Freud could have encouraged her to elaborate the bad object transference and allowed himself to be in the position of the bad object, exciting seducer while interpreting her need to reject him. Freud would have known his own intentions much better than Herr K.'s, and he would therefore have been in a better position to interpret the internal object situation.

A remark by Freud may point to the countertransferential situation that prevented him from becoming the object of Dora's rejection:

> Might I perhaps have kept the girl under my treatment if I myself
> had acted a part, if I had exaggerated the importance to me of her
> staying on, and had shown a warm personal interest in her—a
> course which, even after allowing for my position as her physician,
> would have been tantamount to providing her with a substitute
> affection she longed for. I do not know. [p. 132]

Freud states that he has always avoided acting out a part and
instead practiced the humbler art of psychology, believing that
there must be limits to the use of psychological influence and to
the patient's will and understanding.

This statement by Freud is a reasonable, uncontestable line of
argument, especially his comments on practicing the humbler arts
of psychology and respecting the limits of the patient's own will.
Looked at closely, however, it may suggest a bit of rationaliza-
tion. The question I am raising is whether Freud would have been
merely acting a part or exaggerating the importance to him of her
staying on in treatment had he shown a warm personal interest in
her. The case material indicates that Freud was impressed by
Dora's keen intelligence and astute powers of observation, and
that he also clearly understood that the real objects in her life
victimized her. Could Freud have repressed his personal interest in
Dora and therefore expressed less empathy than her reality situation warranted? It is quite possible that Dora stirred up in Freud
affectionate and erotic feelings simliar to those Herr K. experienced toward her. This would account for his overidentification
with Herr K. At the same time, if Freud had shown more empathy
toward Dora and she had experienced the sense that he had a
positive image of her, it is quite likely that she would have seen
him more directly as the exciting object and directed her rejection
more directly at him. Freud went into this situation knowing
explicitly of her rejection of doctors. Could Freud have been
protecting himself from the rejection of empathy and from assuming the transferential position of the rejected object? His avoidance
in directly dealing with the transference early on speaks to this
view.

These comments are not directed toward Freud's personal psychology. It is human nature to protect oneself by maintaining distance when faced with a rejecting other. If one knows that the other is intent upon rejection, one will tend to feel even more rejected if one treats the other with warmth and kindness and then is pushed away. The person showing empathy in the face of rejection may tend to feel like a fool. Often, the rejector is turning the tables and making the other feel exactly as he has felt when in need of empathy. If the therapist can remember these dynamics and not become self-protective by rejecting the rejector in return, he helps to contain the patient's projection into him "of the fool needing contact." The question this case discussion raises is whether the classical frame and the therapist's aloofness might actually arise out of a reaction to the internal bad object situation and not from a purely scientific, objective standpoint.

Dora decides in her mind before telling Freud that she will terminate from treatment. This decision might have been her way of protecting herself from becoming involved in a dependency that would have given rise to the ambivalent symbiosis. Freud might also have been avoiding the ambivalent symbiosis through a classic analytic stance in which he denied her importance to him.

This case suggests certain dynamics of the internal bad object situation that will be elaborated upon in the vignettes that follow. In many of the cases discussed thus far, an internal rejecting object situation protects the patient from an ambivalent symbiosis. The case of Dora further clarifies the dynamics of ambivalent symbiosis. Underlying Dora's internal rejecting object situation is her symbiosis to the exciting object. The internalization of the exciting object is associated with primitive, sexualized fantasies of incorporation of the part-object phallus/breast. In his paper on "Negation," Freud (1925) writes of the infant's orally incorporating good experience and spitting out negative experience. In the borderline patient's internal object relations, these dynamics come into play as he enters into an ambivalent symbiosis. He fantasizes internalizing the good, pleasurable part-object through sexualized incorporative modes but then must reject that object as it becomes bad because of a fear of merger and loss of autonomy. This constant taking in and spitting out impedes the development of object constancy in which the patient must internalize and integrate both good and bad part-objects.

MICHAEL:
DYNAMICS IN AMBIVALENT SYMBIOSIS

Michael, a young adult patient, shared certain dynamics of ambivalent symbiosis with the famous patient Dora. Michael's girlfriend, Ellen, had gone away on a business trip for several weeks, and Michael was surprised by his reaction to the separation. When Ellen was present, he always wanted to be alone. She would try to talk, but he would want to read, listen to music, or watch a film. On those few occasions when they were together, he would not really listen to anything she said, although he would pretend to. Ellen, in turn, would become angry that Michael had tuned her out and would then reject him. He described his relationship to Ellen as one in which they constantly rejected each other.

Once Ellen went away, Michael was surprised to find that he missed her desperately and could not wait for her to call. The thought that she could separate from him injured his pride. They had agreed that she would call him in three days but he found himself immediately sitting by the phone waiting for her call. When she telephoned at the planned time, he was angry that she had not called earlier and decided that he would not answer the phone and let her worry about what he was doing.

He then found himself extremely attracted to a number of women. He broached the subject of this "strange feeling" because he had not felt particularly sexually frustrated or attracted to these women until Ellen left. He felt that there was some connection between his "strange excitement" and the separation from his girlfriend. He said that he saw each of these women as teasing him, and he felt a need to sexually control them. The sexual fantasies he described related to controlling the woman's desire. He did not imagine his own gratification, but rather focused on heightening and quieting their desires. Some of the fantasies focused on sadistically teasing and sexually enslaving women.

Michael's relationship to the other, like Dora's, was generally characterized by a rejecting mode of object relating. Just as Dora had experienced her symptoms around the fantasy of the exciting object when faced with separation from the external object, Michael experienced his acting-out fantasy of the exciting object when faced with separation from the external object. It seems that the loss of the external object threatens the patient's capacity to maintain the object representation. This threat of internal object loss gives rise to an excited need for the fading object. The rejecting object therefore becomes an exciting object. The patient then tries to control the exciting, rejecting bad and dangerous internal object by sexuality. This sexuality is also a way of attempting to hold onto the fading object.

Michael's history indicated that his mother was unpredictably and alternately seductive and rejecting. Therefore, his own rejecting and seductive characteristics were a way to deal with the bad object through identification. Furthermore, like Dora, Michael had established a general rejecting mode of object relating that defended him against the exciting object situation. The latter emerged with the threat of object loss to both the external and internal objects.

MARCIA

Marcia was a married, middle-aged mother of two grown children. I saw her in treatment for seven years. When she first started treatment, Marcia was agoraphobic, with a poor academic and vocational history. She had made gains by overcoming her phobia, attending school full-time, and then working in a professional capacity.

Marcia had been married for nearly 20 years. She consistently maintained that her husband was not interesting to her sexually, that he was more of a "good mother" than a sexually exciting object. They had had sexual relations rarely during the marriage. At the same time, Marcia expressed attraction to males who were virtually strangers but whom she perceived as cruel and domineering toward women. When I first began to treat her, she would sometimes have a brief sexual affair with a man she described as a "sleaze." At the time, I did not actively explore the details of the sexual interaction. In the course of treatment, Marcia became uncomfortable about her affairs and began to feel that she was placing herself in danger. She therefore fantasized only about cruel men while avoiding intimacy with her husband, who finally told her that he could no longer tolerate their lack of physical intimacy and insisted that they see a marital therapist. They began marital therapy, and Marcia immediately fell in love with the "continental, self-assured, good-looking psychiatrist." She never discussed these feelings during therapy but constantly thought about having sex with the therapist, while going through the motions of fulfilling the prescribed marital tasks.

On occasion in the course of my treatment of Marcia, I would sometimes ask her about her transferential feelings toward me. She would say that she had no intense personal feelings toward me, that she saw our relationship as purely professional. When I attempted to pursue this, she would indicate that she did not find me attractive, that I was not her type. Eventually, when the treatment had reached an impasse, I decided to pursue her rejection more aggressively. I asked her to tell me why I wasn't her type. She essentially said the same thing about me as she always said about her husband. She said that I was too good to her. I did not mistreat or reject her; I just did my job, asking her questions, explaining to her the meaning of her feelings and behavior. She liked men who were actively seductive and rejecting; such men "drove her crazy." Her husband and I were not the type of man to whom she was attracted. The focus of therapy increasingly shifted from her rejection of her husband to her rejection of me. Whereas before she had often seemed somewhat apathetic and disinterested in therapy, sometimes missing sessions and coming late, she now appeared on time for every session. She also became more spirited as she explained that she did not find me good looking, my clothes were "not funky enough," and I was too laid back and passive. These were the very complaints she had verbalized week after week about her husband.

I, in turn, interpreted to her that she was denying her sexual feelings about and dependency upon me. I did not suggest that she was consciously lying, but rather that her devaluation of me, similar to her devaluation of her husband, was the way in which she avoided feelings of dependency and associated sexuality. When she insisted that she preferred the "sleaze" men to me, I wondered if she ever thought about me as a sleaze. She then admitted that on occasion, when I first asked her what she felt about me, she wondered whether I was some dirty-minded sleaze wanting to be stimulated by her. I now asked her to tell me explicitly about her sexual fantasies concerning the cruel, sleazy men. She did not want to, and she doubted my motives for wanting to know. I did not press her to tell me the fantasies but rather asked her to elaborate fully on her view that I was some kind of sleaze who wanted to "get off" on her sexual fantasies. She now fully elaborated the fantasy that I was a sleaze. First, she imagined that I might get off by masturbating as soon as she left, after she had told me her sexual fantasies. Second, she wondered if I might even attack her, throw her on the floor, and rape her. She wanted to know whether she would excite me by telling me her sexual fantasies. When I did not answer in the affirmative or the negative, she said that she could see that she was being ridiculous and, giggling, decided to tell me the fantasies. They focused on a cruel man handcuffing her, ripping off her clothes, throwing her to the floor, and raping her; then she performs fellatio on him. I commented on the similarity to her fear that I was a sleaze who would throw her on the floor, rip off her clothes, and rape her. She then revealed that occasionally she had sexual fantasies about me, particularly that I rape her and that she performs fellatio on me.

She reported that during the week she would sometimes think of me to comfort herself when she felt depressed, but then she would begin to fantasize about fellatio and become extremely anxious. In the following weeks she began to have sexual relations with her husband regularly for the first time in years. At first she forced herself, but then she began to feel excited. She noticed that as soon as she became excited, she would have negative, devaluing thoughts about him and she would become sexually uninterested. Rather than allowing the negative thoughts to turn her off, she began to imagine a cruel, sleazy man making love to her. As she fantasized about the cruel man, his face would sometimes suddenly turn into mine. Then she began to have thoughts during sex about making love to women. The image of a physically large female friend continually entered her mind. This exciting thought greatly disturbed her, and she stopped having sex again. When I asked her whether the female friend reminded her of anything, she said that the friend resembled her mother both physically and in personality. She imagined herself sucking the breast of the friend. As her romantic, erotic, and dependency feelings grew more intense in the transference, she increasingly became enraged at me for just sitting and listening and not enabling her to act out. I reminded her that she had once said that she didn't feel attracted to her husband because he reminded her of a mother. Although she did not fully realize it at the time, she was, in fact, correct.

This patient is dominated by a split-off rejecting object relations unit expressed in her relationship to me and to her husband. This rejecting mode of relating enables her to split off the exciting object relations unit on strange, sleazy men. These men are symbols of the exciting phallic breast. The devalued mother is projected into the husband and me. This splitting serves to protect her from the symbiotic, exciting object dependency needs. I enable her to direct the rejecting devaluing tendencies fully at me and then interpret their defensive function of splitting off the exciting object relationship. As she integrates the exciting and rejecting object unit, the bad mother fully emerges in the transference. Once she begins to direct her dependency needs fully at me, she experiences intense rage because I do not directly gratify those needs. This rage that is activated with dependency and nongratification is much more intense than the original anger associated with the rejecting object situation that splits off the exciting object relation by devaluation. Therefore, the patient defends against a fully activated bad object transference not only because of the dependency and fear of merger but also because of the associated rage.

This wish to incorporate the phallus/breast and to reject it out of frustration is the psychosexual aspect of ambivalent symbiosis. The internalization and expulsion of the internal object is often experienced by the borderline and narcissistic patient through fantasies of sexually incorporating, retaining, or expelling the part-object equivalents of breast, feces, or phallus (Abraham 1924). As Freud (1925) points out, the primitive pleasure-ego tends to incorporate all that is good and expel all that is bad.

This basic proposition of Freud's informs my understanding of the borderline patient's internalized object relations. The borderline patient attempts, in various ways, to take in and maintain a positive self and object unit. However, because of the primitive nature of his object needs, the taking in and holding onto a positive self and object unit is experienced in a regressed, sexualized, part-object mode. Such regressed, primitive object needs threaten the patient with merger, oral devouring, loss of autonomy, and the like. The patient protects himself by turning the good object into a bad one, thereby aggressively expelling it. This is the dilemma the patient faces in activating the ambivalent symbiotic transference.

THE TRANSITION FROM AMBIVALENT TO THERAPEUTIC SYMBIOSIS

The ambivalent symbiotic transference, characterized by primitive sexuality and aggression and described by Searles as the patient and the therapist driving each other crazy, eventually gives rise to the therapeutic symbiosis. In this phase of the transference evolution, sexuality and aggression give way to the holding relationship and ego care. The all-good, comforting, and nurturing self and object unit temporarily dominates psychic life. I believe that this relationship is not preambivalent, but rather that the all-bad object relations unit is split off and projected into the external world outside of the symbiotic relationship. Nevertheless, even though splitting and projective identification are used, this phase serves the patient's development by reinforcing the internalization of the positive self and object unit. In a later phase, the patient will have the opportunity to repossess and integrate the bad and good split-off object relations unit.

Marcia, the last patient described, culminated the ambivalent symbiosis in fantasies about sucking and biting the therapist object's phallus. These modes of relating dominated her interaction in sessions in rapid oscillation. One moment she would express erotic and affectionate feelings; the next moment she would become enraged because I just sat and listened without directly gratifying her. Gradually, the sexual and aggressive fantasies receded as she expressed the wish to be held, comforted, and cared for. At this point she began to experience the external object world as dangerous and insensitive. As she felt increasingly vulnerable to the external bad object world, she increasingly turned to both her husband and me for symbiotic protection. She would say, "Therapy is the only safe haven for me. The world is full of violence and hatred. Look at all the war, crime, pollution, and corruption. I hate to leave here. When I leave, I feel so vulnerable. It's as if someone out there could rob me, rape me, or kill me. When I cross the street I worry that some driver might just go crazy and run me down. I have to think of you to comfort myself and if I can hold on to that, then I'm all right."

Marcia had split off the all-bad aggressive self and object unit into the external world. She gradually became less at the mercy of her persecutory objects as she maintained the all-good symbiotic unit.

Another patient activating the therapeutic symbiotic transference became extremely sensitive to noise. She would startle if she heard someone walking by in the corridor. The noise from an air vent in my office began to drive her crazy. At home, she became highly sensitive to the noise emanating from neighboring apartments. This patient came from an extremely noisy, chaotic household. As she went through this transferential phase, she recalled numerous memories of frightening, violent domestic fights and of family members intruding upon her. She also recalled how noisy and frightening her mother had been. Therefore, this patient's bad internal object was noisy and intrusive.

As her vulnerability emerged to me as a holding object, she projected the internal noisy, intrusive, bad object into the external world. I, in turn, protected her from the persecutory object by my actions. For instance, when colleagues made noise out in the corridor of the clinic, I would tell them to be quiet. I also taped over the noisy air vent with cardboard during our sessions. During the ambivalent symbiotic phase, this patient was extremely sensitive to everything I said. In effect, I was the noisy, intrusive object in the transference. Now, I could say nothing wrong. The very same remarks that had disturbed her months earlier she now heard as comforting or supportive. At the same time, she did not recognize any change in herself but instead believed that I had become more sensitive and less intrusive.

At first I simply intervened by my actions, as just described. Later, as she recalled memories of her intrusive, noisy family, I directly interpreted her sensitivity to noise as a reliving of her relationship to her noisy mother or to the bad mother abandoning her to the noise of the family. I explained that the noise out there triggers the noisy mother in her mind, causing her to feel intruded upon. Thereafter, when noise began to disturb her, she would conjure up a comforting image of me and my remarks about the noisy, intrusive, bad mother and in this way calmed herself. She would literally say to herself, "Oh, I'm going crazy again because all that noise reminds me of how I felt abandoned by my mother and left at the mercy of all the noise and violence in my family." She would then imagine herself being held and comforted by me. Later, she recognized that when noise drove her crazy, it was because she felt abandoned by me as her transference mother. This patient was severely disturbed and had been psychiatrically hospitalized several times for prolonged periods. As she increasingly internalized an all-good symbiotic self and object unit, she gradually became less at the mercy of the projected persecutory object.

11

Intervention during Resolution of Symbiosis

SEPARATION FROM THE BAD OBJECT

This chapter presents cases that focus on patients' separation from the symbiotic transference. Searles (1961) has referred to this phase of the transference–countertransference evolution as the resolution of the symbiosis. This is a prolonged treatment phase, sometimes longer than all of the other phases combined. The focus centers on the patient's mode of separation from the internal bad object activated in the transference. Many higher-level mildly disturbed patients come into treatment at a point at which they have begun to separate from the internal bad object. This chapter focuses on very disturbed patients who achieve this phase of object relations only after a prolonged symbiosis with the therapist, and on less disturbed patients who enter treatment already in the process of struggling to separate from the symbiotic object.

In the symbiotic phase of treatment, the very disturbed patient first undergoes ambivalent symbiosis, in which the split-off all-good and all-bad self and object relations units are projected into the therapeutic relationship in rapid alteration. Gradually, the therapeutic symbiosis becomes dominant and the all-good self and object unit is increasingly projected into the therapeutic relationship, while the all-bad self and object unit is projected into the external world. This splitting strengthens and reinforces internalization of a positive self and object representation unit. The therapist must be a good enough object in reality to reinforce whatever positive self and object unit the patient possesses. Once the patient has secured a positive enough symbiotic unit, he begins to separate from the symbiotic object by projecting all badness into the object and all goodness into the self. Fairbairn (1943) stated that the therapist must be a good enough object in reality for the patient to risk releasing from repression the internal bad object. Therefore, if the patient is able to establish a strong symbiotic bond with the therapist, he will risk fully activating the internal bad object situation in the transference. This step will provide him with the opportunity to separate from the internal bad object and eventually to integrate good and bad self and object units.

Kim

It will be recalled that Kim, discussed at length in Chapter 5, did not attend school or go to work, abused drugs and alcohol, and was involved with a "crack" addicted boyfriend. The earlier chapter illustrated how the therapist repeatedly interpreted Kim's wish to take in poisonous or rejecting or exciting objects instead of the good-mother breast in the transference. Eventually, her acting out diminished and the therapeutic symbiosis became dominant. Remember that Kim bought a parrot who represented the therapist object. The parrot was a fitting twin for the therapist in that she taught it to echo her in the same way that the therapist object sometimes reflected her feelings. The parrot was a transitional object that enabled her to tolerate the physical separation from the therapist. She could comfort herself whenever she wished by taking care of her parrot. Often, she felt as if she were the good, symbiotic mother comforting her infantile needy self.

However, Kim's relationship to her parrot as a substitute transference object points to another aspect of the symbiosis that has important implications for the treatment of such patients. Kim was the symbiotic breast object. She was in complete control. She could place the object in a cage or allow it to fly free. The bird needed her; she did not need the bird. The bird was vulnerable; Kim was omnipotent. Having omnipotent control over the bird enabled her to need me less. Therefore, the symbiotic relationship that Kim had established was unconsciously one in which she had the good maternal breast trapped completely inside of her (inside the cage), and she was identified as the good breast. This state of internalized object relations implied that she was establishing a narcissistic adaptation.

Kim's functioning improved considerably. She stopped taking drugs and abusing alcohol. She found her first full-time job and steady employment. She started to take classes. She continued her relationship with her boyfriend only after he went for help with *his* drug problem and became drug free. However, her narcissistic symbiotic adaptation remained evident in her relationship with him in that she demanded that he place her above all other interests and activities and devote himself exclusively to her. Through the symbiotic transference to the therapist, she had consolidated enough of a pathological grandiose self to enable her to function more autonomously. In her unconscious fantasy, the good breast therapist mother was trapped in her body as a bird is trapped in a cage. She developed a pathological self-sufficiency in which she did not need anyone but expected everyone around her to worship and obey her.

Empathic Frustration

Ferenczi (1930) has referred to a dialectic of technique between "indulgence and frustration" in the treatment of the severely disturbed patient. In general, the therapist should use a predominance of indulgence until the patient secures an internal therapeutic symbiotic relationship. Frustration becomes an important technique during the resolution of the symbiosis. Ferenczi's terms *indulgence* and *frustration* can be somewhat confusing, so I will elaborate on their meanings later.

I indulged Kim by permitting her to call me between sessions, when she was suicidal or in crisis. When she did not come in or call to cancel, I would interpret how she had felt when stood up by her mother and how she was rejecting a dependent bond with me the same way. I would call her to ask what had happened. I was then flexible in rescheduling the missed appointment. At times when she was suicidal or acting out dangerously but could not call me for help, I would call her. When she was in a state of crisis, I was available for extra appointments.

As she became involved in the therapeutic symbiosis, she came for sessions regularly. The first sign of the narcissistic adaptation occurred in a shift of the content of her phone calls. She functioned more autonomously and no longer called me because she was suicidal or in crisis. Instead, she would call with a minor problem and then begin to chat. When I ended the conversation, she was offended. There was a shift in the significance of her complaints. Whereas during the ambivalent symbiosis, she had felt rejected because I ended a dialogue when she was still feeling depressed or dependent, she now felt offended because I did not want to speak to her just for the sake of speaking to her. She wanted me to enjoy hearing from her; she felt that she was doing me a favor. As this situation became elaborated, she would call and ask if I thought that she was gorgeous.

Before the onset of this phase, she would call and describe a delusion about her appearance. For instance, she would say that she had an ugly blemish on her face that needed to be surgically removed. She would then ask if this was so. She would explain that she felt unattractive. When I replied that the problem was not her appearance but the negative self-image that she had projected onto her appearance, she was relieved by my remarks.

In the current phase of treatment, she told me how pretty she was and wanted me to confirm it. When I would neither confirm nor deny it, but instead commented on her self-image, she would become enraged and insist upon direct confirmation of her appearance. Her wish for me to admire her was not so much related to oedipal seduction, but rather was connected to a wish that I mirror the grandiose self; that I serve as a parrot of her omnipotence and narcissism. It was a recapitulation of the early narcissistic relationship to her mother, who often admired her appearance as a narcissistic reflection of herself.

Kim began to break out of the symbiosis by again missing appointments and not calling to cancel. I no longer responded with flexibility by rescheduling, but insisted that we wait until our next scheduled appointment. Once she arrived with only a few minutes remaining of the session. She complained about the inconvenience of the scheduled time and about how far she had to walk to my office. All of these factors reminded her that I was not in reality a parrot in a cage (or a breast within her body), upon whom she could call and whom she could dismiss whenever she wished. I was not always there. She had to wake up early and walk over to see me. In addition to all of this, I interpreted her denial of her need for me as a separate, external person. Despite the fact that she had been late, she became enraged when I ended the session at the appointed time. She later revealed that she wanted me to need her and to be so dependent upon her that I would permit her to stay for as long as she wished. In essence, she wanted to reverse our roles. I should become the dependent, needy, oral child, and she, the all-good, giving, needed breast.

The Therapist Viewed as the Crazy Object

At this point, the all-bad object transference became fully activated. She complained that I was treating her exactly as her crazy mother had. When she was dependent, needy, suicidal, acting out, I was always there, fully available. I would allow her to reschedule appointments. If I did not have another patient waiting, I would permit her to stay for a limited period. If she called me, I spoke to her for as long as she required. Now that she was improving and becoming independent, I was no longer as interested. I did not reschedule, did not allow her to stay if she was late, did not talk to her as long on the telephone. I must like her being dependent and hate her for growing up. I am rejecting her for being independent, just as her mother had rejected her. What about consistency? Did I know that I was being inconsistent with her? Well, what did I have to say for myself? Hadn't I ever read a book about child-rearing? Inconsistency is the worst thing in a parent. She was not trying to tell me how to treat her, but didn't I believe that she should be rewarded for her progress? She admits that it might actually make sense in a certain way that I didn't give her the attention that I used to since she is making progress, but hadn't I ever heard of rewarding progress? Her mother never did, and I'm not much better. I'm so busy. She has so many different numbers at which to reach me. Did I ever think that maybe I'm a little too busy? That I don't have enough time for my patients? Men are vulnerable to heart attacks. She's read that it's not good for men to be so absorbed in their work. She thinks I should slow down, for my own good as well as for hers. When she was little, her mother was busy just as I am. Now her mother always complains about her health. I had better be careful. Why don't I ever tell her how I feel about her? She thinks I have problems with the expression of feelings. Maybe she can help me with this. But she's not going to tell me what she believes I feel about her. She's not falling into that trap. It's just another way for me to avoid discussing my feelings about her. I should go first. And why don't I talk to her on the phone for as long as I used to? Just because she's not suicidal . . .

I comment that the purpose of between-session telephone contacts is for her to be able to reconnect when she's feeling disconnected from her internal relationship with me, not just to have a social chat. Ah, but that's what she wants—a social chat. Poor her—she has an antisocial therapist. And I'm a *social* worker. An antisocial social worker.

The next time she calls, she laughs and says she's calling to reconnect. The internal light bulb of the therapist is just barely flickering. Fading. A dying light. In need of recharging. In a momentary serious vein, she admits that it is difficult for her to express her need for me. It's much easier for her to call to entertain me with chattering.

When Kim is entertaining me, I am her mirror, her parrot, an unconscious breast mother trapped within her body. She is one with me and therefore has no need of the external other. The need for an external good breast would give rise to early oral envy (Klein 1957). Kim would prefer to unconsciously fantasize that she possesses me as a good breast inside of her. She then becomes the good breast to the external other. She can avoid dependency and the consequent envy toward the other. As the good breast, she expects gratitude and envy from the other. The countertransference evoked is that "this patient thinks she is doing me a favor by coming for treatment." As the patient becomes the good breast, the needy, dependent, starving, oral self is projected into the therapist. At other times, the bad, rejecting, unsatisfying, breast mother object is projected into the therapist. The patient's fantasized possession of the good breast served both an adaptive and a maladaptive function. On the one hand, it enables the patient to separate and individuate from the needy self and the bad internal object projected into the external other. On the other hand, it results in a narcissistic adaptation and a schizoid state. The therapist must therefore be inconsistent in technique, sometimes indulging the patient's symbiotic needs by empathic mirroring of his narcissism, and at other times frustrating those needs by interpreting primitive defenses and deliberately not assuming a mirroring function. In not always serving as a mirroring object for Kim's grandiosity, I permitted her to project into me the internal bad object that rewards dependence and rejects autonomy. She was therefore enabled to separate from this internal bad object in the transference.

Justine

Justine, who was already discussed in Chapter 2, achieved a narcissistic adaptation in the symbiotic transference during ambivalent symbiosis, rejected the therapist by comparing him to her previous therapists. In the positive symbiosis, she experienced regressive longings to be held, comforted, and nursed by the therapist mother's phallus. In the negative symbiosis, she experienced oral rage and wished to mutilate and castrate, the therapist's phallus/breast. Through angry distancing behavior and fantasies, she was able to maintain some degree of autonomy and defend against her regressive longing to merge. She gradually developed a therapeutic symbiosis that protected her from the intrusive, bad mother as projected into the external world. During this phase she became extremely sensitive to noise, a reliving of early object experience at the hands of a chaotic mother. She maintained an image of the all-good, comforting therapist that she could draw upon to protect her from intrusion by the bad object.

It will be recalled that she started a job and believed that the therapy would carry her through it. She quit after a short time, feeling weak and overwhelmed. She was enraged at me, saying that I had the honor of being the first therapist, in her long history of treatment, to destroy her faith in therapy. Before, she had believed that therapy would save her, and this faith had kept her going. I had allowed her to be dependent upon me as no other therapist had. I permitted her to call me whenever she needed to and encouraged her to verbalize all of her dependent, sexual, and aggressive feelings toward me. But after all of this, nothing had changed. She still could not work. Her other therapists were wiser for forcing her to be independent in small ways, at least in her relationship to them. I had permitted her to be dependent, and it had not helped. She was simply more dependent. It was clear that she would have to help herself. If she waited for therapy to help, she would be waiting forever. So she found herself a part-time job. Feeling overwhelmed, she wondered whether she should quit. She asked me, but I neither encouraged her to work nor advised her to quit. Her other therapists would have taken the problem apart and lined up all the advantages on one side and all the disadvantages on the other. Then she would be able to see it clearly. I did not provide such help. I just sat there like a blob. Like her mother. Indifferent. Well, she would work, no thanks to me.

Her part-time job became a full-time job. She is improving despite me. I rewarded her dependence. I never encouraged her to be independent. I did not tell her that she should work, and I didn't show any pride in her achievements. I should tell her that I was proud sometimes. Her other therapists would. She thought she was outgrowing me. I knew how to relate to her only when she was dependent. The communication was not the same. My words could no longer comfort her. I was good in a crisis, she would say that for me. But I didn't know what to do with her when she was like this. Sometimes she thought I was afraid of her, the way I never said anything—as if I was afraid that she would cut out my tongue.

She arrives at the next session feeling upset. Her job, which she performs well, is being eliminated. She doesn't know what to do. She's done for. For a moment, I probably look as upset as she does, and I comment on how terrible the situation is. She says that I make matters worse. Why do I have to react? Can't I just sit and listen?

Another time, another crisis. I sit and listen. Her car has broken down. Repairs are costly. She feels like jumping off the roof— figuratively, not literally. Years ago it was literal. But how much can a person take? Maybe she won't come to therapy anymore. Therapy can't help any longer. The environment is impossible, and she can do only so much. *I* can do only so much. Sometimes therapy can't help when the environment is so bad. She no longer has the same faith in therapy that she had fifteen years ago. Therapy used to be the one and only source of hope for her. Her first therapist, fifteen years ago, told her that if she resolved her problems, she could do anything. She had believed him. Now, fifteen years later, she is losing hope. Without hope, she'll have nothing. The only thing left will be to jump off the roof. I have the honor of being the therapist who caused her to lose all hope.

During our next session, she tells me that she is taking a professional licensing exam. She doesn't want to, but she has to. She takes the exam and passes it. She begins to work professionally for the first time. She starts out part time. It works best for her that way. She is doing things a step at a time, as she becomes ready. It's overwhelming. The atmosphere is terrible. She is thinking of quitting. What do I think? If only I'd sort out the pros and the cons. Didn't I care? She knows—it's up to her.

She continues to work, but hates it. She has nothing to look forward to. She's working more hours for more money. She's not happy about this. She doesn't think she's progressing. She's just doing what she must.

Within a few weeks, she is feeling better. The job is not so difficult; she is getting used to it. She's feeling good about herself. Imagine her, a former mental patient, working as a professional, earning a reasonable wage, respected by other professionals. She helped herself in spite of me. Actually, she must admit, I helped a little. She's doing better than she was before. The therapy has changed me as well. I might not want to admit it, but I'm a much better therapist than I was before. She feels she's helped me. I've changed as much as she has—no, even more. Sometimes she feels as if she's the therapist and I'm the patient. She envies me for how much I've changed. But she's changed a little too. I now have to learn how to become a little excited over her achievement.

She often tells me that she is thinking of discontinuing. Maybe she should just stop coming; maybe she should take a vacation from therapy. If she leaves, could she come back? Or would my waiting list be too long? Would I have no time for her? Would my fee become too high? In the beginning of treatment through the symbiosis, I had encouraged her not to leave and interpreted her wish to flee dependency upon me. Now, as she separates, I tell her that it is up to her whether she stays or leaves. As before, I tell her that if she leaves, she's welcome to return. We might have to work out a different time, but I would not abandon her treatment simply because she separated. Sometimes she practices her autonomy by taking vacations from therapy. She then resumes treatment and comes regularly. She says that she's changed herself and her life so much that it frightens her. She feels like a different person. She no longer sees me as representing dependency; instead, I represent autonomy. She says therapy frightens her now because of how autonomous she's become. She had always felt that if she became truly independent she'd have to lose all close relationships. She now sees that she can become autonomous but remain connected and committed in relationships. She does not wish to be emotionally isolated. She can express gratitude to me for helping her while feeling that she mostly helped herself. She can feel dependent without feeling lost in the other. She is starting a new job.

The Patient Attempting to Cure the Bad Object

Justine projected into me the all-good symbiotic object. For a time our relationship protected her from the noisy, intrusive, bad internal mother. She gradually held on to a fantasy of possessing me inside of her as the breast/phallus. She needed constant reinforcement from our external relationship to maintain this omnipotent self and object symbiotic unit. After she had secured the all-good breast/phallus within her, she projected into me the all-bad persecutory breast/feces mother. As she said later, she often spoke to me as if I were "shit." I became the all-bad, symbiotic mother who rewarded her dependence and rejected her autonomy. In devaluing me as feces, she expelled the bad object, practicing her autonomy. For a time she arrived at a narcissistic adaptation, seeing herself as all good and the transference object along with the external world as all bad. During this time she attempted to cure the bad mother (Searles 1986) by treating me. She tried to make me, the mother, more enthusiastic, alive, excited, and less depressed about her autonomy. In the transference, she attempted to cure the depressed mother of her failure in mirroring. She experienced both herself and me as making progress in the therapy. Once she began to perceive me as a good enough, healed, mirroring mother, she increasingly became excited about telling me of her autonomous achievements. Earlier, she had felt depressed and abandoned as she separated, and she therefore perceived me as the depressed, abandoned, abandoning mother. As she became excited, she perceived me as excited. In securing the all-good breast within her and devaluing me as the all-bad object, she also denied her dependency and envy of me as the maternal all-good breast. I did not immediately interpret these primitive defenses but instead wordlessly permitted her to reject me for a prolonged period in order to practice her autonomy.

Narcissistic Adaptation and the Bad Object

I have illustrated the patient's shift from the therapeutic symbiosis to the gradual resolution of the symbiosis. During the therapeutic symbiosis, the patient begins to activate the vulnerable, dependent self toward the therapist as a holding object. The actual external relationship reinforced the internal all-positive symbiotic self and object unit. The patient gradually feels less vulnerable as he unconsciously fantasizes that he possesses the all-good breast. This fantasy leads to a narcissistic adaptation, enhancement of autonomous functioning, and the expulsion of all-bad self and object representations. This therapeutic symbiotic state coincides with Freud's idea that the normal psychic tendency in infancy is to take in all that is good and spit out all that is bad. As will be described later, the borderline patient undergoes an inversion of this process, such that he takes in all that is bad and spits out all that is good. The most severely disturbed borderline patients maintain an identification with the bad internal object and spit out or reject the good internal object. Through undergoing the phase of ambivalent symbiosis, some patients can reach a more normative therapeutic symbiosis in which they take in all that is good in self and object representations and spit out all that is bad. Through this narcissistic adaptation, the patient begins to function more autonomously and to separate from the bad internal object as projected into the transference. With this in mind, the therapist should at first reinforce the internalization of the symbiotic unit by providing mirroring and empathy, and he should accept and tolerate the patient's efforts at separation. Ironically, this therapeutic task sometimes means that the therapist must accept the transference position of being the bad object that rewards dependency and rejects autonomy, thereby allowing the patient to separate from the now-bad symbiotic object in the transference. If the therapist becomes too actively supportive of individuation, the patient can experience the therapist as trying to force him to be autonomous for the sake of the therapist and his narcissism and not for the patient. After accepting the patient's narcissistic adaptation, the therapist must eventually interpret the unconscious fantasy of possession of the good breast as a defense against dependency on and envy of the therapist mother as a separate external object that the patient needs in order to grow further. In this last phase, the therapist helps the patient to integrate the split-off all-good and all-bad self and object representation units (Kernberg 1980).

JONATHAN

The patient, Jonathan, is a young adult who has recently begun a teaching job and is taking related course work. He says, "I must begin the master's program. My new teaching job requires that I obtain a master's degree over the next several years. I have always had a thing about school. I'm scared of it. My greatest phobia. A major conflict. I've always done well, but there's a dreadful fear of failure. The new course is in nineteenth-century American literature. I wasn't a literature major, and many of the students might have majored in literature. I've read all of the authors. But the other students might know so much more. I'm afraid I won't keep up. I don't really want to go for a Ph.D. It's not central. I'll complete my master's because I must, but there's no practical reason to get a Ph.D. I'll probably never get a Ph.D. I feel no need for it."

This monologue is actually an internal two-person dialogue. The patient speaks to a silent object. The evidence is in the denial of the wish to obtain a doctoral degree. The patient talks of the practical necessity to begin a master's program and of his fear of his first course in American literature, and then denies any ambition toward a Ph.D. The question is, Who ever said that he had an interest in a Ph.D.? To whom is he responding when he says that a Ph.D. is not central, that he can live without one, that he will probably never get one? I have made no mention of a Ph.D. Yet he begins to state that he hasn't any interest in one.

I comment that his denial of interest in a doctoral degree sounds like a response, that he sounded as if he was talking to someone who believes that he should have an interest in a Ph.D.

Jonathan responds that his father is always after him to obtain a

Ph.D. His father has a Ph.D. When he told his father that he was beginning the master's course in American literature, the father replied that now he could go on to get a Ph.D.

"And how did that make you feel?"

"Undermined. Like what I was doing now, the course for the master's, wasn't worth anything for itself."

"Merely a stepping stone to a Ph.D."

"Exactly."

"How did that make you feel about pursuing a Ph.D.?"

"Like it's the last thing in the world I want."

"So your father's vigorous efforts to interest you in a Ph.D. have the exact opposite effect. A Ph.D. is the last thing in the world you want."

"School has always been my greatest phobia. This insane need to excel. Must be better than anyone. A 4.0 index. Perfect. This insane need to excel has screwed me. Now I've decided just to get by. What if I only get a 3.0 index? Who cares? What if I never get a Ph.D.?"

The patient's communications express a complicated enactment of internalized object relations. Nearest to his consciousness, the patient's decision to just get by and not strive for a Ph.D. reflects a separation from his father, who insists that he excel and go for a Ph.D. The patient states that his father wants him to do this for his sake and not for the patient himself, so the patient refuses. The father's insistence that Jonathan excel has the exact opposite effect. The father is obsessed with Jonathan's excelling. He wants only the best for Jonathan. The father's monomania for the doctoral degree is a form of splitting. The father does not experience the normal ambivalence that a father often feels toward his son's oedipal competition. He only owns the wish for the son to excel. The wish for the son not to excel is split off and disowned. The son takes in the father's disowned ambivalence. Jonathan correctly reads his father's unconscious wish for his son to fail so that he can remain on top—the only one with the Ph.D. oedipal phallus.

Jonathan rebelled against his father's overtly expressed aspirations for him by never fully living up to his academic potential. The father would compare Jonathan to his male peers who studied hard, just as the father had. The father would say "Look how hard Thomas studies. He's just like I was. Why can't you be like Thomas? You take after your mother. Lazy, just like she is." Jonathan's fellow students thus became representatives of his father. Now Jonathan thinks of how he cannot hope to measure up to his fellow students. In this way, he states that he cannot live up to his father.

In saying that he will not try to excel—that is, that he will just get by, that he will probably never get a Ph.D.—he reassures the internal father object that he will not compete for the oedipal phallus. Instead, he will remain like the "lazy" mother. The father loves the lazy mother even though he often ridicules and abuses her. The father loves Jonathan even though he ridicules and abuses him. The father expects both to be very grateful for his love, for who else but someone as magnanimous as he would love such failures? He often criticizes them and then pities them. Similarly, Jonathan will criticize himself for not measuring up to the more experienced students and then he will pity himself. In this way, he treats himself as the critical, pitying father treats him. The father equates pity with love. When Jonathan pities himself, he feels loved by the internal father. Jonathan would rather remain the father's love object than compete with him.

Jonathan directs his monologue to me. He is informing me that he will not try to excel, that he'll probably never go for a Ph.D. During the course of his treatment, he has raised the question of the Ph.D. on repeated occasions. The problem is always posed in the framework that he can either earn a Ph.D. and become somebody important and successful or never earn a Ph.D. and remain unsuccessful but true to himself instead of his father. I am a therapist with a Ph.D. In the transference, Jonathan reassures his father that he will not compete with him for the oedipal phallus by obtaining a Ph.D. He then becomes depressed and tells me how he is lacking. I as the oedipal father am expected to pity him because of his lack of a Ph.D. phallus. He also believes that I feel guilty because I have one and he doesn't, since he sacrificed his to me. I do not yet interpret all of this but permit him to unfold and enact the transference.

He is lacking in the secrets of phallic knowledge. Castrated of a Ph.D., he needs to take in my knowledge. He is hungry for my gems of wisdom and wants to learn about everything from me. Between the two of us, I possess all of the secret wisdom under the sun. We have dialogues about literature, philosophy, politics, psychoanalysis, sexuality, health, history; all of this is symbiotic communication, a symbiotic enactment of an unconscious fellatio fantasy. He is orally devouring my Ph.D. phallus. The illusion that he has sacrificed his own phallus to me and is now castrated creates the further illusion that he has an insatiable thirst for my phallic knowledge. As he incorporates my knowledge, he increasingly fantasizes that he has captured the phallic object within himself. He imparts this knowledge to anyone fortunate, or unfortunate, enough to listen. He preaches the word of his therapist. At this point he begins to need me less as he clones himself after me.

A shift occurs in the transference. He now no longer thirsts for my words but preaches and lectures to me. For a time, it is like hearing myself talk. He is doing well in his new job and at school, and he is preaching the word to anyone who will listen. At the same time, the negation of the external Ph.D. grows stronger, for what does he need any of the external trappings? He has within him the word of his therapist. He does not need the external Ph.D. phallus. It is trapped inside of him, a part of him; he is it in identification.

On occasion Jonathan begins to feel dissatisfied. He does not have enough money. It is expensive to live in New York; how will he ever move out of his family's home? It is fine to be as smart as one's therapist, but shouldn't he strive for more? He then flagellates himself for being discontented, for feeling a lack, for being envious of those who have it better. At such times, he again becomes needy of my knowledge and mirroring; he needs to hear that he is better than others because he has sacrificed himself in so many areas. He talks about how much more selflessly dedicated he is to helping his students than the other teachers are. They are all superficial materialists like his father. In his efforts to rescue a troubled child, he often gets himself in over his head. He then comes in to me and reports that he is drowning in his self-sacrifice.

He is in need of my omnipotent knowledge to rescue himself and the youngster.

I begin to interpret how in his fantasy, a Ph.D. symbolizes the phallic power of his father. When I first met Jonathan, he was rejecting or negating his own wish to possess the Ph.D. phallus. He recognized that his father was unconsciously threatened by his normal wish to compete, so he sacrificed the phallus to his father and identified with the lazy mother. I explained that he and his father had the pathological illusion that women are weak, castrated, and lazy while men are powerful, potent, and active. To avoid losing his father's love, he identified with his mother and surrendered his competitive strivings. Maintaining the illusion that he was castrated of the Ph.D. phallus, he then needed to take in all of his father's knowledge and power. I showed him how he relived this with me. Most important, once he maintained the symbiotic fantasy that he had devoured my phallic knowledge, he no longer had to envy me as an external object with a Ph.D. or compete with me for it.

I now become the bad father pressuring him to obtain a Ph.D. He has understood my interpretations as statements that all of his achievements amount to nothing, and he should get himself a Ph.D. He says that I have not directly said this, but he can read the messages between the lines. In fact, I must believe that everyone should have a Ph.D.; after all, I got one myself. Why had I gotten a Ph.D., he wondered? For a good while he had not known that I had one. He had liked me better when he believed that I had all of this knowledge without a Ph.D. He actually had learned accidentally about my Ph.D. He had thought I had only a master's degree. Maybe I'm not as secure as I had first appeared. Maybe I really do need society's approval. His father is always like that. Forever flaunting his Ph.D. They visited his father's life-long friend, Tony. His father announced himself to the doorman by saying, "Dr. Marks to see Tony." The doorman called up to Tony and said, "Your doctor is here. Are you sick or something?" His father's Ph.D. is his badge of courage. It's one thing to be proud of a degree, but it's another thing to see it as a sign of manhood. It's his penis, just as I said. You know how guys sometimes see their cars as phallic symbols? His father is like that with the Ph.D.—constantly showing it off. It has a very special meaning in his family. He's talked about it enough with me. I know.

In the course of subsequent sessions it became clear to the patient that his father's perception of and tendency to flaunt his Ph.D. made it a very fitting symbol for childhood oedipal object relations fantasies. His devaluation of the Ph.D. was a defense against his oedipal competitive and envious strivings. Once Jonathan had become conscious of his oedipal competition and envy in the transference and had accepted it, he was able to separate out his real ambitions and interests from his conflicts around the Ph.D. as a symbol. The Ph.D. became just a Ph.D. he could consider on its own merits along with other options.

12

Principles of Intervention and Countertransference Problems

In handling the negative therapeutic reaction, the therapist uses both empathic and interpretive interventions. The negative therapeutic reaction can be attributed to a structural deficit in positive self and object representations and the internal bad object situation. The therapist must provide the patient with an empathic holding relationship so that he can internalize a positive object relationship. When the internal bad object transference becomes defensively activated, the therapist intervenes by empathically interpreting the plight of the bad object.

INTERVENING WITH THE STRUCTURAL DEFICIT

During the out-of-contact phase of patient–therapist interaction, the therapist's interventions are predominantly cognitively em-

279

pathic. The therapist makes the patient aware of the dominance of the negative self and object representations and the deficit in positive self and object representations (personal communication from Dr. George Frank). This initial intervention is similar to Beck's (1979) cognitive technique in that the therapist directs the patient's awareness to the preoccupation with negative thoughts and lack of positive thoughts during depressive, hopeless, or apathetic psychic states. However, this initial cognitive technique is used from an object relations perspective. The patient is engaged in tracking how he does not carry a comforting image of the therapeutic relationship between sessions, especially when he is feeling depressed, hopeless, or apathetic. The patient's all-negative thinking about a particular problem is explicitly attributed to an all-negative image of the self and the other that colors his view of the problem.

FELICIA

Felicia had a latency-age boy who was having behavioral and academic problems. The child was suspended from school, and Felicia had to appear for a conference before he could return. She repeatedly canceled her appointments with the school authorities for reasons that could only be called excuses. In our session, Felicia did not spontaneously express anger, rage, or a sense of persecution in relationship to the school. Rather, she appeared to be indifferent to her son's plight and said that the school problem was the least of her difficulties. She gradually revealed a negative, hopeless view of her relationship with the school authorities. She expressed the conviction that the school authorities did not care, that she would be met by them with accusations, criticism, and indifference; she would therefore avoid this negative experience. Felicia's avoidance of the negative encounter with school was typical of her general behavioral pattern when faced with situational problems. In intervening with Felicia, it was imperative to first acknowledge that school authorities could be critical, accusatory, and indifferent. I then engaged her in looking at how she inevitably has such negative expectations when dealing with people. In this way I was able to demonstrate to her that an internal rejected image of herself and rejecting image of the other color her perception of external reality. I then began to actively explore with her whether there were ever instances when a more accepting image of the other and accepted or valued image of the self color her expectations of reality situations. She acknowledged that the positive self and object representation unit was foreign to her. I wondered whether she was able to use the therapy when she was depressed, apathetic, indifferent.

With Felicia, the dominance of the negative self and object representation unit not only influenced expectations of reality but also contributed to the reality further fitting her projection. For instance, in the case of school, her avoidance of appointments led the school authorities to conclude that she was indifferent and neglectful and to react even more punitively and abusively toward her. Feeling guilty about canceling the appointments, Felicia chose not to explain and felt that she was as bad as the internal and external object accused her of being. Once she was aware of the dominance of the negative self and object representation unit, she became less avoidant and actively faced problematic situations. She would try to keep in mind the positive therapeutic relationship, and if the external authorities were unjustifiably critical, she could distinguish them from the internal object and stick up for herself.

The structural deficit in positive self and object representations results in impairment of ego functioning, particularly in the area of judgment, anticipation, frustration tolerance, impulse control, and regulation of affect. In the case of Felicia, it could be seen that the dominance of the negative self and object representation unit and deficit in the positive self and object representation unit impaired her judgment, anticipation, and frustration tolerance, as was evident in her avoidance behavior with the school authorities. In such a case, the therapist should directly point out to the patient how the internal object relations situation impairs ego functioning. The patient with a structural deficit is unaware that he is missing the psychic functioning capacities. It is necessary for the therapist to point out these capacities until the patient is aware of them; he can then begin to try to actively exercise these ego functions.

As the patient becomes aware of the structural deficit, he will begin to spontaneously and actively explore history in order to account for the inability to internalize a positive object experience.

The patient becomes aware not only of the negative experience that resulted in the negative self and object representation unit but also of the positive experience that was omitted. The exploration of the omitted experience involves the patient's becoming aware of positive self–object functions that he experiences from the self–object transference as requisite for human growth and development. The discovery of the omitted experience is accompanied by the patient's experiencing self-empathy, an internalization of the therapist's empathically making him cognitively aware of the structural deficit.

INTERVENING WITH AMBIVALENT SYMBIOSIS

The patient's beginning internalization of the positive relationship to the therapist activates the bad object situation. The internal bad object does not have to come to life so long as the patient is out of contact with the good object. During ambivalent symbiosis, the therapist interprets the bad object transference as a defense against internalizing the potentially good object transference.

During ambivalent symbiosis, the transference is typically manifested in the hoped-for good object transformed into an exciting object into a rejecting object into a rejected object into a hoped-for good object. The hoped-for good object gives rise to a fear of merger. The wish for merger is expressed in the insatiable need for the exciting object. Insatiable need inevitably gives rise to disappointment and transforms the exciting object into a rejecting object. The rejecting object is rejected in turn. The rejected object gives rise to a fear of object loss, in turn transforming the rejected object into a hoped-for good object, thus giving rise to the repetition of the merry-go-round of hoped-for good object, exciting object, rejecting object, rejected object, hoped-for good object. All of these object relations transformations are the result of the patient's being caught between the longing for and fear of fusion and the wish for and fear of separateness. Patients in ambivalent symbiosis project these object transformations into the transference and into their external object relations.

In making these patients aware of the internal status of the ambivalent symbiotic object, the therapist directs their attention to how they think about the object. For instance, if the patient thinks of the object as rejecting him, the therapist might say, "You were making yourself feel rejected by thinking of the other as rejecting you." In the case of Kim, the adolescent who felt rejected by her drug-addicted boyfriend described in Chapters 5 and 11, I made her aware that she dwelt all day with a rejecting image of her boyfriend.

The therapist also directs the patient's attention to the inevitability of the transformation of the object. For instance, Kim would never say goodbye. When the other departed, she inevitably felt rejected and then rejected the other. I would say, "When you make yourself feel that you cannot live without the other and therefore cannot say goodbye, it will have to follow that you will feel rejected by the other. When you feel rejected by the other, it will invariably follow that you will reject the other. Then, when you think of yourself as rejecting the other, you will inevitably feel all alone. Feeling all alone and abandoned will inevitably create an insatiable need for the other."

Once the patient becomes aware of the transformations of the bad object, I will interpret that the insatiable need for the object will invariably create a fear of being smothered and will therefore give rise to the angry distancing in the rejecting–rejected object configuration.

Empathically Acknowledging Reality while Interpreting the Internal Object Situation

The ambivalent symbiotic patient is often involved with external objects that resemble the exciting and rejecting object. The therapist should empathically acknowledge the patient's distress at being mistreated in the interpersonal situation but should then redirect the patient's attention to the internal infantile object relation.

Marion

Marion complained that her husband had abandoned her to live
with another woman. A year later she remained angry as she
thought of them. One Saturday night, she called her husband
repeatedly, leaving angry, threatening messages on his answering
machine. She then called me, leaving a message on my machine
that she felt out of control. Marion stated that she felt within her
rights to harass her husband. I interpreted that there were two
levels of experience. There was the reality level that she was an
adult with understandable complaints about a man who unem-
pathically deserted her for another woman. But then there was a
question of her infantile rights in that she was reliving the experience of a child who feels left out of the parental coupling and
wants to intrude upon it. Marion then acknowledged feeling left
out of the therapist's life and feeling intrusive in calling for help on
a Saturday evening. The patient became aware that she was living
in a psychic space of feeling left out and wanting to intrude on a
rejecting parental couple and that she had found an external object
whose problems would enable her to enact the internal situation.

The Displacement of the Ambivalent Symbiotic Transference

The patient may displace the insatiable need for the exciting object
into external objects outside of the therapy. These patients will
direct the hoped-for good object, exciting object, rejecting object,
rejected object sequence toward objects in their lives. The therapist will initially be viewed as an ideal coach to help the patient
deal with the bad objects, but eventually the therapist will be
placed in an impotent position.

The therapist interprets that the patient's dependency needs
have been excited in the therapy and that he is turning to others to
fulfill them. He inevitably feels rejected by the others. The therapist then explains that in feeling rejected by the others, the patient
can eventually create an image of the therapist as useless because
the therapist cannot change the others. These interventions will
inevitably result in a therapeutic symbiosis.

INTERVENING WITH
THERAPEUTIC SYMBIOSIS

During this phase the patient increasingly projects the good object relations unit into the transference and the bad object relations unit into external reality. However, the relationship to external reality improves in that the internalized good object serves as a buffer between him and the bad object. The patient now becomes less sensitive to the inconveniences of external reality.

In this phase, the therapist's interventions are increasingly empathic; this permits the patient to idealize the object in the transference and mirror his separation from the bad object and his internal individuation. The therapist should not interpret splitting at this point, but should instead allow the patient to internalize him as a good object. Sometimes during this phase, the patient will analyze or further separate from the bad object by discussing and analyzing the bad objects of his everyday life. The phase is "symbiotic" in that the therapist enters the patient's object world, seeing it from his viewpoint. A certain rhythm of communication develops specific to the intersubjective interaction between patient and therapist. The therapist's keeping time to the rhythm can be seen as an intervention crucial to the development of the therapeutic symbiosis.

The Rhythm of Symbiosis

Diane, the Hispanic single parent discussed in Chapter 7, was severely abused as a child, had difficulty maintaining regular employment, and had to leave her apartment by late June. When the deadline came to move, Diane did not have enough money to rent an apartment. She sent her son to her family out of state and stayed with a friend, hoping to save enough money to find an apartment by autumn.

As the deadline approached, she felt as if she were going crazy. What will happen if she can't find an apartment by the time her son returns? What if she loses her job? People are fired for no reason. She used to go through life on automatic, never worrying about these things. She guesses it all caught up with her. She calls me to say that she can't take it anymore. Her son is demanding a two-bedroom apartment. She's lucky if she can afford a one-bedroom apartment. She is fed up. Cannot take it anymore. She does not want to talk any longer. Goodbye.

She is looking for an apartment. All of the buildings in the area are going co-op. Old, dilapidated buildings. She doesn't have enough money yet to rent an apartment. She is just practicing, seeing what's out there. But there is nothing. Her married lover calls. He has connections in real estate. He sends her to look at an apartment. It's small, and the rent is high. If she takes it, she will not have a penny left over. She wants to have a bit of a cushion in case she loses her job.

She has forgotten about her son. She should write or call to let him know that she's okay. She continues to pound the pavement for an apartment. Nothing. She doesn't have enough money anyway. In my capacity as a social worker, I call social service agencies, real-estate brokers. Nothing. She is correct. August is passing by. Pounding the pavements. The heat is scorching. The Bronx is a wasteland of apartments. They do not want children in Queens and Westchester. Again and again and again. No children allowed. The new slogan: Back to the Bronx. Every so often I mention Brooklyn. Neither she nor I knows Brooklyn, but I recall vague rumors that cheap apartments are to be found there. So when I feel that something should be said, some sort of good advice proffered out of hopelessness, anxiety, a sense of futility, the need to do or to say something, mention is made of Brooklyn. Maybe this is where the cheap apartment that accepts children and doesn't require a broker's fee exists. She asks, Brooklyn Heights? I answer, Rumor has it that Brooklyn Heights is expensive. Diane smiles. I learn to keep my suggestions to myself. Containing anxiety.

What do other people do? Maybe she should ask her family for help. Could it be that they never help because she never asks? She calls. The answer is no. Her mother can't help because she just contributed toward her sister's new car. No one can help because each did something else with his money. No, the problem was not that she never asked. She never asked for a good reason. We discuss her anger at her family for never helping. Diane calls such discussion "talking trash" and says that she enjoys it. We analyze the problems of everyone in her family. Talking trash about those folks again. That's what we do in therapy. Talk trash about the family, work, friends, and neighbors, the city, the nation, the world. Learning how to talk trash in therapy. It just goes to show you—the majority of the people in the world suck. That symbiotic time of the treatment during which all the world—with the exception of Diane and me—is poisonous, malevolent, and destructive.

This case illustrates the rhythm of symbiotic relatedness. Searles (1986) has commented on the sense of suspense and ongoing crisis that often arises in the patient–therapist interaction during intensive therapy with the borderline patient. In keeping time to the patient's rhythm of communication, the therapist allows himself to serve as a container for the patient's suspense, crisis, and unmanageable anxiety (Bion 1984).

Diane has projected her internal bad objects into a difficult external reality. In "talking trash" about her environment, she begins to create some distance and separateness from her bad objects. The symbiotic relatedness with me serves to buffer Diane from the persecutory objects and enables her to manage a difficult environmental situation. It is difficult to distinguish whether the point of view about her life is a central aspect of symbiotic relatedness. It is not merely that the therapist understands or joins the patient's point of view. Rather, in allowing himself to be used as a container by the patient, the therapist also gives rise to his own stream of unconsciousness, and a rhythm eventually develops, reflecting an intersubjective view of both patient and therapist.

INTERVENING WITH THE RESOLUTION OF THE SYMBIOSIS

As the patient internalizes the good object in the transference, he becomes less dependent on the external therapist. The internal bad object is now fully projected into the therapist to foster separation. The patient begins to objectify and further separate from the bad object by analyzing the therapist. The patient will sometimes induce the therapist to fail him and then analyze and attempt to cure the bad object in the transference. The patient may now manifest increased autonomy by arriving late for sessions, no longer calling the therapist between sessions, and sometimes requesting temporary vacations from therapy. The therapist should not now interpret such distancing as a defense against dependency (as he would have during ambivalent symbiosis) but should rather remark on how the patient is trying to need the therapist less in striving for autonomy.

After the patient has become sufficiently autonomous, the therapist should interpret the patient's view of the therapist as all bad as a defense in recognizing his dependence on and envy of an *external* good object. This intervention differs from the interpretation of the defense against dependence during ambivalent symbiosis in that during that phase, the therapist focuses on the patient's defense against dependence on the therapist as an *internal* good object (focusing on the transformation of the hoped-for good object into an exciting, then rejecting, then rejected object). Now the therapist intervenes by interpreting the patient's narcissism as a defense against dependence on and envy of the therapist as a *separate* external object. In this way, the patient begins to integrate positive and negative internal object relations units and to further recognize his separateness.

Countertransference

The management of countertransference is inherently related to effective intervention. Each phase of patient–therapist interaction gives rise to its own particular transference–countertransference dilemmas. The out-of-contact patient is often fixated at a practicing-subphase level of ego development and a paranoid–schizoid level of object relations. An analogy can be drawn between the verbal presentation of the adult patient and the behavioral activity of the child patient. In session, the adult patient verbally describes the chaos of his life, the initiating and rejecting of housing, employment, and interpersonal situations. The child patient will initiate and then reject various play activities, exhibiting hyperactivity, destructiveness, and chaos. With both the child and the adult, the therapist is often drawn into limit-setting, structuring, and ego supportive techniques.

The Countertransference Reaction of Engulfing the Patient

Kernberg (1975) has questioned the therapeutic value of ego supportive techniques in the treatment of the borderline patient. He has stated that environmental manipulation, direction, suggestion, advice, and reassurance will serve to increase the patient's splitting off of the good and bad object transference. I agree with Kernberg on this point and would add that the severely disturbed patient induces the therapist into using generalized limit-setting and ego supportive techniques in order to transform the therapist into the engulfing bad object.

Mahler (1975) emphasizes that practicing-subphase behavior originates not as a result of the flight from the bad object, but rather as a normative developmental phase of the ego in separation–individuation. Therefore, the out-of-contact patient is defensively using practicing-subphase behavior as a paranoid–schizoid flight from the engulfing object. The patient presents chaotic, disorganized, destructive, and hyperactive behavior that induces in the therapist an increasing tendency to set limits, provide organization and structure, and lend his strong ego to the patient's fragile, weak ego. In the treatment of the adult patient, the therapist will often increasingly assume the position of manager of the patient's chaotic life. With the child patient, the therapist will often try to limit the youngster's chaotic, hyperactive, and destructive behavior.

The therapist often feels that the patient is "asking" him to set limits because the patient cannot control himself. At the same time, the patient increasingly rebels from the limit-setting and perceives the therapist as engulfing. By inducing the therapist into using generalized ego-supportive techniques, the patient avoids exercising his own ego functioning and furthering his autonomy. He also maintains a tie with the bad, engulfing object through the vigorous cycle of inducing and then rejecting engulfment. As the therapist is increasingly transformed into the engulfing object, he may also experience impairment of his own ego functioning with the patient, particularly in the areas of judgment and frustration and anxiety tolerance. The therapist will often become increasingly frustrated and anxious, setting limits when it is not necessary and then giving up in disgust and not setting limits when it *is* necessary.

Permitting the Patient to Practice

In the treatment of the out-of-contact patient who exhibits practicing-subphase behavior, the therapist can remain effective by assuming the developmental position of the practicing subphase mother instead of the engulfing object. In this developmental position, the therapist attempts to catalyze growth by permitting the patient to "practice" and by setting limits only when the patient is in real danger. In the treatment of the adult patient, the clinician empathizes by listening to the patient's adventures in changing housing situations, jobs, and interpersonal relationships as preliminary efforts in autonomous functioning. The therapist may also empathically interpret the patient's need to flee from the engulfing object in order to preserve his autonomy. The therapist should not become the engulfing object by interpreting the patient's fear of commitment or by becoming anxious about the patient's unstable life and attempting to help him manage it.

Searles (1979) has stated that in the treatment of the out-of-contact patient, the patient and therapist can advance to a phase of therapeutic symbiosis only if the therapist can permit himself to enter the patient's internal psychic world as opposed to imposing his own psychic world on the patient. Winnicott (1958) has written about the developmental importance of the mother's permitting the child to be alone in her nonintrusive presence. As the therapist listens to the out-of-contact adult patient's adventures as practicing phenomena, the patient will feel that he is being left alone in the presence of the witnessing therapist. Gradually, he will become increasingly interested in letting the therapist into his life. He will begin to look forward to recounting his adventures to the therapist. Eventually, he will even think of the therapist during his adventures. In this way, the therapist will gradually become an internal witness in therapeutic symbiosis. The patient's paranoid–schizoid flight from the engulfing object will be transformed into practicing-subphase behavior in the presence of a developmental witness. The child engaging in chaotic, hyperactive, daredevil behavior, a paranoid–schizoid flight from the engulfing object, will increasingly begin to practice his autonomous motoric competence in the presence of the mirroring therapist.

The therapeutic stance that I am advocating for the out-of-contact patient implies that the therapist is always psychically active in exercising his autonomous ego functioning of anxiety and frustration tolerance, impulse control, and, especially, judgment. Like the mother of the practicing child, the therapist must exercise judgment in knowing when to run after and limit the child who is darting into danger and when to tolerate his own anxiety and frustration in allowing the child to practice. In assuming an approach of either setting generalized limits or never setting limits, the therapist avoids exercising his own autonomous ego functioning in determining when the patient is practicing and when he is truly in danger. Setting generalized limits and never setting limits are two sides of the same coin—or two faces of the same bad object countertransference: the engulfing object and the abandoning bad object.

Countertransference and Ambivalent Symbiosis

The ambivalent symbiotic interaction between patient and therapist is fraught with its own particular transference–countertransference issues. Beginning therapists working with severely abused children who activate an ambivalent symbiotic transference experience a common countertransference reaction. The child patient is initially pleasurably stimulated by meeting a warm, friendly thera-

pist with a room full of toys. The child, who has been severely
deprived and abused, requests particular games or toys. The therapist provides, within reason, what the child requests. However,
the child increasingly begins to express disappointment with what
is provided. The toys may not be exactly what he wants; he may
ask for one game, but when it is provided, he might wish he had
another. Or the paints may not be exactly the colors that he wants.
Then the child might complain of not having enough time in the
session. The therapist senses that the child is disappointed. The
countertransference problem is that the therapist is having trouble
being in the position of being the one who disappoints the child.
The therapist either becomes overgratifying in an effort to avoid
disappointing the child or avoids placing himself in a position of
being disappointing to the child (and disappointed in the child) by
no longer providing the child with anything in which to be
disappointed. In both instances, the therapist attempts to avoid
accepting the transference role of the bad object who excites and
then disappoints (rejects) the child.

I have discussed how the ambivalent symbiotic patient transforms the therapist into the hoped-for good object, exciting object, rejecting object, rejected object, hoped-for good object, and
so on. Beginning therapists often experienced pleasurable stimulation in being cast in the position of hoped-for good object, a
transference role that is syntonic with the professional image of
the therapist as an empathic, helpful object. However, once the
patient begins to project into the therapist exciting rejecting and
rejected objects, the therapist often experiences such roles as alien
and tends either to remain the hoped-for good object or to abort
all such roles by withdrawing from the patient. In supervision, I
have found that therapists usually become better able to accept the
bad object transference roles when they can understand that they
are still being helpful to the child even when cast in the transference role of the disappointing (exciting and rejecting) object.

The appearance of the disappointing object in the transference
is actually a positive prognostic sign because it implies that the
child patient has enough internal good object experience to expect
help; expectations imply hope and the belief in a good object in

which to be disappointed. In addition, and most important, the disappointing object serves an essential therapeutic purpose in that the patient transforms the hoped-for good object into a disappointing object in order to protect himself from merging with a too-good and idealized object and losing his autonomy. The acceptance of the bad object role must be distinguished from the acting out of that role. The therapist accepts the role by behaving as he did initially, by providing play materials that are reasonable, and by allowing the child to experience his disappointment.

Accepting the bad object role does not mean that the therapist in any way deliberately enacts the bad object role, but rather that the therapist does not actively try to avoid being perceived in this role. The therapist who will have the greatest difficulty in accepting the bad object transference is one whose own internal bad object situation becomes activated by the patient's transference and projected into the patient. For instance, such a therapist might have had a parental object whom he could never please. This situation can be referred to as a bad object countertransference, and it is one with which the therapist himself may need further treatment to resolve.

The ambivalent symbiotic patient may project not only unwanted object but also unwanted self representations into the therapist. In such situations, the therapist will sometimes unknowingly enact the patient's presenting problem in the countertransference. This countertransference problem can be illustrated with a brief clinical experiment that I have sometimes conducted in supervision workshops. A number of violently abused youngsters were referred to an inner-city clinic because of extremely defiant behavior toward all authority. The referral sources would complain that the youngsters disregarded authority and refused to obey rules, regulations, or instructions. The children would often relate to their therapists as if they were the abusive parents and the therapists were the abused, unwanted children. They would not designate roles for themselves and the therapist to play, but instead appeared to believe in the reality of the abusive relationship into which they cast the therapist. In other words, the child would *not* say to the therapist, "Let us play that I am the mean teacher and you are the child." Rather, in the course of playing a game with the therapist, the patient would begin to become verbally domineering and harshly abusive, and would act as if he believed that his abusive behavior was warranted by the therapist's badness and incompetence. The patient's belief in the reality of the transferential feelings therefore has a borderline—as opposed to a "let's make believe," neurotic—quality.

Role Playing of the Transference–Countertransference

I would sometimes present an interaction I had with one such child patient to one of the therapist participants in the child therapy workshop. I would simply tell the therapist that I would enact the role of a violently abused youngster referred for defying authority, and he (the therapist participant) would play the therapist. Playing the role of the child, I say to the therapist participant, "Let's play catch." I then throw a rubber ball to him to invite him to play. As we play, I proceed to verbally abuse him for not throwing or catching the ball correctly. For a duration of not more than five minutes, I berate him for never catching or throwing the ball correctly. No matter how he throws or catches the ball, I tell him he has not thrown it correctly. If I drop it, I blame him for throwing it incorrectly. After five minutes of this play, I miss his throw and let it roll behind me. I order him to chase it and bring it to me. Most therapists whom I've engaged in this play invariably refuse to retrieve the ball.

At this point I end the play and ask the therapists what they experienced emotionally and cognitively during the five-minute interaction. Almost all of the therapists stated that after only about one minute of our interaction, they felt as if they were in the child's role instead of the therapist's role they were designated to assume. They began to feel very anxious and became clouded in their judgment as to whether they were throwing the ball incorrectly and somehow misunderstanding my commands or whether I was deliberately finding fault with everything they did. After several minutes, most of the therapists were pretty sure, but not certain, that they were not throwing or catching the ball incorrectly. By the time I ordered them to retrieve the ball I had missed, they were feeling very anxious, but defiant. The therapists usually did not want to retrieve the ball, because they felt that they would appear too submissive to themselves, to me, and to the other participants. They also felt that I might verbally abuse them further for being so submissive in following my instructions in retrieving the ball, but that I would also verbally abuse them for their refusal. Usually, the therapists felt that it was better to be abused for defiance than for submission.

After the therapists expressed their subjective experience in this interaction, a discussion ensued among the participants focused on whether the therapist was correct or incorrect in not retrieving the ball. All of the participants were struck by how, after only five minutes of such interaction, the therapist participant had repeated the child's presenting problem of defiance. The participants in the group expressed a great deal of confusion and uncertainty as to whether the therapist participant was (1) correctly setting limits and introducing reality so that the patient did not actually believe in the role play or (2) merely acting out the role of the abused, defiant self-representation being projected into him by me in the role of the patient. The participants also said that they had often experienced identical interactions with many of their own child patients and had reacted exactly as the therapist had responded in the role-playing with me.

The therapist was essentially enacting the abused and defiant role of the self-representation projected into him, when he refused to obey the child patient's command to retrieve the ball. If the therapist wordlessly retrieves the ball or follows the command of the child patient as if he (the therapist) were a robot, the patient will become *more*, not *less*, aware of the playful, symbolic role-playing nature of the interaction as opposed to the reality of the interaction for the very reason that the therapist did not take the verbal abuse seriously, as if it really hurt or as if the therapist were, in a way, really threatened by the child patient's attack. In this way, by not taking the abusive attack *seriously*, the therapist conveys to the patient his understanding of the internalized symbolic play of the interaction without overtly reminding the patient of the unreality or role-playing quality of the play. Even more important, I understand the patient's abusive attack as his identification with a rejecting object in attempting to defeat his own efforts to have the therapist serve as an extension of the self. On the one hand, the child patient is demanding that the therapist serve as an extension, or self–object, of the self. On the other hand, he does so in such a rejecting and abusive fashion that he induces in the therapist an opposition to serving as a self–object. Once the therapist defies the child patient, he is then transformed from the abused and rejected child into the rejecting parent object. In this way, the child patient maintains his tie to the rejecting bad object. The therapist in actuality defies the bad object by serving as an extension to the child. As the therapist serves as an extension of the child patient in the face of the assault of the bad object, the patient will increasingly form a symbiotic attachment to the therapist. It is absolutely imperative that as the therapist serves as an extension to the child, he do so only within the limits of reality and reason. Therefore, if a child were to ask me to retrieve the ball and hand it to him and I did so, and he threw it again and asked me to retrieve it again, I would do so. But if he demanded I run and make a great effort to retrieve it, I'd only play at running, deliberately not exerting myself in chasing it.

Turning the Therapist into a Slave

Earlier, in Chapter 6, I discussed the case of Robert, a youngster who would order me about and call me a slave. Sometimes, during our interactions, I experienced a countertransference reaction of wanting to tell him to do it himself, that I was not his slave. His abusive behavior called forth rejecting object reactions in me. He would change rules in midplay and set it up so that I failed. I sometimes felt like calling to his attention the fact that he cheated and that I was doing the activity correctly. When he had me do exercises, I sometimes wanted to show him that I could do them, and at other times I wanted not to do them at all. I usually performed these activities despite these feelings, but only to the point at which I began to feel tired, or only to the point of doing the exercise with a reasonable degree of concentration. This permitted him to project into me the unwanted inadequate self-representation and the inattentive, rejecting object representation. While following his instructions, I never tried to do so well as to be "beyond reproach." I served a "containing function" for his unwanted self and object representations and associated affects as he attacked me as the inadequate child and inattentive mother, and I tolerated these attacks without retaliating or acting as if I did not have to prove that I was not inadequate. He gradually began to permit his own vulnerability and sense of inadequacy to emerge in the transference to the holding object.

One of the developmental problems for this youngster was that his parents never served as an extension of the self, but rather expected him to serve this role. For instance, his mother demanded his undivided attention but never provided him with attention. Both of his parents would often say, if he asked them to do anything for him, "I'm not your slave." Their rejection of his developmental need to experience a sense of omnipotence resulted in the fact that he could not surrender infantile omnipotence, so he increasingly demanded that others serve him as "slaves." He also internalized his parents' refusal to be "slaves" by his own refusal to follow any instructions, rules, or regulations. Therefore, the internal rejecting object was one who refused to be a "slave," and he experienced any expectation that he obey rules, no matter how appropriate, as slavery, just as his parents had rejected even his age-appropriate needs and expectations as efforts to make them into slaves. In this sense, slavery is psychically equivalent to engulfment and loss of autonomy. During the symbiotic phase, the parents probably experienced his need that they serve an extension function not as the normal need of a child, but rather as the demand of a parent that they obey. This idea relates to Searles's view that borderline parents often transfer into the child images of their own internal parents. He says that such parents often relate to their children as though the children were their parents.

How to Serve as an Extension of the Child's Self

The neurotic or more highly structured youngster will often ask the therapist to enact a role, such as good guy or bad guy, witch or savior, slave or master. In such cases, it is explicitly understood that the assumption of such roles by child and therapist is only play. In contrast, the severely borderline youngster often does not play in such a sublimated, secondary-process, symbiotic fashion. Rather, the child will simply begin to treat the therapist as a slave, witch, good guy, or bad guy without identifying such behavior as role playing. The therapist can keep such interactions in the realm of symbolic play instead of reality by enacting the role exactly as the child suggests, so long as it does not hurt the child or the therapist.

Therefore, if a child directs me to play the slave by picking up objects from the floor, I will do so exactly as he wishes without adding any visible enthusiasm, resentment, or emotion to the behavior. If a child scolds me and then tells me to scold him back, I will ask him exactly what he wants me to say and I will then repeat his words. I add nothing spontaneous of my own to this behavior but follow his instructions as if I were an automaton. In using this technique, I do not have to artificially remind the youngster that we are only playing or that I am only asssuming a role, because the fact that I enact the role in the precise words and tone of the youngster's directions keeps our interaction in the realm of the transitional play space. By acting as if I am a puppet in the child's play, I serve as an extension of the child's self (Seinfeld 1989).

When the child expresses dependency needs through the rejecting, abusive object by, for instance, ordering the therapist to pick up after him, the child provokes the therapist to reject his dependency needs in turn. If the therapist does so because he is not comfortable assuming the transference position of slave, then the child will see the therapist as a rejecting object and will reject the therapist in turn. In this way, a rejected self-rejecting object relationship dominates the transference–countertransference and prevents the child from taking in the therapist as a holding object.

If the therapist responds to the child's commands as dependency needs and serves as an extension of the child's self, then the child's vulnerable self begins to emerge in relationship to the holding object.

The Therapeutic Frame

In the treatment of the adult ambivalently symbiotic patient, the therapeutic frame often becomes the avenue by which the therapist serves as an extension of the patient's self or as a holding object. Earlier, I mentioned my agreement with Kernberg concerning his rejection of supportive techniques that involve directing the borderline patient in his life activities. However, in his discussion of the mutual exclusiveness of interpretive and supportive techniques, Kernberg does not distinguish between supportive techniques that aim to strengthen the patient's self and object images and supportive techniques that attempt to direct the patient in the management of his daily life. Supportive techniques that aim to strengthen self and object representations have a valuable place in the handling of the negative therapeutic reaction. Giovacchini (1979) has described such techniques as nonverbal interpretations of the impairment of object constancy. Sending a postcard during a vacation or permitting phone contact between sessions (within reasonable limits) would be examples of such nonverbal interventions aimed at strengthening object constancy. Especially during the out-of-contact and symbiotic phases, the therapist must establish a balance between providing a secure-enough analytic frame to ensure that the patient will activate transferential projections while also providing enough flexibility to strengthen positive self and object representations. Fairbairn (1943) stated that the therapist must be a good-enough object in reality for the patient to risk releasing the bad object from repression. In assuming the position of a good-enough object in reality, the therapist can serve as a suitable container for the projection and building of a hoped-for good object. As I have repeatedly shown, during the ambivalent symbiosis, the hoped-for good object inevitably becomes an exciting and rejecting (or disappointing) object. Therefore, if the therapist avoids becoming a hoped-for good object, he will also avoid becoming an exciting and rejecting object. By refusing to strengthen the patient's positive self and object representations, the therapist can remain "nothing at all to the patient" and in this way avoid being the hoped-for good object that becomes a disappointing object.

Generally, during the out-of-contact and symbiotic phases, the therapist provides a more flexible frame (within the context of regularly scheduled, dependable appointment times for a fixed length) in order to strengthen positive self and object representations. He provides greater abstinence and neutrality during the resolution of the symbiosis as the patient increasingly separates from the bad object in the transference. Ferenczi's (1928) recommendation that the therapist of the severely disturbed patient provide both indulgence and privation may be relevant here.

The Therapist Viewed as Failing the Patient

In the resolution of the symbiosis, the patient will inevitably experience the therapist as failing him. The patient may induce the therapist to fail him, or he may interpret the therapist's behavior or interventions as failing him. One patient whom I had treated for several years would react to any interference in her daily efforts to individuate as a major catastrophe and as an obstacle to her progress. She would present to me her utter despair and wish to give up because some unavoidable event in her daily life had interfered with her plans and progress. If I empathized with her plight, she saw in me the mother who was falling apart and couldn't handle her anxiety. If I remained neutral, she saw me as uncaring, as not supportive of her autonomy. If I interpreted the transference, she remarked that I was doing her thinking for her. In fact, all of the reactions she attributed to me were experiences of her actual early object relations. In this way, she found, objectified, and separated from the bad object in the transference. Searles (1975) has described how the patient may both drive the object crazy and endeavor to cure the object through the transference. In the countertransference, the therapist may feel that he is being driven crazy, that he is not helpful to the patient, or that he is even destructive. It is essential that, throughout this phase, the therapist accept the transferential position of the crazy, bad object permitting the patient to analyze him and separate from him without withdrawing or retaliating.

The child patient increasingly internalizes a positive self and object representation unit through the symbiotic transference; he will no longer experience limit setting and empathy as engulfing and will become better able to take in the therapist in both limit-setting and empathic functions. During the resolution of the symbiosis, the therapist should gradually become a separate object and less of an extension of the child. It is during this phase that the therapist will set limits on the child's abusive or destructive behavior in order to increasingly introduce reality and not simply to protect the child from danger. The therapist may also choose to disobey the child's commandments as a way of introducing reality and separateness. However, if the child has had a sufficient therapeutic symbiosis, his demands for the therapist to serve as an extension often spontaneously lessen; or if the therapist does refuse him, he will on some level understand that the therapist does so in order to enhance his autonomy and not merely to reject him.

Some Special Important Problems in Technique

As previously noted, during the symbiotic phases of the transference, the therapist on occasion permits the patient to split off and project the all-bad object into external objects and to analyze the bad object. The patient thereby further separates from the bad object, using the therapist and the analyzing function as a buffer. However, the therapist must eventually shift the focus to the internal nature of the object—for instance, by focusing attention on what the patient has the object do to himself and what he does to the object in his mind.

I had a patient who always described how her sister tortured her. At one point she went away on vacation for several months and had no contact with the "bad" sister. Yet she constantly thought of her in rage and self-pity. I shifted from an empathic to an interpretive approach by asking her why she brought the hated sister along on her vacation. I then began to focus on how she used her sister's image to torture herself in her mind. If the therapist altogether avoids eventually shifting the focus from the external to the internal object, he is placing himself in the countertransferential position of being the only good object in the patient's life.

Once the patient becomes fully aware of the internal nature of the bad object, it is important that the therapist demonstrate to the patient that the internal object is not merely a replica of the original external object or objects but a combination of the actual external object and the particular developmental level of the patient which influenced his perception of the external object. The therapist initially explores with the patient the attributes of the patient's early external objects that resemble the patient's internal object. But then the therapist also explores how the patient's view of the object can also be the result of his early level of cognitive, ego, and psychosexual development in combination with the attributes of the actual external object. In taking into account the developmental position that influenced his perception of the object's actual behavior, the patient develops a more integrated view of the object.

One last transference–countertransference dilemma is that of the patient who manifests a negative therapeutic reaction by (unconsciously) creating a crisis that gives rise to an urgent need that gives rise to a desperate behavioral reaction that temporarily settles the crisis but creates the groundwork for a new crisis. Diane, the patient whom I discussed earlier, is an example of a patient who manifests the negative therapeutic reaction through the repeated creation of crisis. In the countertransference, the therapist will tend to feel increasingly hopeless, ineffectual, and powerless. It may become difficult for the therapist to think beyond the crisis, and both patient and therapist will see the crisis and the patient's reactions as inevitable. In such transference–countertransference situations, it is essential for the therapist to maintain his capacity to think and to avoid becoming totally drawn into the patient's crisis-creating projective identifications. It is especially important for the therapist to interpret the internal bad object situation's impossible omnipotent demands. Diane would often limit her options as she set impossible deadlines for herself that then created pressure for her to search desperately for unsatisfactory jobs and housing. During such crises, it is imperative for the therapist to maintain the capacity to determine which demands on the patient are created by the actual external situation and which are created by the internal bad object situation.

This book has attempted to show that the bad object transference, traditionally considered an insurmountable obstacle to treatment, actually has therapeutic value in allowing the patient the opportunity to separate from the bad object in the transference-countertransference situation. The therapeutic value of the negative therapeutic reaction derives from considering the bad object transference as a recapitulation of the early developmental vicissitudes of the bad object. Toward this end, the author has related phases of the bad object transference to phases of early development. The therapeutic approach to the bad object transference is one that combines empathic response with interpretive intervention.

References

Abraham, K. (1919). A particular form of neurotic resistance against the psychoanalytic method. In *Selected Papers of Karl Abraham*, pp. 303–311. New York: Brunner/Mazel, 1927.

——— (1924). A short study of the development of the libido, viewed in the light of mental disorders. In *Selected Papers on Psycho-Analysis*, pp. 137–156. New York: Basic Books, 1953.

Adler, G. (1985). The primary basis of borderline psychopathology: ambivalence or insufficiency? In *Borderline Psychopathology and Its Treatment*, pp. 3–13. Northvale, NJ: Jason Aronson.

Adler, G., and Buie, D. (1979). The psychotherapeutic approach to aloneness in the borderline patient. In *Advances in Psychotherapy of the Borderline Patient*, ed. J. L. LeBoit and A. Capponi, pp. 433–448. New York: Jason Aronson.

Asch, S. (1976). Varieties of negative therapeutic reaction and problems of technique. *Journal of the American Psychoanalytic Association* 24:383–407.

Bach, S. (1985). Perspectives on self and object. In *Narcissistic States and the Therapeutic Process*, pp. 153–176. New York: Jason Aronson.

Basch, M. F. (1980). Differential diagnosis choice of treatment: borderline disturbance. In *Doing Psychotherapy*, pp. 110–120. New York: Basic Books.

Beck, A. T. (1979). *Cognitive Therapy of Depression*. New York: Guilford.

Bion, W. (1984). *Learning from Experience*, pp. 31–37. London: Maresfield.

Blanck, G., and Blanck, R. (1974). *Ego Psychology: Theory and Practice*. New York: Columbia University Press.

—— (1979). *Ego Psychology II: Psychoanalytic Developmental Psychology*, pp. 176–209. New York: Columbia University Press.

—— (1986). *Beyond Ego Psychology: Developmental Object Relations Theory*. New York: Columbia University Press.

Campbell, J. (1949). *The Hero with a Thousand Faces*, pp. 49–148. Princeton, NJ: Bollinger Series.

Eckstein, R., and Wallerstein, J. (1954). Observations on the psychology of borderline and psychotic children. *Psychoanalytic Study of the Child* 9:344–369.

—— (1955). Vicissitudes of the internal image in the recovery of a borderline schizophrenic adolescent. *Bulletin of the Menninger Clinic* 9:86–92.

—— (1962). Special training problems in psychotherapeutic work with psychotic and borderline children. *American Journal of Orthopsychiatry* 32:569–583.

Eissler, K. (1953). The effect of the structure of the ego on psychoanalytic technique. *Journal of the American Psychoanalytic Association* 1:104–143.

Eliot, T. S. (1922). The wasteland. In *The Complete Poems and Plays. 1909–1950*, p. 40. New York: Harcourt Brace Jovanovich.

Fairbairn, W. R. D. (1940). Schizoid factors in the personality. In *Psychoanalytic Studies of the Personality*. London: Routledge and Kegan Paul, 1952.

—— (1941). A revised psychopathology of the psychoses and psychoneuroses. In *Psychoanalytic Studies of the Personality*, pp. 28–58. London: Routledge and Kegan Paul, 1952.

—— (1943). The repression and return of bad objects (with special references to the war neuroses). In *Psychoanalytic Studies of the Personality*. New York: International Universities Press, 1965.

—— (1944). Endopsychic structure considered in terms of object relationships. In *Psychoanalytic Studies of the Personality*, pp. 82–136. London: Routledge and Kegan Paul, 1952.

—— (1958). On the nature and aims of psychoanalytic treatment. *International Journal of Psycho-Analysis* 39:374–385.

Ferenczi, S. (1928). The elasticity of psycho-analytic technique. In *Final Contributions to the Problems and Methods of Psycho-analysis*, pp. 87–101. New York: Brunner/Mazel, 1955.

—— (1930). The principles of relaxation and neocatharsis. In *Final Contributions to the Problems and Methods of Psycho-analysis*, pp. 108–125. New York: Brunner/Mazel, 1955.

Finell, J. S. (1987). A challenge to psychoanalysis: a review of the negative therapeutic reaction. *Psychoanalytic Review*.

Freud, A. (1946). Introduction to the technique of analysis of children. In *The Psychoanalytic Treatment of Children*, pp. 3–14. New York: International Universities Press.

Freud, S. (1905). Fragment of an analysis of a case of hysteria. In *Collected Papers*, vol. 3, pp. 13–146. New York: Basic Books, 1959.

—— (1916). Some character types met with in psychoanalytic work. In *Collected Papers*, vol. 4, pp. 318–344. New York: Basic Books, 1959.

—— (1917). Mourning and melancholia. In *Collected Papers*, vol. 4, pp. 152–172. New York: Basic Books, 1959.

—— (1918). From the history of an infantile neurosis. In *Collected Papers*, vol. 3. New York: Basic Books, 1959.

—— (1923). *The Ego and the Id*, p. 39. New York: W. W. Norton.

—— (1924). The economic problem in masochism. In *Collected Papers*, vol. 2, pp. 255–268. New York: Basic Books, 1959.

—— (1925). Negation. In *Collected Papers*, vol. 5, pp. 181–185. New York: Basic Books, 1959.

—— (1937). Analysis terminable and interminable. In *Collected Papers*, vol. 5, pp. 316–357. New York: Basic Books, 1959.

Giovacchini, P. (1965). Maternal introjection and ego defect. *Journal of American Academy of Child Psychology* 4:279–292.

——— (1967). The frozen introject. *International Journal of Psycho-Analysis* 48:61–67.

——— (1978) Psychoanalytic treatment of the alienated patient. In *New Perspectives on Psychotherapy of the Borderline Adult*, ed. J. Masterson, pp. 3–39. New York: Brunner/Mazel.

——— (1979). *Treatment of Primitive Mental States*. Northvale, NJ: Jason Aronson.

——— (1982). Structural progression and vicissitudes in the treatment of severely disturbed patients. In *Technical Factors in the Treatment of the Severely Disturbed Patient*, ed. P. Giovacchini and L. B. Boyer, pp. 3–64. New York: Jason Aronson.

——— (1986a). The transitional object and the psychoanalytic paradox. In *Developmental Disorders*, pp. 73–100. Northvale, NJ: Jason Aronson.

——— (1986b). Object constancy and mental representations. In *Developmental Disorders*, pp. 101–132. Northvale, NJ: Jason Aronson.

Greenson, R. R. (1965). The working alliance and the transference neurosis. *Psychoanalytic Quarterly* 34:155–181.

Grotstein, J. (1985). *Splitting and Projective Identification*, p. 164. New York: Jason Aronson.

Guntrip, H. (1969). *Schizoid Phenomena, Object Relations and the Self*, pp. 87–114. New York: International Universities Press.

Heisenberg, W. (1958). *Physics and Philosophy*. New York: Harper & Row.

Jacobson, E. (1964a). The fusion between self and object images and the earliest types of identifications. In *The Self and the Object World*, pp. 33–48. New York: International Universities Press.

——— (1964b). The child's finding of his sexual identity and the building up of his ego. In *The Self and the Object World*, pp. 70–86. New York: International Universities Press.

——— (1969). The child's discovery of his identity and his advance to object relations and selective identifications. In *The Self and the Object World*, pp. 49–69. New York: International Universities Press.

Joyce, J. (1986). *Ulysses*. New York: Vintage Books.

Kafka, F. (1937). *The Trial*. New York: Alfred A. Knopf.

Kernberg, O. (1975a). The syndrome. In *Borderline Conditions and Pathological Narcissism*, pp. 3–48. New York: Jason Aronson.

——— (1975b). General principles of treatment. In *Borderline Conditions and Pathological Narcissism*, pp. 69–110. New York: Jason Aronson.

—— (1978). Contrasting approaches to the psychotherapy of borderline conditions. In *New Perspectives in Psychotherapy of the Borderline Adult*, ed. J. Masterson, pp. 77–119. New York: Brunner/Mazel.

—— (1980). *Internal World and External Reality*. New York: Jason Aronson.

—— (1984). Transference management in expressive psychotherapy. In *Severe Personality Disorders*, pp. 112–130. New Haven: Yale University Press.

Klein, M. (1923). Early analysis. In *Love, Guilt and Reparation and Other Works, 1921–1945*, pp. 77–105. New York: Delta, 1975.

—— (1927). Symposium on child analysis. In *Love, Guilt and Reparation and Other Works, 1921–1945*, pp. 139–169. New York: Delta, 1975.

—— (1940). Mourning and its relation to manic depressive states. In *Love, Guilt and Reparation and Other Works, 1921–1945*, pp. 344–369. New York: Delta, 1975.

—— (1945). The Oedipus conflict in the light of early anxieties. In *Love, Guilt and Reparation and Other Works, 1921–1945*, pp. 370–419. New York, Delta, 1975.

—— (1946). Notes on some schizoid mechanisms. In *Envy and Gratitude and Other Works, 1946–1963*, pp. 1–24. New York: Delta, 1975.

—— (1955). The psychoanalytic play technique: its history and significance. In *Envy and Gratitude and Other Works, 1946–1963*, pp. 122–140. New York: Delta, 1975.

—— (1957). Envy and gratitude. In *Envy and Gratitude and Other Works, 1946–1963*, pp. 136–275. New York: Delta, 1975.

Knight, R. (1953a). Borderline states. In *Psychoanalytic Psychiatry and Psychology*, ed. A. P. Knight and C. R. Friedman, pp. 99–109. New York: International Universities Press, 1954.

—— (1953b). Management and psychotherapy of the borderline schizophrenic patient. In *Psychoanalytic Psychiatry and Psychology*, ed. R. P. Knight and C. R. Friedman, pp. 110–122. New York: International Universities Press, 1945.

Kohut, H. (1971). *The Analysis of the Self*. New York: International Universities Press.

—— (1977). *The Restoration of the Self*. New York: International Universities Press.

—— (1984). The self psychological approach to defense and resistance. In *How Does Analysis Cure?* ed. A. Goldberg and P. Stepansky, pp. 111–151. Chicago: University of Chicago Press.

LeBoit, J., and Capponi, A. (1979). *Advances in Psychotherapy of the Borderline Patient.* New York: Jason Aronson.

Mahler, M. (1975). *The Psychological Birth of the Human Infant*, pp. 225–234. New York: Basic Books.

Masterson, J. (1976). *Psychotherapy of the Borderline Adult: A Developmental Approach*, pp. 13–27. New York: Brunner/Mazel.

—— (1981). *The Narcissistic and Borderline Disorders*, pp. 133–140. New York: Brunner/Mazel.

McDougall, J. (1980). *Plea for a Measure of Abnormality.* Madison, CN: International Universities Press.

Ogden, T. (1986). *The Matrix of the Mind: Object Relations and the Psychoanalytic Dialogue.* Northvale, NJ: Jason Aronson.

Olinick, S. (1964). The negative therapeutic reaction. *International Journal of Psycho-Analysis* 45:540–548.

—— (1970). Negative therapeutic reaction report on panel. *Journal of the American Psychoanalytic Association* 18:655–672.

Rinsley, D. (1980). *Treatment of the Severely Disturbed Adolescent.* New York: Jason Aronson.

—— (1981). Object relations theory and psychotherapy with particular reference to the self-disordered patient. In *Technical Factors in the Treatment of the Severely Disturbed Patient*, ed. P. L. Giovacchini and L. B. Boyer, pp. 187–216. New York: Jason Aronson.

Rosenfeld, Harold. (1987). Narcissistic patients with negative therapeutic reactions. In *Impasse and Interpretation*, pp. 85–104. London: Tavistock.

Searles, H. (1958). Positive feelings in the relationship between the schizophrenic and his mother. In *Collected Papers on Schizophrenia and Related Subjects*, pp. 216–253. New York: International Universities Press.

—— (1959). The effort to drive the other person crazy—an element in the aetiology and psychotherapy of schizophrenia. In *Collected Papers on Schizophrenia and Related Subjects*, pp. 254–283. New York: International Universities Press.

—— (1961). Phases of patient-therapist interaction in the psychotherapy of chronic schizophrenia. In *Collected Papers on Schizophrenia and Related Subjects*, pp. 521–559. New York: International Universities Press.

—— (1972). The function of the patient's realistic perceptions of the analyst in delusional transference. In *Countertransference and Related Subjects*. New York: International Universities Press.

—— (1975). The patient as therapist to his analyst. In *Countertransference and Related Subjects*, pp. 380–459. New York: International Universities Press.

—— (1977). The development of mature hope in the patient–therapist relationship. In *Countertransference and Related Subjects*, pp. 479–502. New York: International Universities Press.

—— (1978). Psychoanalytic therapy with the borderline adult: some principles concerning technique. In *New Perspectives on Psychotherapy of the Borderline Adult*, ed. J. Masterson, p. 43–73. New York: Brunner/Mazel.

—— (1979). Development of mature hope in the patient–therapist relationship. In *Countertransference and Related Subjects*, pp. 479–502. New York: International Universities Press.

—— (1986). *My Work with Borderline Patients*. Northvale, NJ: Jason Aronson.

Seinfeld, J. (1989). Therapy with a severely abused child: an object relations perspective. *Clinical Social Work Journal* 17:40–49.

Sours, J. (1978). The application of child analytic principles to forms of child psychotherapy. In *Child Analysis and Therapy*, ed. J. Glenn, pp. 615–648. New York: Jason Aronson.

Spitz, R. A. (1965). *The First Year of Life*, pp. 180–194. New York: International Universities Press.

Stolorow, R. D., and Lachmann, F. M. (1980). *Psychoanalysis of Developmental Arrests*. New York: International Universities Press.

White, M. T. and Weiner, M. D. (1986). The grandiose self: a wellspring of rage or achievement? New York: Brunner/Mazel.

Winnicott, D. W. (1958). The capacity to be alone. In *The Maturational Processes and the Facilitating Environment*, pp. 29–36. New York: International Universities Press.

—— (1960a). The theory of the parent–infant relationship. In *Maturational Processes and the Facilitating Environment*, pp. 37–55. New York: International Universities Press, 1965.

—— (1960b). Ego distortion in terms of true and false self. In *Maturational Processes and the Facilitating Environment*, pp. 140–152. New York: International Universities Press, 1965.

—— (1963). Dependence in infant care, in child care, and in the psychoanalytic setting. In *Maturational Processes and the Facilitating Environment*, pp. 249–250. New York: International Universities Press, 1965.

—— (1978). *Through Paediatrics to Psycho-Analysis*. London: Hogarth Press.

Zetzel, E. (1966). The analytic situation. In *Psychoanalysis in the Americas*, pp. 86–106. New York: International Universities Press.

Index

About the Author

Jeffrey Seinfeld, Ph.D., is Associate Professor at New York University School of Social Work and a private consultant to the Jewish Board of Family and Children's Services. Dr. Seinfeld received his training at Hunter College of Social Work and New York University School of Social Work. He has authored and co-edited works in the fields of psychotherapy and clinical social work, including *The Empty Core: An Object Relations Approach to Psychotherapy of the Schizoid Personality*, and *Interpreting and Holding: The Paternal and Maternal Functions of the Psychotherapist*. Dr. Seinfeld is in the private practice of psychotherapy in New York City.